THE CAMP AND THE CITY
TERRITORIES OF EXTRACTION

JEANNETTE SORDI, LUIS VALENZUELA, FELIPE VERA

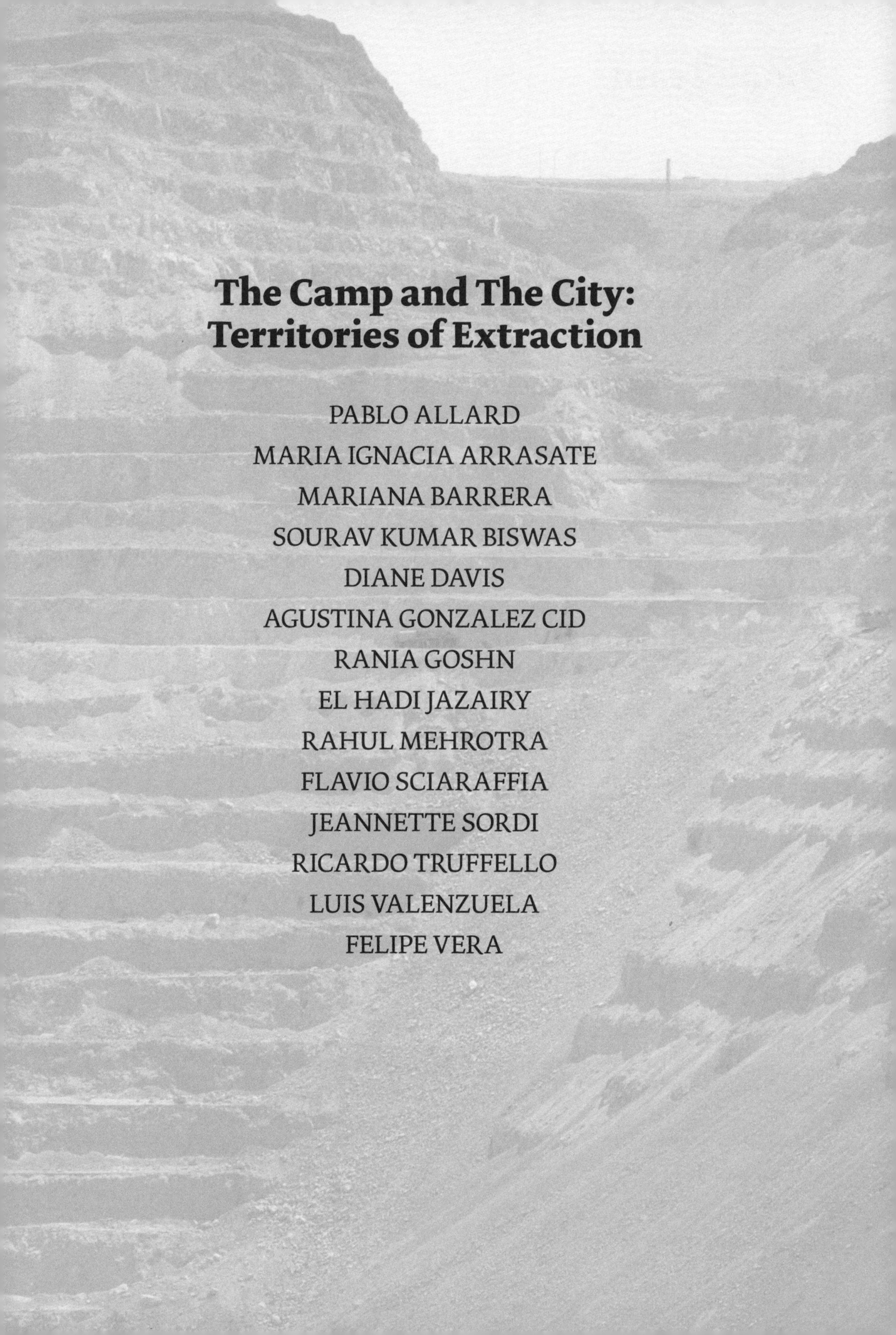

The Camp and The City:
Territories of Extraction

PABLO ALLARD

MARIA IGNACIA ARRASATE

MARIANA BARRERA

SOURAV KUMAR BISWAS

DIANE DAVIS

AGUSTINA GONZALEZ CID

RANIA GOSHN

EL HADI JAZAIRY

RAHUL MEHROTRA

FLAVIO SCIARAFFIA

JEANNETTE SORDI

RICARDO TRUFFELLO

LUIS VALENZUELA

FELIPE VERA

Book Team

Authors
Jeannette Sordi
Luis Valenzuela
Felipe Vera

Editor and research coordinator
Agustina González Cid

Copy Editor
Stephanie Carwin

Maps and research assistants
Manuel Bianchi
Serena Dambrosio
Mónica Fontana

Texts by
Pablo Allard
Maria Ignacia Arrasate
Mariana Barrera
Diane Davis
Agustina González Cid
Rania Goshn
El Hadi Jazairy
Sourav Kumar Biswas
Rahul Mehrotra
Flavio Sciaraffia
Jeannette Sordi
Ricardo Truffello
Luis Valenzuela
Felipe Vera

The authors appreciate the support by
CODELCO - Corporación Nacional del Cobre, Chile; COES - Centre for Social Conflict and Cohesion Studies (Chilean grant CONICYT/FONDAP/15130009)

The project involved the collaboration of
Harvard University Graduate School of Design; Harvard University David Rockefeller Center for Latin American Studies; Universidad Adolfo Ibáñez DesignLAB; Centro de Inteligencia Territorial at Universidad Adolfo Ibáñez; Centro de Ecología, Paisaje y Urbanismo at Universidad Adolfo Ibáñez

Acknowledgments

Creating a publication such as this one requires both the engagement and support of numerous people and institutions including, but invariably exceeding, the names listed here. This book is a result of a series of research approaches and debates within a framework that we have informally named the 'Research Project on the Camp and the City.' We sincerely hope this book triggers a conversation that challenges the notion of permanence as the only condition in the city.

We must first acknowledge and thank Codelco´s Executive President, Oscar Landerretche, who enthusiastically supported the idea of such a scope of research of mining and the City of Calama. We extend a special thanks to a large number of Codelco´s professionals who followed and helped throughout the process represented by Vice President, Corporate Affairs and Sustainability, Patricio Chavés, and the former Vice President, René Aguilar. This publication would not have been possible without their generous support.

We are also tremendously grateful to the Graduate School of Design at Harvard University who supported the Research Project in 2014 and 2015, which generated many of the ideas represented in this volume. We are grateful to the Dean of the Graduate School of Design, Mohsen Mostafav, and the Chair of the Urban Planning and Design, Rahul Mehrotra, for supporting the project and encouraging further research. Additionally, we would like to thank the David Rockefeller Center for Latin American Studies at Harvard University. In particular, we would like to thank Ned Strong, Director of the DRCLAS program, for his commitment and support.

Furthermore, we are grateful for the generous support of the Center of Territorial Intelligence and the Center for Landscape, Ecology and Urbanism at the Design Lab of Universidad Adolfo Ibáñez. We thank them in particular for their generosity and commitment for supporting design research and the exploration of complex issues related to architecture and the city.

During the process of putting this volume together we were very fortunate to have XXX Editions, which has established an important space for architecture and urbanism publications over the last few years. In addition to their bookmaking expertise, we benefited from the inspiring collaboration with the editor-in-chief Massimiliano Scaglione and his team, as well as the thoughtful insights provided by his team. We are very pleased with the graphic identity of the content of this publication that produced a beautifully designed volume.

Additionally, many students had a vital role in fostering the conversations that led to this book. We thank the students who participated in the advanced research seminars at the Harvard Graduate School of Design taught by Luis Valenzuela. We also thank the students who pursued their studies on this topic, such as: Pedro Aparicio, Maria Arroyo, Kate Cahill, Jaime Daroca, Mikela De Tchaves, Arianna Galan, Agustina González, Joyce Lee, Namik Mackic, Julie Mercier, Maïlys Meyer, Alica Meza, Althea Northcross, Davi Parente Schoen, Catalina Picón, Margaret Scott, Sam Wright; and with the teaching and research assistants Flavio Sciaraffia, Adriana Chavez and Mariano Gómez Luque.

At the School of Design from the Universidad Adolfo Ibáñez, the following students participated very enthusiastically: Vicente Alessandri, Elisa Barrios, Valentina Barrios, Patricio Cardenas, Marisol Carrillo, Hang-Man Cheung, Alejandro Diaz, Vicente Fagalde, Jose Manuel Gomez, Francisco Iglesias, Tomas Iturrieta, Nicolas Kersting, Josefina Leon, Victoria Lopez, Valentina Nash, Agustin Olave, Charlotte Odette, Daniela Prato, Sylvana Quest, Santiago Ruiz, Diego Silva, Fabianna Tarsetti, Maximiliano Toledo, Jorge Trepat, Josefa Vargas, Fernando Velazquez and Sofia Wenborne.

Furthermore, many faculty and doctoral fellows provided thoughtful insights that nourished the content of this book during these academic seminars and discussions. We especially thank Pablo Allard (Dean School of Architecture at Universidad del Desarrollo), Jose Miguel Ansoleaga (Codelco), Patricio Aroca (Universidad Adolfo Ibáñez), Magdalena Balcells (Codelco), Solano Benitez (Architect), Patricio Chavez (Codelco), Ignacio Errazuriz (Cámara Chilena de la Construcción), Eugenio Garcés (Faculty at Universidad Católica), René Huerta (Municipality of Calama), Rahul Mehrotra (Director of Planning and Urban Design at Harvard University Graduate School of Design), Sandra Miranda (Aramark), Nicole Norel (Universidad Adolfo Ibáñez), Rodolfo Reygada (Calama PLUS), María Alejandra Rivera (Municipality of Calama), Osvaldo Rojas (City of Calama), Hugo Romero (COES Researcher), Josefina Valdés (architect at MUVA), Esteban Velásquez (Mayor of Calama) and Javier Vergara (Architect at Ciudades Emergentes).

We hope this collective effort will bring a new perspective on temporality and the city, one that can trigger more powerful and yet nuanced discussions on urbanism. Mostly, we specially thank the people of Calama; this book is especially aimed at helping them have a better quality of life.

Prologue   **10**
Oscar Landerretche

The Camp and The City: Territories of Extraction   **20**
Jeannette Sordi, Luis Valenzuela, Felipe Vera

TERRITORIES OF EXTRACTION

01   **Towards an Ephemeral Urbanism for Extraction:**   **22**
The Camp and The City as Spatial Paradigms
Felipe Vera, Rahul Mehrotra

02   **Resource Territories:**   **62**
Hassi Messaoud Oil Urbanism
Rania Ghosn, El Hadi Jazairy

03   **Resource-led New Towns and Challenges to Sovereignty**   **84**
Diane E. Davis, Mariana Barrera

04   **Coping with Complexity:**   **102**
Experiences in Post-Disaster Recovery
for Extractive Towns in Chile
Pablo Allard, Maria Ignacia Arrasate

05 The Functional Relationship in Mining Territories: **136**
Calama's Cluster Case, Chile
Ricardo Truffello, Luis Valenzuela

06 A Landscape Approach for Calama's Oasis: **158**
Negotiating Landscape Conservation,
Agricultural Livelihoods and Mining
Flavio Sciaraffia, Sourav Biswas

07 Landscape Rules: The Calama Recreation Game   **182**
Jeannette Sordi

08 Conflicting Spaces in New Territories of Extraction   **204**
Luis Valenzuela

THE CAMP AND THE CITY
Calama as a Camp   226
Agustina González Cid

Calama as a City   260
Agustina González Cid

The Landscape of Extractive Urbanization   260
Jeannette Sordi, Luis Valenzuela, Felipe Vera

Contributors   306

Prologue

Oscar Landerretche

Excerpt of a speech given in London, October 2015

We all know the enormous contribution that mining has made to technological and industrial development. We must always keep in mind that the technological opportunities and challenges that we confront actually contain enormous potential for emerging economies. These challenges can mobilize local entrepreneurship, technology, and science in ways that can actually generate a multiplier effect on growth and development. Of course, we must always invest in research, design, and science with a business perspective and keeping the long-term strategic interest of our business in mind; however, let's not lose sight that it may be very much in our long-term interest to be perceived as a well for progress, modernity, science, technology, and innovation. In my view, this perception can generate a much more powerful and lasting "social license," a "license for growth and development."

If you are fortunate enough to glide over our country in daytime and look down, you will see how we have transformed the landscape, moved mountains, opened craters, created lakes, constructed and abandoned cities in the middle of the mountains and the deserts, interwoven the landscape with networks of energy and water and tailings and acid and rivers of molten rock. It's amazing, exciting, dramatic, and heroic. It's wonderful, so wonderful, the power of science and technology, the energy of finance and capital that we may learn to be infatuated with it, it may seduce us, and it may become the subject of worship.

What can we do to prepare for next time so that we can bring humanity and society along with us in the wonder of this transforming world that, nonetheless, must still be there, for them, in the end, with most of the things that they expect and remember?

Rio Loa valley, Atacama desert, Jeannette Sordi, 2015

Atacama desert extraction landscape, Serena Dambrosio, 2015

Loa River valley cultivation, Serena Dambrosio, 2015

View of Calama's airport from the Indigenous Cemetery, Jeannette Sordi, 2015

The Camp and The City: Territories of Extraction

Jeannette Sordi, Luis Valenzuela, Felipe Vera

Cities are fundamental structures that support and foster the most intense expressions of human life that, in order to operate, deploy several layers of infrastructure on broader and extended territories, expanding their effects clearly beyond their administrative limits. Urbanization metabolizes territories surrounding cities as well as territories that are located far beyond the centers themselves and provide the needed resources and goods. Landscapes of extraction are probably one of the most evident examples of this: whole regions are exploited for their resources in order to ensure the development of others.

However, while it is becoming evident that these territories could be considered as part of the urbanization process itself, they are still very marginal in the agenda of urban designers, planners, regional administrators, and political institutions. Actually, the fact that these territories are considered as subordinated to cities, or as an extension or side effect of them, makes it so that they are not paid enough attention as places for living themselves - cities and landscapes that clearly need ad hoc models and strategies to be understood and qualified as such. Territories of extraction are in a way the negative of cities: they are what ensures the development, prosperity, and consolidation of cities, but are themselves the emblem of deployment and precariousness. No matter the size and legal definition of a settlement - whether it is a town, a city, or a metropolis - if it is part of the extraction economy it is usually considered a "camp," a temporary living hub that is part of the overall extraction industry and infrastructure.

With this in mind, *The City and The Camp: Territories of Extraction* aims to not only focus on a particular field of action for urban design and planning, but also to set a platform for investigating relatively unexplored tensions that appear in such extractive contexts. The city and the camp in a way represent two sides of the same phenomenon, the development of urbanization, but while the first is assigned the dignity of being defined by itself, camps are usually considered the byproduct of specific functions and situations, temporary and dislocated by definition. The essays included in this book explore these problematics from a range of different perspectives.

At the very center of the discussion is the twofold dimension that configures these landscapes. Looking at the ecological aspect for instance, on the one hand, these territories are a fundamental keystone for the same creation of the urban; while on the other, they simply devastate huge portions of ecological systems, disrupting their inner equilibrium, and imprinting them with permanent, almost irreversible, effects. Or thinking about the configuration of their institutional framework: it is disappointing to see how extraction territories are rarely capable of capitalizing on the creation of wealth that they efficiently support, as they usually get trapped in clientelist dynamics that in many cases generate a near dissolution of sovereignty. Rather than promoting the installation of more compensative and long-term visions capable of ensuring the development of these precious areas, public institutions often allow major corporations to govern the territory freely without any interference.

Another, no less important, discussion that forms part of this book and is implied in its title is the complex dialectic between the structure of the camp and the structure of the city as diverse paradigms of space production and operation. Is it possible for urban settlements in contexts of extreme efficiency to emerge not just in the form of camps, but as cities that articulate more complex cultural and economic layers that ensure a certain quality of life? The way in which functionality, morphology, and public life appear in settlements located in territories of extraction, as well as the footprints of extraction "sites," seem to introduce (given its increasingly bigger scale and its pervasive presence) a particular set of conditions that almost isolate these settlements from the very notion of "the city," making it easier to relate them more to the structure of the camp. Precisely because they retrofit a system where the urban is thought of as an engine for the realization of complex processes taking place way beyond their physical scope, which are negotiated beyond the scale of the city. Indeed, extraction sites are constantly being internally reconfigured by logistical operations on the landscape, which are very precisely articulated transformations conceived to "absorb" as much as possible of whatever resource is available on the territory. To this, apparently the structure of "the city" might present more problems, and therefore the structure of "the camp" as the main expression of settlements appears. Yet, there is a potential embedded in extraction operational modes and the logic of the camp, which is the opportunity to take advantage of the high level of infrastructure of the first and the temporality of the second. We are indeed imagining that, as they approach the end of their original productive cycle, mining infrastructures and camps can be actualized in new strategies for moving forward. Imagining the reabsorption, reinvention, and disassembly of these incredible physical and human resources as a reversible cycle that, instead of trash, leaves a real legacy behind.

The book is constructed along two main tracks and objectives. The first aim is to articulate a discussion about territories of extraction in order to set up concepts and provide a general overview of their common challenges throughout different landscapes. The second is to generate a more specific and evidence-based discussion by looking closely at the city of Calama, in Chile, as a case in which the challenges that appear in extractive territories are extreme and therefore offer the ground for the development of a more projective critical view. Calama is the major enclave of the northern mining region of Chile and has historically faced the challenges of big mining cities. After what was called by Alejandro Aravena the "social tsunami," many actions were taken toward the articulation of a more sustainable development model for the city and its metropolitan area. In this way, it has recently taken care of what was called its "historical debt," identifying, designing, and today implementing a series of projects that react to the current demands of citizens and of the environment in broader terms. These investments in the city are diminishing accumulated deficits of service provision and environmental assets, and for this an unprecedented institutional catalyzer was put in place: Calama PLUS, or *Calama Plan Urbano Sustentable*. Through this process, consensus has been created with respect to the need of moving forward with a sustainable and productive long-term development. In this sense, the initiatives led by Calama PLUS, the inclusive commentary dialogue articulated by it, and the agenda of projects that have been agreed upon through compromise between private and public partnerships, have suggested the idea that the clientelistic relationship between stakeholders present in the territory could change. Calama PLUS set the basis for the definition of a new paradigm based on compensation and ecological conservation that could ensure the quality of the territory in the future.

The challenge today, however, is about how to overcome the reactive attitude by which previous problems were tackled, moving forward with the articulation of a long-term vision, in which instead of reacting to the present requirements of the city in its quotidian condition, some shared long-term solutions are created, via the discussion and evaluation of possibilities and the elaboration of development scenarios. This is a very complex challenge, but a very necessary one as well. In order to advance towards a more sustainable development of Calama and the region served by this urban cluster, it is critical to include multidimensional themes as a priority in the discussions, understanding their role as a process integrated into the urban and territorial system.

In fact, Calama today provides the world with almost one tenth of the copper it needs, but it does so at the expense of its environment. In order to reverse this dynamic, it is not enough to pay older accumulated "urban debts," but to actually advance towards the changing of the paradigm into a compensatory one in real time. Calama presents the same challenges and questions that other landscapes of extraction present. For instance, questions such as: Can these infrastructures be re-utilized? Can their settlements survive, and find a purpose of their own? Can the landscape be remediated by the activation of new programmatic and productive activities? In other words, can efficiency make room for environmentally responsible protocols, and for a projective strategy of re-utilization? After all, artifacts are automatons designed to perform a very specific set of operations. Therefore, design has an agency that could make a difference, i.e. by inserting new rules into the system. Design-related disciplines can play a critical role in the reformulation – or the design – of processes of extraction, but only if their disciplinary apparatuses mobilize their intelligence towards a real understanding of the complexity and implications that lie behind such processes. Ephemeral Landscapes of Extraction have to be designed, not for the sake of efficiency, but especially for the sake of legitimating and incorporating the territories they exploit into the category that they remotely sustain: the city.

The contributions present in this book aim to trigger discussions that will help to answer these and other questions that appear when dealing with territories of extraction.

As framed by Felipe Vera and Rahul Mehrotra's essay, it is very important to be able to recognize the structure of the camp and the structure of the city, even beyond what is commonly recognized as camp and as city. A meaningful discussion should thus be undertaken in order to understand the real nature of both. What are the conditions that define the camp and the city? It doesn't have to do either with their temporality or materiality, but what are then the issues and challenges? As Vera and Mehrotra claim, sometimes it seems that settlements supporting extractive territories are not cities, but rather camps struggling to fulfill their aspiration of becoming cities, an aspiration that is rarely – if ever – accomplished because, as they claim, camps in contexts of extraction are inherently acts of consumption.

Rania Goshn and El Hadi Jazairy explore the meaning of territory as the inevitable partner of resource metabolism. As they claim, territory is the form of power over geography that interweaves political processes, material metabolism, and spatial form, becoming the object and site for the negotiation of the state's extractive capital and the state's public expenditures. Through the case study of Hassi Messaoud – a North African oil-extraction site critical for Europe's supplies – they interrogate whether it is possible to conceptualize the landscape of resources (or *paysage*) by recentralizing the country (*pays*) and the worker of the land (*paysan*) in the organization of nature's metabolism.

Diane Davis and Mariana Barrera's essay aims to unfold how extractive new towns manage urban and governance challenges, particularly with respect to the distribution of infrastructure and services, with what implications for the willingness and capacity of private firms to stay put, and with what effect on the urban quality of life of its residents. In resource-led towns, where private companies operate as functional equivalents of local government and planning agencies by taking responsibility for basic infrastructure and prioritizing town needs, citizens are not equally well served, urban spaces become divided, and larger developmental aims are easily compromised. Focusing on two different "experiments in urbanization" – Añelo in Argentina and Tete in Mozambique – Davis and Barrera develop a preliminary understanding of how resource-led new towns manage these challenges, highlighting the benefits and risks of company-led investments in the development of extraction regions.

Pablo Allard offers a review of the challenges and lessons learned in post-disaster planning and implementation efforts of three Chilean towns related to different extractive industries: the case of the town of Chaitén (salmon industry) destroyed by a volcano eruption in 2008, and the towns of Dichato (fishing and tourism) and Constitución (forestry) severely affected by the 2010 earthquake and tsunami. Building on the three cases, and unfolding the difficulties in developing resilient urban recovery master plans given the complexity of post-disaster recovery, fragmented sectorial agendas, and processes embedded in the public investment system and centralized decision-making practices in Chile, the essay showcases the innovations and design-based strategies implemented to cope with such challenges.

Ricardo Truffello and Luis Valenzuela's work aims to redefine the cluster of Calama, claiming that the several mining centers depending on it are actually part of the same enclave. The objective is to generate evidence – through network analysis modeling the interaction between the urban and productive territory – of the territorial characteristics of a complex mining cluster. In particular, the analysis of the enclave aims to characterize the level of functional dependency between the mines and the cities (or camps), analyze the relation between mining activity and urban development (including future projections to 2020 and 2070), and determine the dimensions of the territorial occupation of the mining industry. The final objective is thus to propose and articulate a territorial vision that, going beyond a limited understanding of the problems as regarding either the city or the mine, can inform future decisions and territorial development.

The essay by Flavio Sciaraffa and Sourav Biswas focuses instead on the oasis of Calama, at once highlighting how the lack of planning and policy instruments has been preventing a proper management of the oasis in conjunction with urban processes and mining activities – endangering agricultural and indigenous livelihoods, the fading cultural-historical heritage – and the untapped opportunities of the Oasis as a landscape element for an extreme-desert urban environment. Taking into account the current land regulation in Chile, and the specific conditions of the place, the paper unfolds methods and principles stemming from Landscape Ecology and Landscape Planning, stressing their suitability to address complex socio-ecological issues involving multiple stakeholders and systems such as Calama's Oasis.

Jeannette Sordi takes the "collection of populations" that live in Calama as a starting point to define the multiple scales, interests, and needs that characterize extraction territories, highlighting the need to outline scenarios for the region that can coexist with mining and survive within it. Considering landscape as the entity comprising all the genetic, dynamic, and functional relations through which the components of a territory get connected to each other, the essay suggests that landscape may also be the hinge with which this territory can exude its potential. Landscape is seen as a medium that would allow considering the aforementioned collection of disparate populations and project its transformation into a community. Landscape as the framework within which each population could outline its own rules, narrative, and objectives; play its own game.

Luis Valenzuela's article takes a careful look at some of the new geographies that arose in Latin America in the late 1980s to early 1990s as a result of the changes in the relationships between political, economic, and social factors in the extraction industry. As he claims, the traditional mining model has evolved into a modern extractive business model, whose impact and complexity keeps increasing, and which now involves global mining companies, international mining outsourcing companies, and national service companies. Under the mining boom, the articulation and tension of the uneven geographies in the growth of natural resource extraction settings permanently submerge the real needs of daily life in local contexts, where social conflicts arose linked to the unequal territorial welfare, on one side due to spatial inaccessibility to public services and infrastructure, and on the other side, due to the concentration of poverty.

Altogether, these articles offer insights on the complexities and challenges presented by territories of extraction, which are exacerbated by the binary contraposition of the camp and the city. These essays are complemented with a series of maps and more projective interpretations of the territory of Calama and its region, which are the result of an applied research project developed as a collaboration between the Center of Territorial Intelligence and the Center for Ecology Landscape and Urbanism at Universidad Adolfo Ibañéz and the Harvard Graduate School of Design. Rather than giving a closing argument to this discussion, the aim of this book is that of triggering a significant conversation that will shed some light on the analysis and intervention within extractive territories, bringing back the quality of urban life and all its nuances to the center of attention.

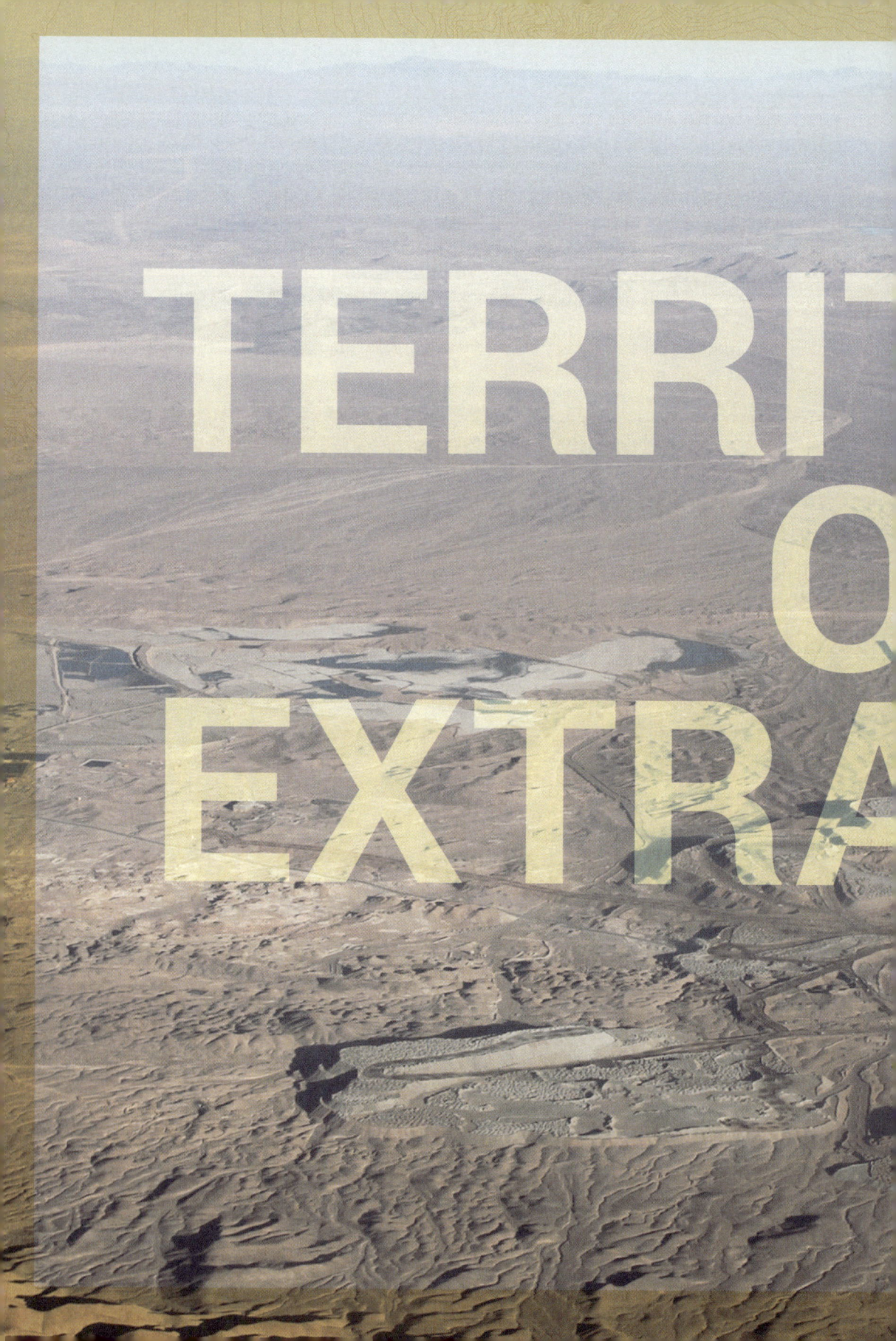

Chuquicamata, Jeannette Sordi, 2015

Towards an Ephemeral Urbanism for Extraction:
The Camp and The City as Spatial Paradigms
Felipe Vera, Rahul Mehrotra

> *Friday, May 17, 2002, Chuquicamata.*
> I look around the giant dining room where we are eating a scrumptious Chilean lunch – shellfish and *congrio* eel and perfectly chilled white wine, talking about the production of copper at the largest open-air mine pit in the world [...] I look past the adept waiters and desserts and cake being lavished on the diners at other tables, out onto the looming mountain outside that will soon descend upon all this, these lush chairs that we are sitting on, these luxurious chandeliers that hang above us [...] I tell myself that it can't be true that this entire facility, and the town itself, which stretches out on all sides, with its streets, its hospitals, its police station, all, all of it will lie beneath a colossal mound of *ripio* – rubble, yes, billions of tons of refuse from the mine of Chuquicamata. *Desert Memories*, Ariel Dorfman.

On Saturday, September 1, 2007, at noon, the city of Chuquicamata closed its doors after almost ninety-two years of operation. The closing initiated a process of depopulation and disinvestment that would end up in the burying of the city that Ariel Dorfman mentions in the passage above. This historical enclave located 1,600 kilometers north of Santiago, Chile in the middle of the Atacama Desert developed a city that evolved to host more than 24,000 people. Most of the dwellers were workers in the biggest open pit mine in the world, who lived in Chuquicamata with their families. At the time of the closing, the authorities declared that the settlement was already "part of Chilean memories" and that some specific parts, such as the historical center – including a theater, a public square, a church, some schools, etc. – would be among the only parts of the city that would not lie under *ripio* (rubble). A few years later, having the colossal mound of *ripio* as a background and the city converted into an abandoned ghost town, more than 50,000 people gathered in the square for the evening in order to celebrate, with fireworks, the hundred years of its foundation. It was an act of optimism, in that they hoped that this celebration would revive the memory of the city and bring it alive, attracting everybody to what had recently been converted into an empty camp!

Walking the empty streets and observing the town's high quality urban design, one cannot believe the city's demise. Today, ironically, the city is composed of empty historical buildings juxtaposed with the interminable pile of debris from the mines. In any case, this is a rude reminder that this case highlights and challenges some of the preconceptions and conventions of urban design and planning in extreme contexts, especially in contexts of natural resources extraction. Furthermore, when we think that Chuquicamata town is only one case among a huge range of cases of temporary cities built in support of the exploitation of natural resources, not only in mining, but also in a series of other extractive activities such as oil extraction, forestry, and others, one understands the colossal scale of the field, and perhaps the problem. There is an interminable array of cities, towns, and other types of settlements that are scattered all over the globe following similar temporary patterns of spatial occupation. The scope of extractive activities, like the ones at play in the Yanacocha mine in Peru, having more than 10,000 temporary dwellers, the Maritsa Iztok Mines in Bulgaria, the Motru Coal Mine in Romania, or Salvador and Pelambres in the north of Chile, generate a whole constellation of diverse sorts of temporary settlements around the globe dealing with the complexity of environmental consequences and incredibly large-scale operations that constantly modify the topography of a temporary landscape at a territorial scale. Settlements supporting such activities are, in a way, able to be conceptualized as exceptions within the territory. Not exceptions in the sense of difference, but exceptions in the sense of what is not continuous and therefore as that which allows greater levels of readjustment in its modes of operation and growth. The materialization of a state of exception in these cases introduces many contradictions or unresolved tensions, which in a way need to be explored and discussed carefully, especially through the lenses of urban design and planning knowledge. For instance, many of these cities are designed, operated, and discussed as camps, while in the imaginary of their inhabitants they are actually experienced and perceived as living, transcendent, and permanent cities. These perceptions in turn create aspirations in their citizens that often cannot be fulfilled under the limitations of their true agendas. Many such aspirations are not realized due to the fact that the lifecycle of these settlements can only extend as long as the duration of the extractive activity, following the availability of the resource. In extraction, if one thing is clear, it is that when nothing is left, it is time to move on. Therefore, many of these cities are born and grow, trapped in the logics of extraction, knowing that they have a certain or predictable expiration date, a fact that irrevocably imprints and limits the complete deployment of their potential as urban systems and cultures. Exaggerating the urban dynamic of cities, and situating ourselves within a larger temporal span, we might imagine extractive territories as a platform, on and in which temporary settlements for extractive activities appear and disappear as a series of temporary reconfigurations of natural and man-made metabolization, creating ephemeral occupations in the territory.

In these exceptions, the urban does not necessarily adhere to its traditional quest for permanence, but is rather a pulse, assembling and disassembling itself in a reversible manner according to the flows of the material extracted, market demands, and supply of resources. Some of these scattered settlements would last for twenty years, others for hundreds. Some would get dismantled after the extractive operations are over, while others would be just emptied, being left for time to erode them. Only a few will be reconverted or reinvented into something different than a mining settlement, evolving into a more complex structure, developing new economies, and escaping from this logic of the broader landscapes of extraction.

Some of the traditional urbanism categories and values blur when one analyzes the urban environment that emerges from these contexts. Many questions appear when one discovers the real complexity of these clusters. What kind of urbanism is appropriate for these urban structures if we consider the underlying logics that rule them? Are they just productive machines that are part of the extractive apparatus, or do they represent the opportunity to develop something else? Should they embrace the fact that they are born with an expiration date, building an imaginary that recognizes this fact, or should they aspire to become cities, investing in the construction of thick memories, urban narratives, and transcendental significations? Abstracting the questions a bit more we could ask: how should we refer to these settlements? What are they in reality? How can one call them camps if many of them – like Chuquicamata, for instance – are in their material presence perceived and lived in as cities? How could we treat them or design them as camps if complete lifecycles of people, from birth to death, are played out within their buildings? Or, on the other hand, how can we call them cities if, when one analyzes the functional patterns that drive them, one finds that they follow more the structure of a camp that that of a city? How do we assert that they are actual cities if, when probed, they seem to be more like camps in which "the urban" seems to appear by accident? How can we call these settlements cities if one finds that so many of them are just abandoned after operations in the mines are over? Or, considering that the city is by default the place in which democracy and freedom have found their more radical forms of expressions, how can we call cities urban structures that usually tend to reduce the flow of life to its more basic elements, sustaining them in nearly their barest state and keeping them functional for productive activities? How is this different from the figure of the camps in their more crude expression? How is this not similar to an understanding of the camp as instrumental apparatus for a biopolitical management subjugated to the needs of an outsider?

These are some of the questions that emerge when examining the many settlements that are developed in support of extractive activities. Many of these contradictions and open questions are resolved after analyzing the form of life in these settlements. However, this not only refers to the city in terms of its built form but rather to a particular form of life supported by a cohesive as well as shared set of relationships that appear when extraction is the chief driver for development. In this sense, the logic of extractions and contradictions that come with them not only emerge in cities that are strictly or exclusively created for supporting extraction but also in the urban condition more generally. They also appear when extraction as a form of life migrates or connects with pre-existing or adjacent settlements. An example of this might also be the series of phenomena that are still happening after the relocation of Chuquicamata's population inside the adjacent city of Calama. This town also began as an agriculture town situated in what was the biggest oasis of the Atacama Desert and that, by the time of the relocation, was a city struggling with the challenges of embracing a development model strongly fueled by the mining industry. While it is true that the tensions between the imaginary of the camp and that of the city were then already strongly present in this case. However, they clearly increased after the aforementioned displacement and relocation process. To have more than a third of the population using the city as a dormitory, built and paid for by the mining industry, generated a growth of the urban form that was only capable of supporting basic conditions of bio-productive life or what has been described by Agamben as "bare uses." The set of relationships installed in this city has for years operated at a scale that went beyond the scale of Calama, in which very little of the capital allowed for a proper allocation in the spaces that were supporting their operations. Naturally, this fed the anxiety within its population and the emergence of more sustainable (and perhaps "sacred") forms of life. The lack of investment then added to a very insipient history of improvement in the quality of the urban environment and a progressive privatization of the spaces that supported public life, creating several tensions and social confrontations. At a certain point, people went out into the streets to demand a more sustainable model of growth, capturing the attention of authorities and mining industry.

As a result, many actions were taken to avoid what was starting to be called the "social tsunami." However, none of these actions really tackled the basic problems of Calama. Being a city driven by logics of extraction, there was indeed a fundamental contradiction – a citizenship that demanded a model of growth for the city, and an economy that needed to instead just perpetuate a huge mining camp. Of course, a lack of shared vision or the impossibility of creating one is really the heart of the problem, and the avoidance of the question – whether this settlement was going to be treated as a camp, or if it was a going to be treated as a city – will continue to exacerbate the tensions. For only by confronting this larger question could both the citizens and the owners move towards a resolution in the long-term and create more effective strategies for urban design and planning in response to the real dynamics of this condition.

In the city today, one feels this unresolvable tension – rather opposite to what one experiences when within the boundaries of Chuquicamata. Patterns of spatial occupation, the predominance of privately owned public space, and an almost insipient public life all remind one of being in a camp in an extremely stark way, rather than in a city. In cases like this, the question is then: how can we call this settlement a city if its growth really follows the logic and structure of the camp? What is then the course of action to negotiate the best future for such a settlement? Or what are the steps to convert, revert, empower, intensify, thicken, or just change the urban dynamics in order to make the settlement align with the aspirations of the citizens?

Like Calama, many other extraction sites remind us that under certain conditions the boundaries between the camp and the city blur. There are actually moments in which settlements, which are recognized formally and institutionally as cities, are in their true nature actually camps. This gets manifested in the patterns of space occupation, in the structure of their governance and institutional frameworks, as well as in the programs of their buildings and the morphology that their urban grain. In fact, going further and taking a very radical position, Giorgio Agamben argues that, "We must expect not only new camps but also always new and more lunatic regulative definitions of the inscription of life in the city. The camp, which is now securely lodged within the city's interior, is the new biopolitical *nomos* of the planet."[1] In this regard, one could argue that on some occasions, cities supporting extractive territories might be clear examples of such a "new biopolitical *nomos*" that according to Agamben is transforming the contemporary city across a broad spectrum. In this sense, there are tremendous implications in advancing towards a deep understanding with regard to the true nature of these types of settlements that are akin to camps. Many nuances emerge by exploring these conditions, issues of governance, and cultural heritage, as one tries to identify whether it is the structure of the camp or the city that drives growth and transformation.

On the one hand, the camp as a paradigm operates in a much more fluid way than the city. Despite its seemingly fragile appearance, it incorporates systems embedded with a great degree of elasticity and flexibility that are able to adapt to transformations within the environment. Like other ephemeral settlements, the extractive camp has the capacity to be constructed within a short period of time, also offering the possibility of being deconstructed at the same speed, often by just inverting the construction process. The camp as a configuration of settlements allows spaces to be actively created in response to the flows of people, transportation, goods, and communication, allowing a certain efficiency in fulfilling the basic needs of urban space. Within the camp paradigm, lightness, however, is not always desirable. Material lightness is often accompanied with the thinness of institutions, the predominance of the private, and the absence of any element that does not serve the quest for efficiency and

---

1. Giorgio Agamben, "The Camp as Nomos," in *Homo Sacer: Sovereign Power and Bare Life*, trans. Daniel Heller-Roazen (Stanford: Stanford University Press, 1998), 96.

productivity. In the camp, at different levels there is a lack of advocacy with regard to the rights to the city, because the city as a value is actually not present in the minds of those who set the rules. Camps, like cities that mimic the structure of the camp, are often manifested as unsustainable conditions that would not be allowed or easily accepted within cities. Going further along this line of argument, Agamben suggests that, "If the essence of the camp consists in the materialization of the state of exception, and in the subsequent creation of a space in which bare life and the juridical rule enter into a threshold of indistinction, then we must admit that we find ourselves virtually in the presence of a camp every time such a structure is created."[2]

In this sense, it is crucial to be able to recognize each of these structures when analyzing an urban system. But can we make a binary distinction as suggested by Agamben? Could we extrapolate from this argument that the urban is the result of resource extraction under the form of the camp, or at least that it is inscribed and governed under its logics? Are both these structures guided by opposed and irreconcilable logics? Are camps, or cities in contexts of natural resource extraction, really always meant to be consumed, destined to obsolescence and disappearance? If we accept these elements, we would then have to argue that settlements supporting extractive territories are destined then not to be cities, but rather camps struggling to fulfill their aspiration of becoming cities. An aspiration that is rarely – if ever – accomplished, perhaps because camps in the contexts of extraction are inherently acts of consumption.

There are clearly some evident distinctions that quickly come to mind when one has to choose between referring to a settlement as 'city' or a 'camp'. One, for instance, is the different temporal dimension associated with the camp versus the city – meaning whether the settlement can be considered a permanent or a temporary configuration, with the temporary more clearly alluding to the camp and permanent often associated with a city. One would also assume that if the settlement were impermanent, it would be built by default with light materials, like fabric or bamboo, or even recycled containers, while if it were constructed from more robust materials, like bricks or concrete, it would allude to being a city. One would then naturally assume that it would have the aspiration of being a more permanent configuration. This distinction, however, is not that clear when it comes to sites in contexts of extraction.

To loop back to Chuquicamata, which was built out of very solid materials and conceived as a very robust but impermanent mining camp. Even if many of its buildings were constructed with the latest technological features and were meant to last for many years, it was destined to be abandoned at a certain point. Another distinction

---

2. Giorgio Agamben, "The Camp as Nomos," 98.

that comes to mind might be the level of specificity that, as a settlement, a camp and a city have. One would presume that besides its materials, a camp would be mostly made out of residences, having an urban fabric with a less programmatic complexity. A refugee camp, for instance, would have the repetition of a similar basic unit of residential dwelling as the main componzent of its configuration. Public units would almost be absent, and the thickness of the fabric would not allow outside spaces to be recognized as public and accessible gathering spaces, unless crowds or events are held in the open. The same happens in a traditional mining camp, where efficiency-seeking public programs are usually incorporated as two or three basic programs, which are also very much related to keeping the bodies at work functional, meaning a gymnasium and bars. Chuquicamata, however, did not follow this pattern. It had a highly complex set of programs ranging from theaters to public squares. Some of the most important artists of the country went there to perform in its spaces. In addition, its public amenities were made to a very high standard, like its hospital, which was among one of the best in the country.

Thus, the initial distinctions we use for defining what a camp and what a city are, while in common language seem to be very straightforward and clear, are not that distinctive when looking closely at forms of camps that supersede the scale of a cluster or basic unit like the tent. In other words, binary distinctions such as permanent versus temporary or simple versus complex are in a way reductive when thinking about urbanism in contexts of extraction, as they mostly emanate from aesthetic considerations. Therefore, it is perhaps more productive to ask ourselves about the true nature of both configurations in order to be able the to recognize the structure of the camp and the structure of the city when we confront these readings. In doing so, one could argue that both their more radical and extreme manifestations are completely opposite paradigms of space production. They are extremely diverse in nature and often get aesthetically equalized in spite of their ontological differences. It is almost as if both camps and cities were often confused because, in cataloguing them, unproductive preconceptions are often used without taking into account deeper and more important elements of their real inner nature, distinguishing only using images of the permanent versus the ephemeral. In other words, cataloguing on a visual bias what looks like it is constructed to endure in time and be resilient and long-lasting versus what seems to be constructed for holding a temporary state of exception and being quickly disassembled, eroded, or absorbed is a limited method. For rather than their level of complexity, the materials from which they are made, or any set of particular attributes, that which really defines cities and camps is their different nature. In fact, there is a deeper distinction, a less evident one that relies on their modes of operation in the contexts in which they are immersed and on reading the real purpose that they fulfill or sustain.

In order to introduce a more nuanced discussion relating to these operational modalities and to overcome blind descriptions – dazzled perhaps by the evidence of external attributes – one would have to articulate the question of nature, of its deep structure, and to discuss what we really mean when we recognize something as a city and how that is different from what we would recognize as a camp. How do we find the right plane of comparison? For years, the nature of the city has been discussed in different ways, while the nature of the camp is in a way a more recent discussion. The nature of the city, for instance, has been discussed through attributes like morphology, readability, scale, and other such features. Mumford, for example, argues in *The Disappearing City*[3] that the true nature of the city relies exclusively on the significance of its form and its legibility. He argues that when modernity broke the correspondence between meaningful cultural significance and functionality, it actually dissolved the essence of the city, allowing the emergence of another shapeless and denaturalized construction. He was reacting to two forms of what he recognized as the 'anti-city' that were on the rise. On one side, he saw a city that was the product of the serial reproduction of buildings and, on the other side, the city with no borders, developing in horizontal extension. The appearance of suburbia as a predominant form was a case in point. Several years after that, the city as he knew it was absolutely transformed. Paradoxically, over the years the two models implicitly criticized by him would become the urban condition by default: either 'super-urbanism' as the urbanism of extreme densities, or 'sub-urbanism' as the urbanization of landscape. Today, form is no longer a code in which the essence of the city can be recognized. Cities became formless, and it is the same weakness of their form that in such a case is really their strength.

Another and perhaps more useful approach to set the ground for comparison might be the arguments proposed by Luis Wirth. In his piece, "Urbanism as a Way of Life," Wirth writes, "A sociologically significant definition of the city would seek to select those elements of urbanism which mark it as a distinctive mode of human life group."[4] He writes this essay trying to define the impact of new configurations of the urban on the systems of relations and the interactions of the people who inhabit them. He says that, "The contemporary world no longer presents a picture of small isolated groups of human beings scattered over a vast territory as Sumner described primitive societies," and thus he recognizes that things have changed but he places the nature of the city within the set of social interactions. Although he is aware that the built environment is undergoing major changes, for him these are not the transformations

---

3. Lewis Mumford, *The Disappearing City* (New York: Pantheon Books, c. 1986).
4. Louis Wirth, "Urbanism as a Way of Life," *The American Journal of Sociology,* 44(1) (Jul. 1938).

would affect the very nature of the city; instead, this would be ontologically a set of particular social relations that appear after given conditions of the built form, even if scale or morphology are defining the tone, type, and prototypes of relationships that appear within the urban fabric. Hence the true nature of the city would not be an issue of attributes like scale or morphology, but instead would be tied to the social and to the underlying principles that drive social transformations. The city would be in this sense a point of convergence of a series of vectors deployed as a gradient in the territory, defining different environments in which social relations can happen. In other words, for Wirth "cityness" is defined as a subtle entity, even perhaps an intangible one, which happens to rest on and use a physical structure that rather than determining interactions only supports them. In this sense the city, understood as a container for interactions, would not be the origin of the social fabric but rather a result of it.

In the same way, this is what happens when we think of the nature of camps; like the nature of cities, these would not then rely on their material attributes. It would not be density, size, or the accumulation of wealth that would define them. From Wirth's perspective, the condition of the city would not be a result of its architecture, the character of its buildings, or the product of their role in the economy, but rather ontologically the city would be a social phenomenon that evolves as the social modes of interaction evolve, then transforming the physical vessel that sustains them. In extending this argument, a true understanding of both types of settlements, the city and the camp, would then rise perhaps from a reflection on what Harvey eloquently calls the bridge between "sociological imagination" and "spatial consciousness" or "geographical imagination," as a much more nuanced reading of the camp and the city as spatial production paradigms, allowing a more politicized, culturally meaningful, and operative conceptual construction to frame this discussion. In order to construct such a deep reading of both the city and the camp as paradigms, it is useful to recall Arendt's expression of *"vita activa,"* which establishes three distinctions of human activities. She categorizes any human activity as (1) "labor," which refers to those activities, supporting biological processes proper of the human body; as (2) "work," which refers to the non-natural activities that allow people to construct an artificial world – different from the natural one – in which they are immersed; or as (3) "action," being the only activity that happens between people without the mediation of things or matter, the human condition of living in pluralities, that allows the emergence of the political condition of life. According to Agamben, camps would be – in their more radical condition, that of refugee camps – biopolitical spaces that can only host what he calls "bare life," which one could interpret as the proliferation of what Arendt denominates "labor," over "work" and "action;" This gets very clear when one looks at the balance between public and private space in current mining camps supporting the activities in the mining cluster of Calama. Design can certainly mediate the emergence of these diverse types of activities. For instance, when looking at current mining camps one can clearly identify a subjugation of "action" in the spirit of the supporting of "labor" and "work."[5]

Thus one could argue perhaps that within the city, the paradigm of space is configured in a way in which "labor" and "work" serve the proliferation of "action," whereas within the camp paradigm, "action" and "work" are in place mostly for supporting "labor." The predominance of labor over action is what seems to characterize the camp as a space production paradigm. It is in this sense that we can contextualize and understand what Agamben means when he says, "Today it is not the city but rather the camp that is the fundamental biopolitical paradigm of the West."[6] This does not refer to the fact that the physical materialization of cities is becoming lighter – which it is – or that the metabolism of cities is accelerating – which is also true –and therefore buildings are becoming more impermanent. It does not mean that cities aesthetically resemble camps, which would be a rather shallow expression. This actually means that the nature of human activities within the urban realm is changing and moving towards the supporting of 'labor' as the predominant human activity, rather than the fostering of 'action' in the political sense described by Arendt, as the stronger expression of the human condition. This transformation of the urban space is more evident and clear when we look at the challenges posed by landscapes of extraction, where efficiency is the predominant value. Similarly, Agamben's comments, which refer to this own thesis of the acknowledgement of this transformation, "throws a sinister light on the models by which social sciences, sociology, urban studies, and architecture today are trying to conceive and organize the public space of the world's cities without any clear awareness that at their very center lies the same bare life."[7]

Ephemeral Urbanism of Extraction as a category implies a highly efficient system that maximizes productivity, optimizes processes, and produces automated and standardized results. It is the perfect embodiment of the paradigm behind every extraction activity: efficiency. Indeed, it is efficiency that not only drives the layout of the site and the organization of the logistics, the spatial configuration, and the processing of the resources once they are already extracted, but also the same efficiency that constructs the conditions for bare life to be predominant and for "action" to retreat as secondary human activity. Harvey's sociological imagination or Wirth's urbanism as a way of life, along with any expression of the urban, in contexts of extraction are

---

5. To go further into depth on this subject, see Hannah Arendt, *The Human Condition*, 2nd rev. ed. (Chicago: University of Chicago Press, 1998).
6. Giorgio Agamben, "The Camp as Nomos," 176.
7. Ibid, 102.

in a way filtered through the efficiency matrix, and therefore are "distilled" or even "deprived" from their "citiness" in order to fulfill their main purpose: to accommodate people for a limited period of time, providing minimum levels of comfort and human interaction.

In a way, as counterparts of cities, camps have been seen as discreet transitory spaces outside the urban realm, even when they are located inside the urban fabric, as in the case of massive transactional markets or slums. In fact, the notion of informality has relegated the idea of the camp just to its aesthetic expression. As the spaces of the impermanent, camps have occupied relatively secondary spaces, as pieces of land that are usually equated with the basic and precarious. However, the camp itself, as the materialization of the state of exception, has transcended the boundaries of temporary use as the space in which the efficiency matrix has subjugated "action," blurring the indistinctive threshold of what is juridically permitted and ethically acceptable. It is within this context that we are challenged by the need to develop tools for intervening and thinking about these non-permanent configurations – tools that will propel us to establish a productive understanding of the aspirations that define the patterns of growth and use and the emerging form of occupation in the broader global territory. Design must find a way to return to this space of human "action," of meaningful political intervention in these productive landscapes that define the category of Ephemeral Urbanism for Extraction.

01. Añelo, Argentina; 02. Pabellón del Inca Hotel, Chile; 03. María Elena, Chile; 08. Salar de Olaroz, Argentina; 09. Chuquicamata, Chile; 10. Morococha Mine, Peru; 11. Escondida, Chile; 12. South Belridge Oil Field, USA; 16. El Salvador, Chile; 17. Tierras Bajas Project, Bolivia; 20. Macaé, Brazil; 21. Pico Truncado, Argentina; 22. Guerrero Negro, Mexico; 25. Hull-Rust-Mahoning Mine, USA; 27. Athabasca Oil Sands, Canada; 29. Yanacocha, Peru; 32. Cerrado Soy Fields, Brazil; 33. Betze-Post Mine, USA; 34. Louisiana Offshore Oil Port, USA; 35. Potash Phosphate Mine, USA; 36. Donnie Oil Extraction Wells, USA; 37. Orinoco Belt Oil Fields, Venezuela; 41. Chevron Oil Refinery, USA; 46. Arctic Oil Extraction, Arctic; 49. Cerrejón, Colombia; 53. San Cristóbal Mine, Bolivia; 54. Alaska Ranger, Alaska; 55. Diavik Mine, Canadá; 60. Carajás Mine, Brazil; 62. Exuma, The Bahamas; 64. El Bagre Gold Mine, Colombia; 66. Bakken Oil Fields, USA; 74. Kidd Creek, Canada; 76. Greighton Mine, Canada; 77. Kennecott Mine, USA; 84. Bonneville Salt, USA; 85. Arizaro Salt, Argentina; 86. Uyuni Salt, Bolivia; 88. Cantarell, Mexico

42 | Felipe Vera, Rahul Mehrotra

18. Norilsk, Siberia; 24. Bor Undur Mine, Mongolia; 44. Ulan Bator, Mongolia; 47. Mirny Mine, Russia; 48. Kai Xin Factory Trawler, China; 59. Kumtor Gold Mine, Kyrgyzstan; 92. Samotlor, Russia; 96. Priobskoye, Russia; 104. Samotlor, Russia; 105. Fedorovo-Surguts, Russia

Towards an Ephemeral Urbanism for Extraction | **43**

04. Kiruna, Sweden; 05. Kimberley Mine, South Africa; 06. Chevron Oil Refenery, South Africa; 13. Nahalal, Israel; 14.Oil Rocks, Azerbaijan; 23. Creil, Netherlands; 26. Sandiola Gold Mine, Mali; 30. Obuasi Gold Mine, Ghana; 38. Gartzweiler Surface Mine, Germany; 39. Ffos y Fran, United Kingdom; 40. Belchatow Coal Mine, Poland; 43. Jubail, Saudi Arabia; 51. Orapa Diamond Mine, Botswana; 56. Tapline, Saudi Arabia; 57. Garzweiler Mine, Germany; 58. Catoca Mine, Angola; 61. GreenLand, Greenland; 65. Morila Gold Mine, Mali; 67 Mponeng Gold Mine, South Africa; 68. TauTona Gold Mine, South Africa; 69. Savuka Gold Mine, South Africa; 70. Driefontein Gold Mine, South Africa; 71. Kusasalethu Gold Mine, South Africa; 72. Moab Khotsong, South Africa; 73. South Deep Gold Mine, South Africa; 75. Noligwa Gold Mine, South Africa; 80. Venetia Diamond Mine, South Africa; 81. Grib Diamond Mine, Russia; 82. Jwaneng Diamond Mine, Botswana; 87. Ghawar, Saudi Arabia; 89. Sufaniyah, Saudi Arabia; 90. Rumaila N&S, Irak; 91. Greater Burgan, Kuwait; 93. Ahwaz, Irán; 94. Zakum, Abu Dhabi; 95. Azeri-Chirag-Guneshli, Azerbaijan; 97. Bu Hasa, Abu Dhabi; 98. Marun, Irán; 99. Raudhatain, Iran; 100. Gachsaran, Iran; 101. Qatif, Saudi Arabia; 102. Shaybah, Saudi Arabia; 106. Zuluf, Saudi Arabia

44 | Felipe Vera, Rahul Mehrotra

07. Grasberg Mine, Indonesia; 15. Mount Whaleback Mine, Australia; 19. Fish Farm, Hong Kong; 28. Duri Oil Field, Indonesia; 31. Marine Acquaculture, China; 42. Seaweed Farms, Indonesia; 45. Ranger Mine, Australia; 50. Super Pit Gold Mine, Australia; 52. Udachnaya, Russia; 63. Oyu Tolgoi Copper Mine, Mongolia; 78. Yubileyny Diamond Mine, Russia; 79. Argyle Diamond Mine, Australia; 83. Botuobinskaya Diamond Mine, Russia; 103. Saertu, China

Towards an Ephemeral Urbanism for Extraction

omething is clear, is that
t is time to move on

1. TIMELINE_EXTRACTION

CASE NAME	AREA (KM2)	PEOPLE
1. Añelo, Argentina	2,5	5.000
2. Pabellon del Inca hotel, Chile	0,5	1.800
3. Maria Elena, Chile	7,5	4.600
4. Kiruna City, Sweden	16	18.148
5. Kimberley Diamond, S. Africa	0,04	1.800
6. Chevron Oil Refenery, S. Africa	2	4.600
7. Grasberg Mine, Indonesia	9	19.500
8. Salar de Olaroz, Argentina	350	350
9. Chuquicamata, Chile	8	25.000
10. Morococha, Peru	0,7	5.000
11. Escondida, Chile	54	8.000
12. South Belridge Oil Field, U.S.A.	630	400
13. Nahalal, Israel	3	907
14. Oil Rocks, Azerbaijan	190	5.000
15. Mount Whaleblack, Australia	20	8.000
16. El Salvador, Chile	2	8.697
17. Tierras Bajas Project, Bolivia	250	250.000
18. Norilsk, Siberia	32	1.800
19. Fish Farm, H. Kong	11	21.000
20. Macae, Brazil	1.216	212.433
21. Pico Truncado, Argentina	11	21.000
22. Gerrero Negro, Mexico	16	13.054
23. Creil, Netherlands	23	1.600
24. Bor Undur Mine, Mongolia	144	8.510
25. Hull-Rust-Mahoning, U.S.A.	13	16.361
26. Sandiola Gold Mine, Mali	302	1.500
27. Athabasca Oil Sands, Canada	60	8.000
28. Duri Oil Field, Indonesia	324	7.000
29. Yanacocha, Peru	51	2.303
30. Obuasi Gold Mine, Ghana	1,5	5.700

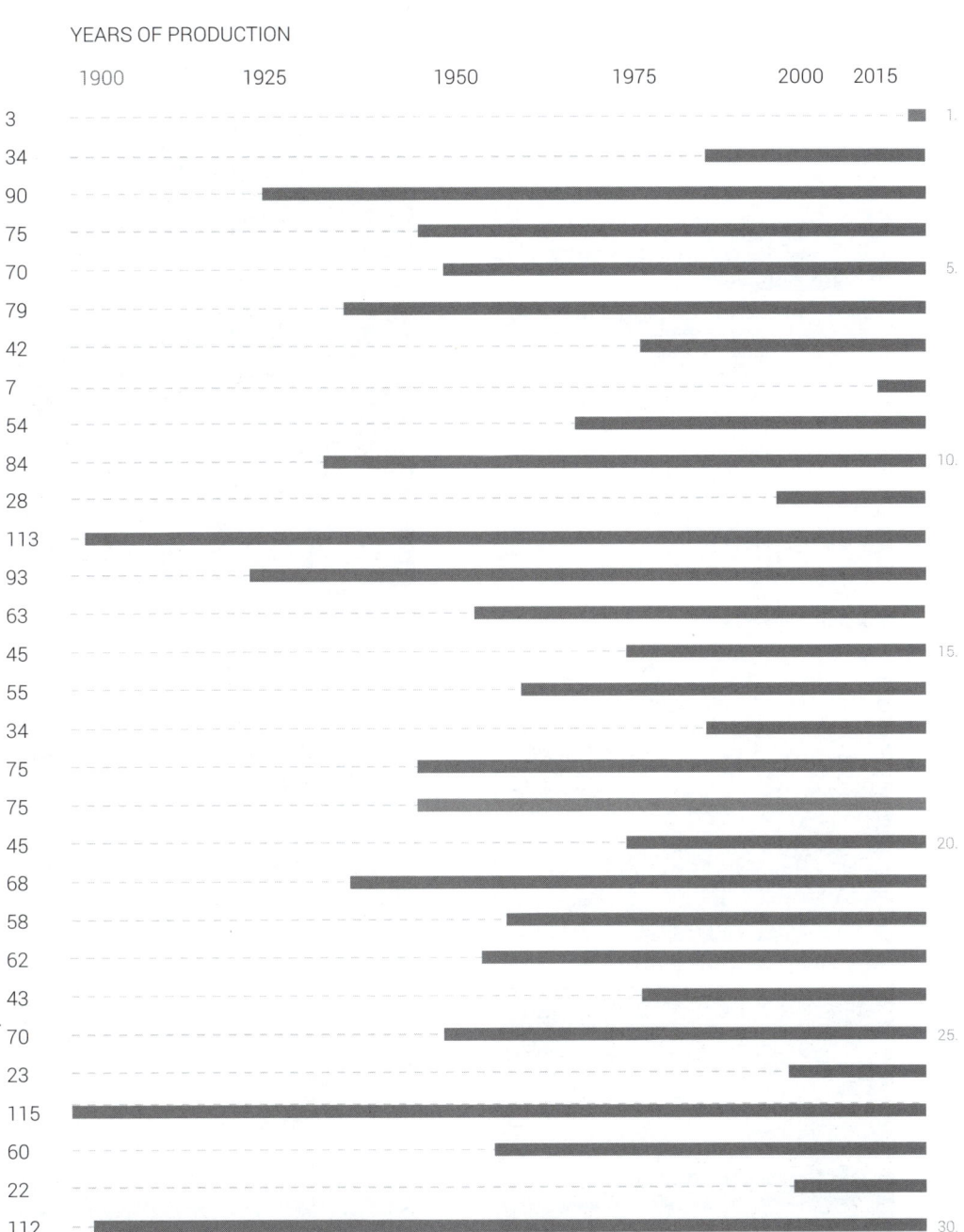

Towards an Ephemeral Urbanism for Extraction | 49

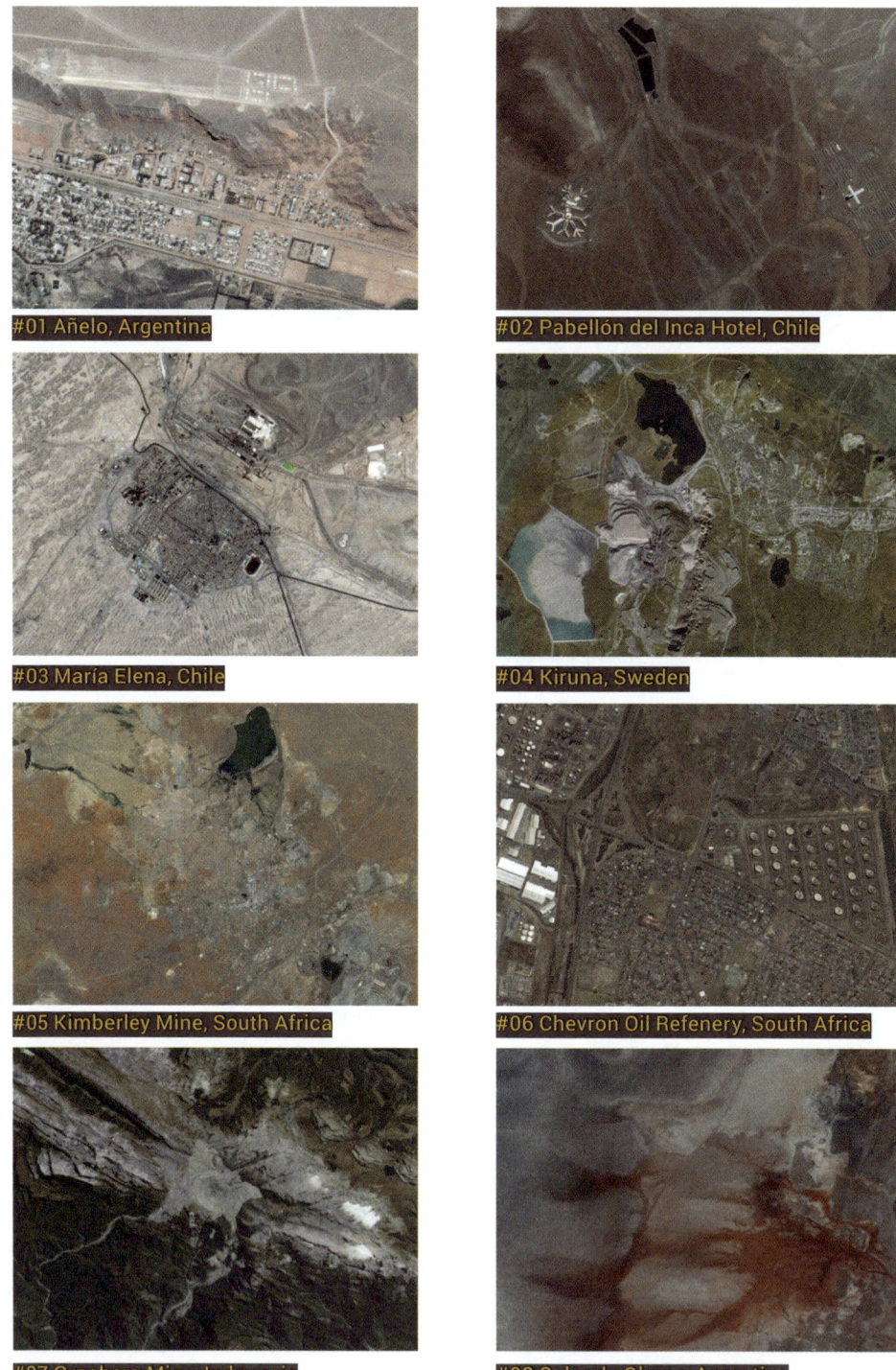

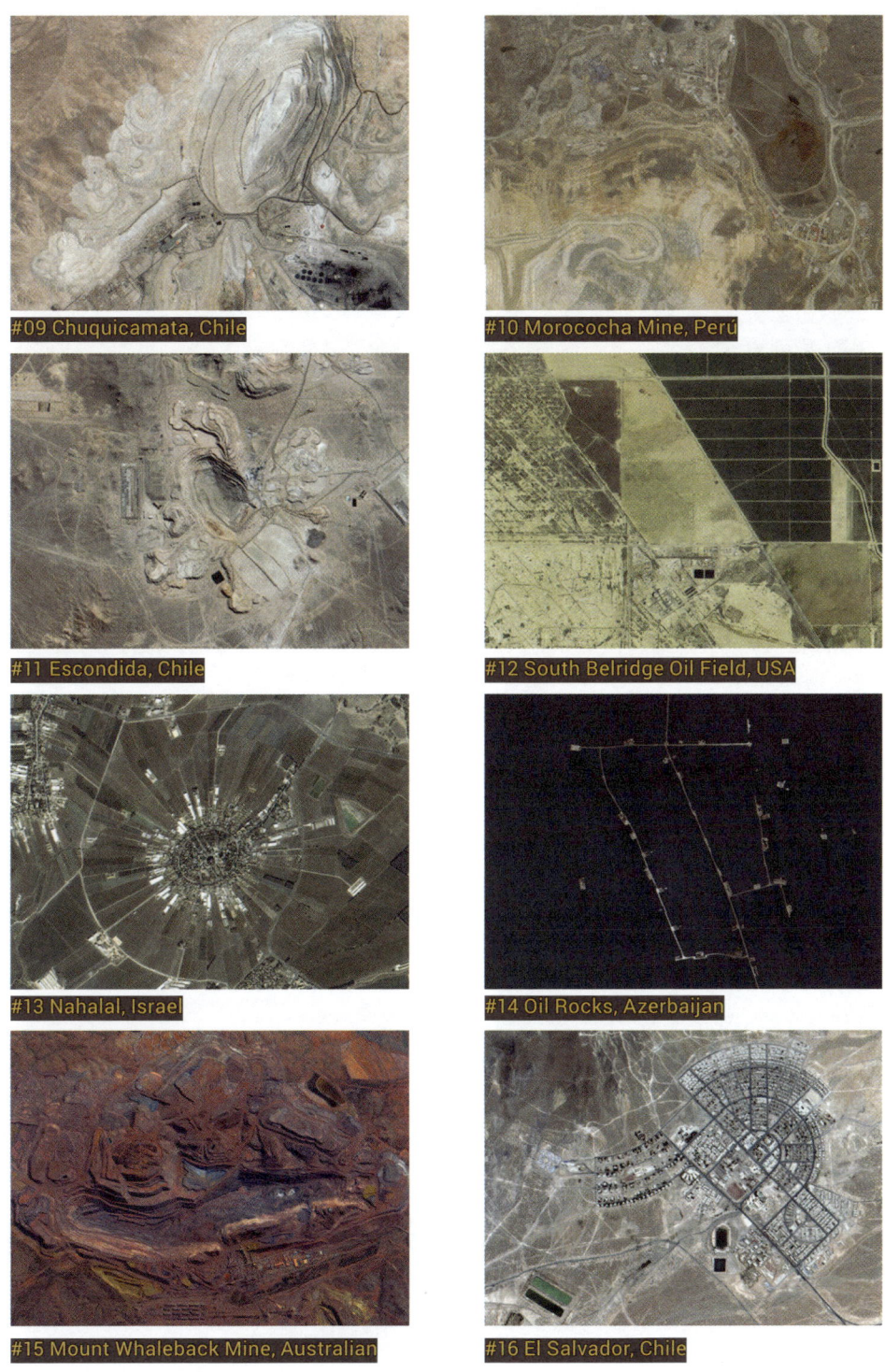

Towards an Ephemeral Urbanism for Extraction | 51

Name **Añelo**
Location **Neuquen, Argentina**
Area **2.5 km2**
Population **5000 dwellers**
Duration **3 years**

Añelo, where YPF launched its shale oil project, doubled its population in 3 years. Today, it has 5,000 inhabitants, and it is expected to grow up to 30,000 in 15 years. The expansion initiative involves a 250 hectares industrial park and an urban project.

#01

Name **Pabellón del Inca Hotel**
Location **Collahuasi, Chile**
Area **0,5 km2**
Population **1800 dwellers**
Duration **34 years**

This settlement, located in the Chilean altiplano at an altitude of 3,850 meters, belongs to Doña Inés de Collahuasi's mining company. It has all the necessary facilities for its inhabitation, and its design included a landscape intervention.

#02

Name **María Elena**
Location **Chile**
Area **7,5 km2**
Population **4600 dwellers**
Duration **90 years**

Situated on land purchased from the Treasury in 1924, the plant was inaugurated in 1926 with the sodium nitrate extraction system patented by the Guggenheim Brothers, which replaced the Shanks system. Its layout was made based on the flag of the United Kingdom.

#03

Name **Kiruna**
Location **Sweden**
Area **16 km2**
Population **18148 dwellers**
Duration **75 years**

Añelo, where YPF launched its shale oil project, doubled its population in 3 years. Today, it has 5,000 inhabitants, and that number is expected to grow up to 30,000 in 15 years. The expansion initiative involves an industrial park (250 hectars) and an urban project with a budget of Kingdom.

#04

Name **Kimberley Mine**
Location **South Africa**
Area **0,04 km2**
Population **1800 dwellers**
Duration **70 years**

Kimberley is the capital of the Northern Cape province in South Africa and is known as the 'Diamond City' due to its proximity to the mine where operations started in the 1870s. From 1871 to 1914 almost 50,000 miners worked on the excavation.

#05

Name **Chevron Oil Refinery**
Location **Cape Town, South Africa**
Area **2 km2**
Population **4600 dwellers**
Duration **79 years**

The Caltex/Chevron Refinery in Cape Town is one of the largest in South Africa with an output of 100,000 barrels per day. The proximity of the complex and residential areas resulted in the implementation of stringent environmental restrictions.

#06

Name **Grasberg Mine**
Location **Indonesia**
Area **9 km2**
Population **19500 dwellers**
Duration **42 years**

The Grasberg mine is the largest gold mine and the second largest cooper reserve in the world. It is located in the Papúa province, Indonesia, and it has 19,500 employees.

#07

Name **Salar de Olaroz**
Location **Argentina**
Area **350 km2**
Population **350 dwellers**
Duration **7 years**

The Salar de Olaroz mine is one of the largest lithium mines in Argentina. The mine is located in northern Argentina in the Jujuy Province. The Salar de Olaroz mine has reserves amounting to 619 million tons of lithium ore grading 0.2% lithium resulting in 1.21 million tons of lithium.

#08

Name **Chuquicamata**
Location **Chile**
Area **8 km2**
Population **25000 dwellers**
Duration **54 years**

Inaugurated in 1882, Chuquicamata is the largest open copper mine in the world, and it belongs to the Chilean government company Codelco. The growth of this mine forced the displacement of the population in the adjacent town.

#09

Name **Morococha Mine**
Location **Perú**
Area **0.7 km2**
Population **5000 dwellers**
Duration **84 years**

Morococha is a town that originated at an altitude of 4,700 meters. Four centuries after its creation it will apparently disappear as a result of all of the extraction activities of its natural resources.

#10

Name **Escondida**
Location **Antofagasta, Chile**
Area **54 km2**
Population **8000 dwellers**
Duration **28 years**

Escondida is a copper mine located at an altitude of 3,100 meters in the Atacama Desert, Chile. This mine, whose construction started in 1988, is the largest extractor of copper in the world.

#11

Name **South Belridge Oil Field**
Location **Belridge, California, USA**
Area **630 km2**
Population **400 dwellers**
Duration **113 years**

The Belridge Oil Compound is a large oil field located in northwestern Kern Country in San Joaquin Valley, California. Discovered in 1911, it is one of the largest oil producers in California and by 2008 had accumulated 1.5 billion barrels of oil.

#12

Name **Nahalal**
Location **Israel**
Area **3 km2**
Population **907 dwellers**
Duration **93 years**

Nahalal is the first cooperative agricultural community composed of individual farms, called moshav. Nahalal is based in concentric circles, with the urban zone in the center and the fields and parks on the exterior.

#13

Name **Oil Rocks**
Location **Azerbaijan**
Area **190 km2**
Population **5000 dwellers**
Duration **63 years**

There are a number of massive artificial peninsulas extending offshore from the Azerbaijani city of Baku. The most famous of these is known as Oil Rocks, an offshore metropolis of semi-abandoned oil extraction platforms in the Caspian Sea.

#14

Name **Mount Whaleback Mine**
Location **Pilbara, Australia**
Area **20 km2**
Population **8000 dwellers**
Duration **45 years**

This iron mine is located in the Pilbara region in Western Australia. The mine is majority-owned by BHP Billiton which is the second-largest iron ore mining company in the Pilbara.

#15

Name **El Salvador**
Location **Chile**
Area **2 km2**
Population **8697 dwellers**
Duration **55 years**

El Salvador, originally a mining town, is located between the Andes range and the Atacama Desert, at an elevation of 2,300 meters. Its economy is based on copper mining and while at its peak it had a population of 24,000 inhabitants; today it has just around 7,000.

#16

Towards an Ephemeral Urbanism for Extraction

Añelo
Type: Oil

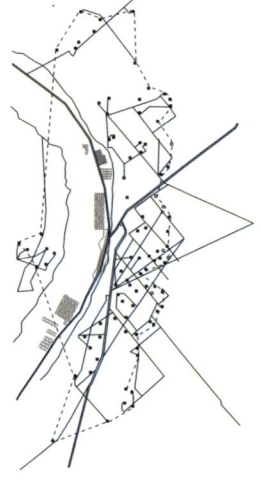

Pabellon del Inca Hotel
Type: Oil

Maria Elena
Type: Nitrate

El Salvador
Type: Copper

Tierras Bajas
Type: Agriculture

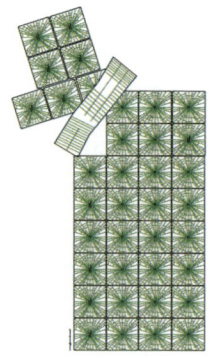

Athabasca
Type: Oil

Mahoning
Type: Iron

Kimberley
Type: Diamond

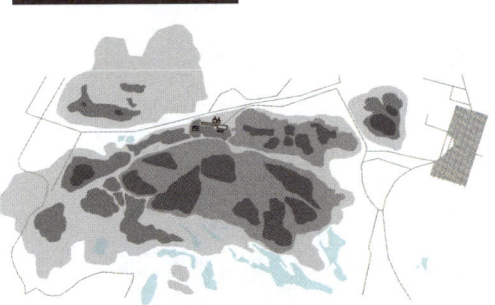

Duri Fields
Type: Oil

China Acquaculture
Type: Acquaculture

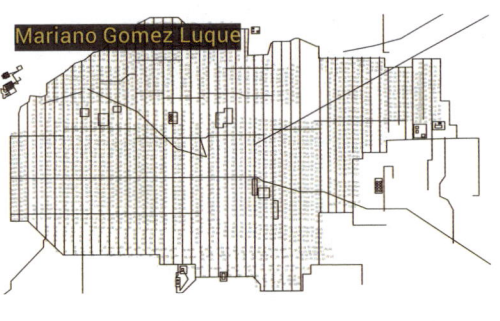
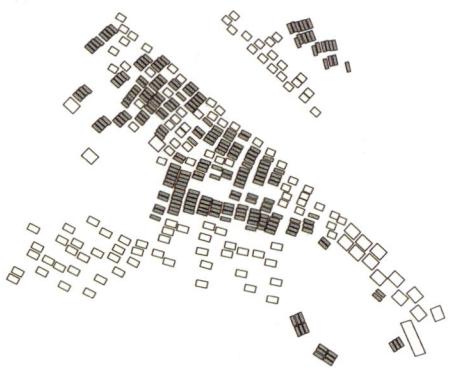

Nahalal
Type: Agriculture

Oil Rocks
Type: Oil

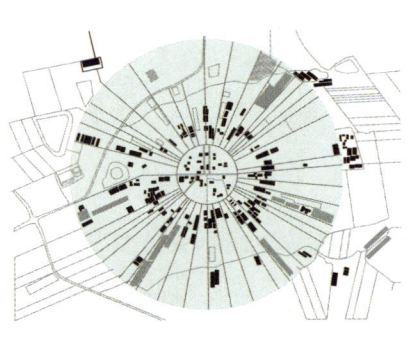
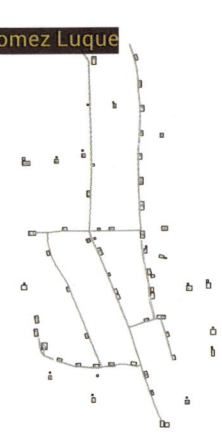

Towards an Ephemeral Urbanism for Extraction

Diavik Diamond Mine, Canada

Seaweed farm, Indonesia

Before operations

After operations

María Elena, Chile

01. Town, and the extraction facilities near it.
02. Territorial scars.
03. Logistic landscape of extraction.
04. Town plus logistic landscape plus connectivity network.

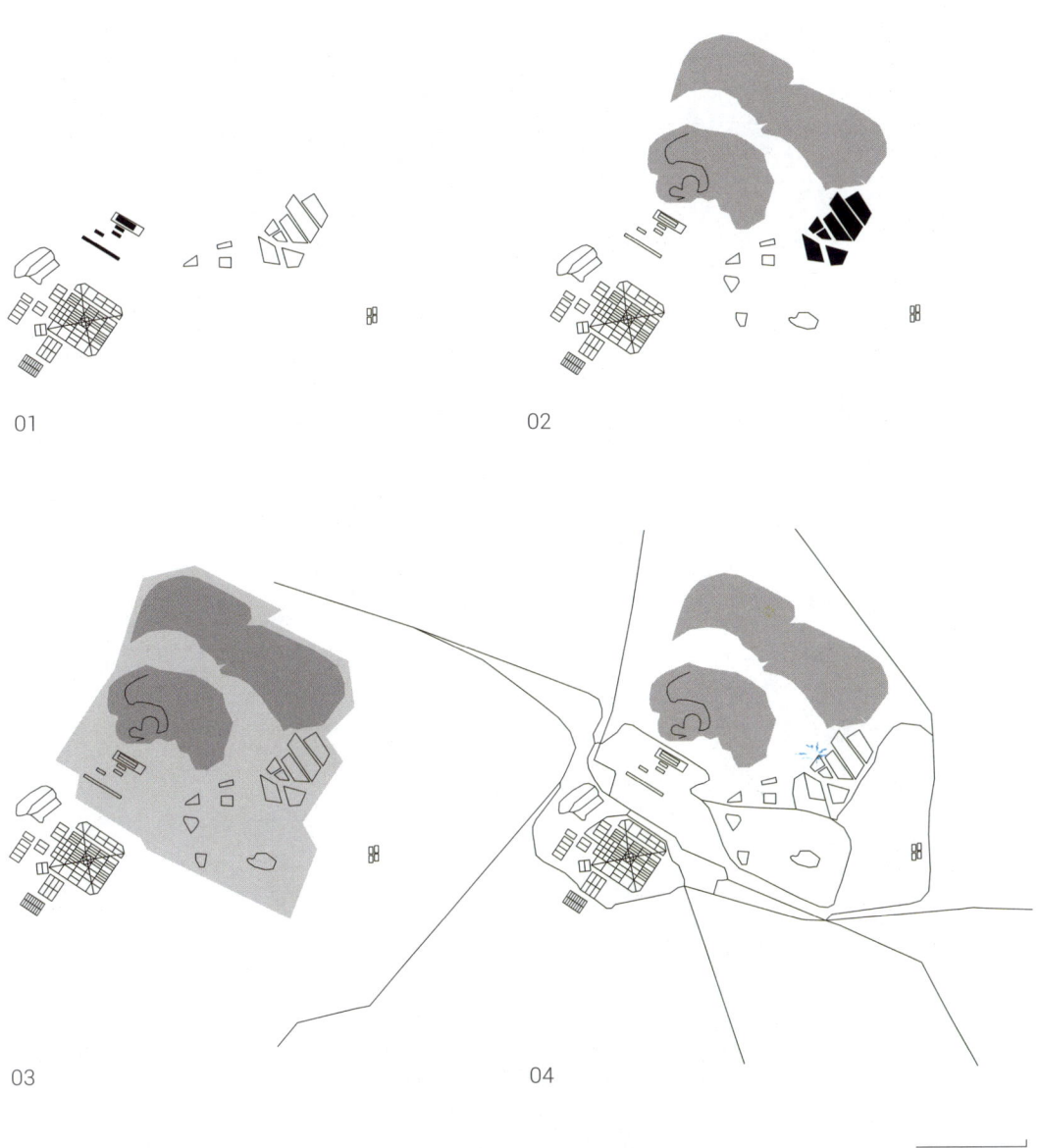

Mariano Gomez Luque

Towards an Ephemeral Urbanism for Extraction | **61**

Nahalal, Israel

01. General geometry plus extended parcels.
02. Radial segmentation plus buildings.
03. Connectivity network.
04. Full system.

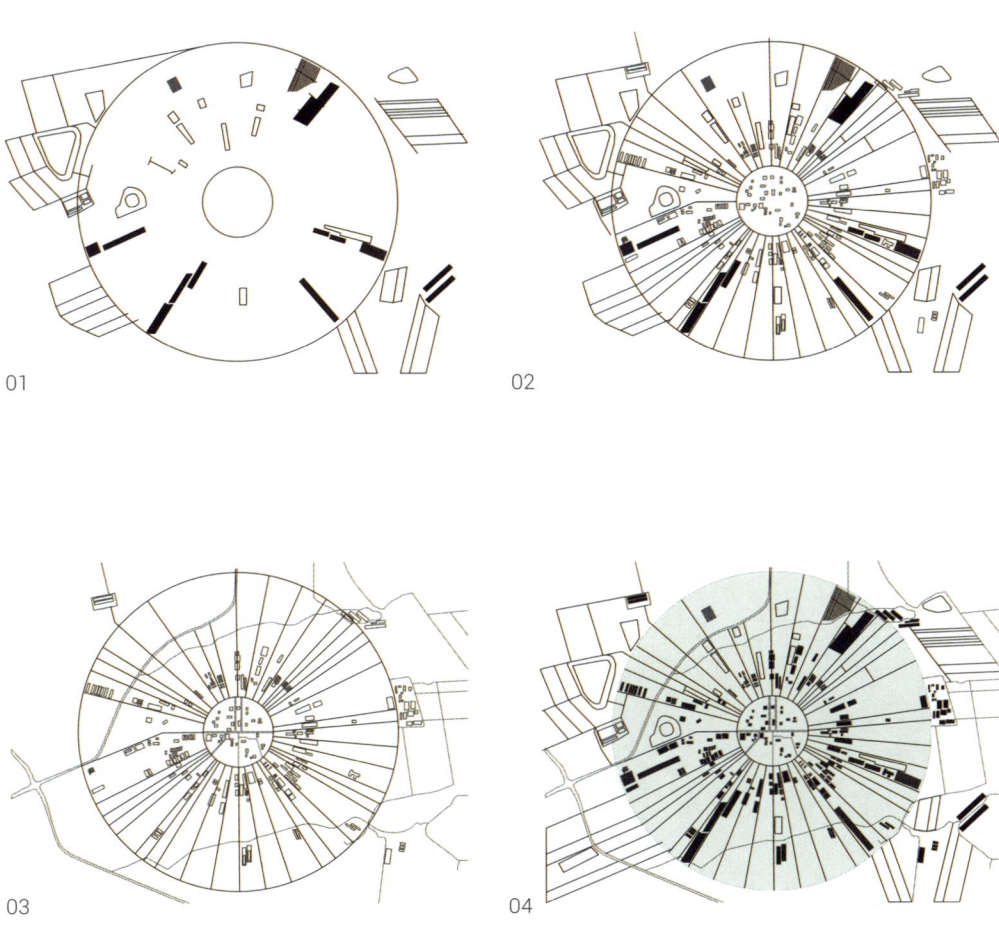

Mariano Gomez Luque

Towards an Ephemeral Urbanism for Extraction | **63**

Pabellón del Inca Hotel, Chile

01. The Hotel and its logistic site. Distance: around 1 Km.
02. Infrastructure of extraction deployed on site.
03. Main connection system, and site excavated.
04. Full system: the Hotel as a "residential" terminal of extraction activities, articulated via a network of circulation paths.

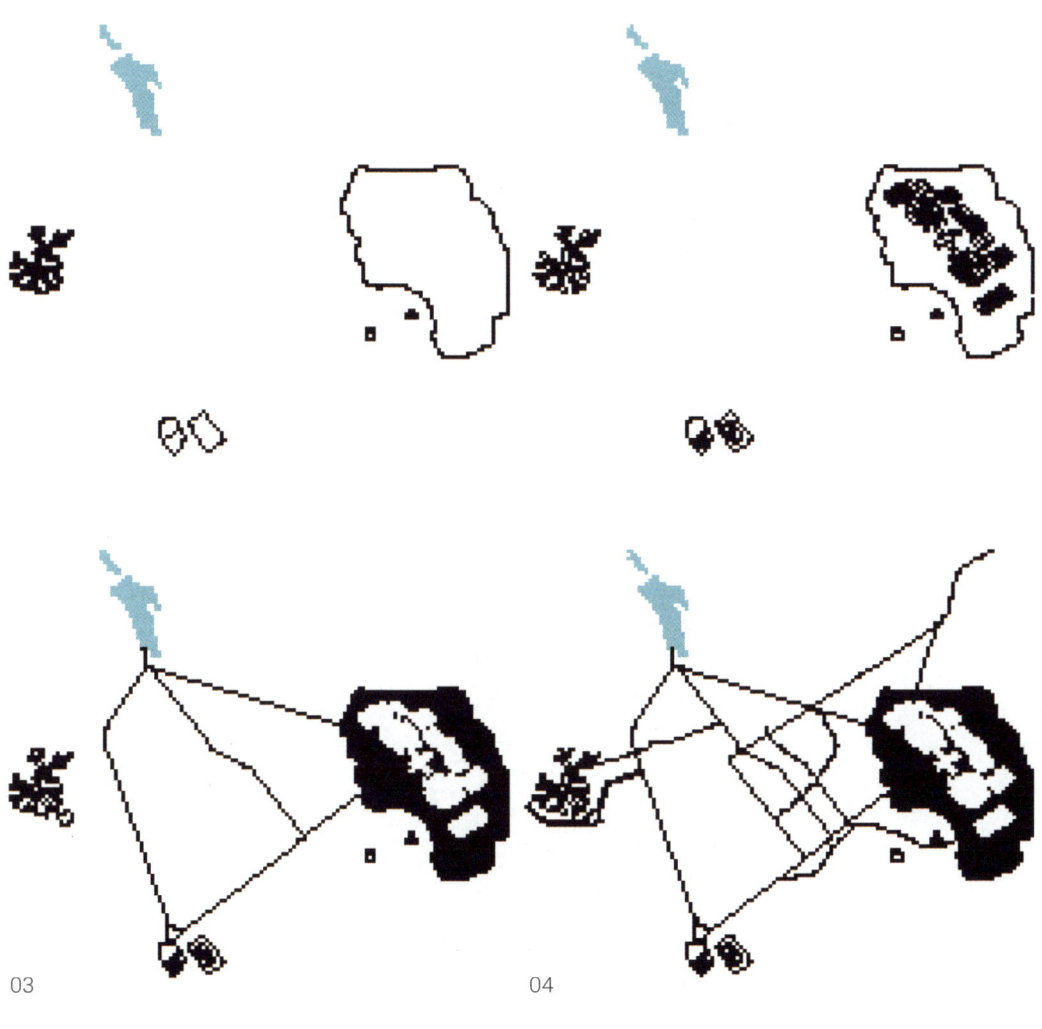

Mariano Gomez Luque

Towards an Ephemeral Urbanism for Extraction

Calama's landscape, Agustina Gonzaléz Cid, 2015

Resource Territories:
Hassi Messaoud Oil Urbanism
Rania Ghosn, El Hadi Jazairy

View of Hassi Messaoud_Bases-Vie

From Resource Metabolism to Resource Territories

In *Homo Geographicus*, Robert Sack notes that, "We humans are geographical beings transforming the earth and making it into a home, and that transformed world affects who we are."[1] He adds that the consequences of our geographical agency are more pressing because we are now "geographical leviathans." This geographic perspective informs our relations with the Earth's forces and materials, or what we call "resources". Parts of nature are thus abstracted as a thing that can be bought and sold – reducing its qualities to its exchange value.

The economy of natural resources requires the de-territorialization and re-territorialization of products from the extraction hole to the whole world,[2] or what has been conceptualized as metabolism. Promulgated by discoveries on the vascular system, the "ideology of circulation" drew on physiological analogies but also mirrored the accelerating mobility conditions of capital, people, resources, and information.[3] By the mid-nineteenth century, architects and planners began to speak of the city and of the territory mobilizing the scientific analogies of metabolism and circulation as key to spatial organization. Terms such as "hybrid natures" and "cyborg cities" have contributed to probing the legacies of modernist divisions between the human and the nonhuman, the social and the material, the city and nature. They convey the imperative for a simultaneous consideration of the production and reproduction of nature and power, for "Once we begin to speak of people mixing their labor with the earth, we are in a whole world of new relations between people and nature."[4] The modern transformation of the city, highly dependent on the mastery of territorial resources, was thus linked with the representation of cities as consisting of and functioning through complex networks of circulatory systems, the veins and arteries of which extended across the land and were to be freed from all possible sources of blockage.[5] While all very significant, such concepts remain insufficient, however, for theorizing the political relations that underpin the harvesting of the earth's materials and the formation of urban settlements.[6]

---

1. Robert Sack, Homo Geographicus (Baltimore: Johns Hopkins University Press, 1997), 1.
2. Gavin Bridge, "The Hole World: Scales and Spaces of Extraction," New Geographies 2: Landscapes of Energy, ed. Rania Ghosn (Cambridge, MA: Harvard GSD, 2010), 43–50.
3. Richard Sennett, Flesh and Stone: The Body and the City in Western Civilization (New York: W.W. Norton, 1994).
4. Raymond Williams, "Ideas of Nature," Culture and Materialism: Selected Essays (London: Verso, 1980), 76.
5. Erik Swyngedouw, "Circulations and Metabolisms: (Hybrid) Natures and (Cyborg) Cities", Science as Culture, 15(2) (2006): 105–121; Erik Swyngedouw and Kaika, Maria, "Fetishizing the Modern City," International Journal of Urban and Regional Research, 24(2) (2000): 120–138.
6. Erik Swyngedouw, "The City as a Hybrid: On Nature, Society and Cyborg Urbanization," Capitalism, Nature, Socialism 7 (1997): 65–80; Erik Swyngedouw, "Circulations and Metabolisms: (Hybrid) Natures and (Cyborg) Cities", 105–121; Matthew Gandy, "Rethinking Urban Metabolism: Water, Space and the Modern City," City 8(3) (2004): 363 – 379.

Donna Haraway reminds us that discourses of biology and organisms have "a plot with a structure and function [...] fashioned into factual truth, with intentionality in narration."[7] Biological metaphors instrumentalize the image of the objectivity of science to ideologically explicit ends, in particular as they naturalize the politics of accumulation and circulation.

They favor homeostasis, or a condition of balance of flows, to dismiss blockage, friction, and violence as the necessary corollaries of circulation. The image of objectivity that such scientific analogies perpetuate blurs the boundary between scientific rationalization and social control,[8] between the political economy of circulation and the emergent forms of territorialities. Rather than the annihilation of territory by circulatory networks, this chapter makes clear that territorial organization is necessary to insure the metabolism of resources.[9]

Resource Territories
Through the case study of Hassi Messaoud's oil urbanism, this chapter asserts territory as the inevitable partner of resource metabolism. As the largest single item in international trade, both in value and weight, oil requires a large technological system to extract, transport, and deliver. The exploitation of oil resources is grounded in forms of territories; it is enabled by a large infrastructural system to extract what is deemed "valuable matter" from the earth and by the sovereign's authority to legitimatize rights and demarcate zones of operation. Often operating in peripheral areas, regions that until the deployment of the industry were isolated from central power and unconnected to national and regional networks, the extractive logistics of resources "develop" the frontier by deploying roads, ancillary services, and security posts. Resources are not only spatially produced, but also produce new spatial configurations. Resource outposts attract people with their opportunities for labor and other economic mobility; their associated structures of work, housing, and health and social services give a specific material shape to people's lives. The resource system fixates itself in space and, in the process, materializes a territory – simultaneously epistemological and geographical – that harnesses its own geography of places and relations. Within this framework, the resource system is a "technical zone," a set of coordinated but widely dispersed regulations, calculative arrangements, infrastructures, and technical procedures that render certain objects or flows governable.[10]

---

7. Donna Haraway, Primate Visions (New York: Routledge, 1989), 4.
8. Matthew Gandy, "Introduction," Concrete & Clay: Reworking Nature in New York City, (Cambridge: MIT Press, 2002).
9. David Harvey, Spaces of Capital: Towards a Critical Geography (Edinburgh: Edinburgh University Press, 2001), 328.
10. Andrew Barry, "Technological Zones," European Journal of Social Theory 9.2 (2006): 23–53. Gavin Bridge "Global Production Networks and the Extractive Sector: Governing Resource-Based Development," Journal of Economic Geography (2008): 389–419.

Historically, the management of natural resources has been mediated and enabled through the consolidation of power over nature in the form of the concession territory, a right granted by a central political authority to extract value. Territory is the form of power over geography that interweaves political processes, material metabolism, and spatial form. The Oxford English Dictionary shows that in the late sixteenth and early seventeenth centuries, "population" referred to "a peopled or inhabited place."[11] The subsequent construction of population as an object of government dissociated population from place in favor of territory as a geographic appellation that ties the governor to the economy and security. It is "a rendering of space as a political category: owned, distributed, mapped, calculated, bordered, and controlled,"[12] and as such is *reformed* with every claim over space. "The relation to the earth as property," as Marx claims in the *Grundrisse*, is hence "always mediated through occupation of the land and soil, peacefully or violently."[13] In *Terror and Territory*, Stuart Elden draws on two etymologies of territory; *terra* "piece of earth," a terrain that sustains and nourishes the people and *terrere* "to frighten," a place from which people are warned off, and which is closely associated with the maintenance and survival of the state over its territory.[14] The linkage between "terror" and "territory," as William Connolly insinuates, "is more than merely coincidental [...] To occupy territory is to receive sustenance and to exercise violence."[15] Territory becomes the object and site for the negotiation of the state's extractive capital and the state's public expenditures.

In rentier economies, which derive all or a substantial portion of their national revenues from the rent of resources, the management of resource metabolism is entrusted to the sovereign. The notions of territory and sovereignty are thus intertwined with the state's control of economic resources embedded in its land, operationalized to govern population and to settle and secure the national territory. This is particularly significant for a socialist rentier state where the government relies completely on its oil revenues to cover public expenditures, not least its investment in housing, education, and the military. Far from leading to consensus and cooperation, commodified nature becomes at times an item of contestation inserted into often deeply unequal and unsettled sets of social relations, in which the state holds the monopoly of both violence and resources. Rather than abolishing or transcending the violence

---

11. Stephen Legg, "Foucault's Population Geographies: Classifications, Biopolitics and Governmental Spaces," Population Space Place 11 (2005): 137–156.
12. Stuart Elden, "Governmentality, Calculation, Territory," Environment and Planning D: Society and Space 25(3) (2007): 562 – 580.
13. Karl Marx, Grundrisse: Foundations of the Critique of Political Economy (New York, Vintage Books, 1973), 485.
14. Stuart Elden, Terror and Territory: The Spatial Extent of Sovereignty (Minneapolis: University of Minnesota Press, 2009), xxviii-xxix.
15. William Connolly, "Tocqueville, Territory, and Violence," Challenging Boundaries: Global Flows, Territorial Identities, ed. M. .J. Shapiro and H. R. Alker (Minneapolis: University of Minnesota Press, 1996), 141 – 64.

necessary for extracting resources, the character of rentier economies bestows thus the role of landlord upon the state. Hence, the contradiction between the territory of the resource and that of the sovereign is not abolished, but is taken to a higher level as "capital now faces the territory of the nation-state as the external obstacle to be conquered and internalized."[16] The co-production of resources and the social order highlights resource geographies as sites where actors negotiate their political rationalities. From this perspective, territory is understood as a constitutive dimension of production, a tool for government, and a stake of contestation in itself. Rather than being eroded by metabolic flows, territory is reordered by resource economies. How does the state negotiate the circulatory imperatives of the "least possible friction in space" with the territorial imperatives or promises of resource systems to fix population and settlement in place?

North African Energy Imaginaries

A growing body of architectural visions is engaging resource territories and imaginaries. Over the last decade, AMO/OMA has explored the possibilities of a new energy policy in Europe in relation to climate and security concerns. Amongst these projects, *Roadmap 2050* was initiated by the European Climate Foundation to develop a practical plan to reduce Europe's CO_2 emissions by 80 percent by 2050. Towards this new architecture, AMO contributed graphic narratives about the geographic, political, and cultural implications of a zero-carbon power sector. The envisioned project rests on a specialized and networked regionalism. The new continent, European, is redefined by its energy sources; Ireland and the western half of England are the "tidal states," while the eastern half forms part of the "isles of wind." Former Yugoslavia is reunited as "Biomassburg", and for our interests, most of Spain, Italy, Greece, and some of North Africa become "Solaria." The rendering of Solaria, "Parisian Energy from Sahara Sun," abstracts one side of the Mediterranean in the icon of the Parisian metropolis – the Eiffel Tower – and the North African side in a caravan of camels traveling across a field of solar panels.[17] (Fig. 1)

The rendering echoes earlier imaginaries and energy geographies, in which North Africa has fuelled the fantastic and materialist aspirations of Europe. As early as 1920, the German architect and engineer Herman Sorgel conceived Atlantropa, a project for a 35-kilometer-long hydroelectric dam across the Strait of Gibraltar, which presented the Mediterranean South as a huge power plant that could ensure energy and economic security for an enlarged Europe, as a counterweight to rising American and Asian power. The project remained on paper. The energy relations between North and South materialized later in the century with a set of pipelines underneath the

---

16. Mazen Labban, *Space, Oil, and Capital* (London: Routledge, 2008), 53.
17. For a more detailed reading of Roadmap 2050, refer to Rania Ghosn, "Energy Regions: Production without Representation," *Journal of Architectural Education* 68(2) (2014): 224-228.

Mediterranean that connected the oil and gas fields of Africa to European markets. The images are as such reminiscent of earlier environmental imaginaries, in which the productive hinterlands are within the flows of production in relation to cities in the North, and yet outside of representation and of the body politic.

Hassi Messaoud
Beyond the binaries of North-South, the following case study examines forms of oil urbanism in the Algerian Sahara, and in particular that of a site critical to Europe's oil supplies, in order to reflect on the organization of territories of extraction. (Fig. 2)

The history of Hassi Messaoud could be read as a mediation of the relations of resources, population, and security in the sovereign's organization of territory, the contradictions of which are formalized on the extraction site. Hassi Messaoud refers to both Algeria's largest oil field and the township that developed in relation to the hydrocarbon industry in the Sahara Desert. (Fig. 3) Since oil was first discovered in 1956, central authorities have changed the administrative status of Hassi Messaoud, with every generation of urbanism responding to a persisting territorial question: What is the appropriate form of settlement of an industrial site that plays a strategically important role in oil flows and ensures a large part of the national economy?[18] From its establishment by the French colonial administration through the two decades following independence in 1962, Hassi Messaoud was an industrial center managed by oil companies. Following the Algerian government's desire to settle a permanent population in the Sahara, the 1984 administrative zoning changed the status of Hassi Messaoud from an industrial center to an incorporated town with an elected assembly. Over the following decades, it became the archetype of a dual-town, with a series of corporate "bases-vie" walled off from other town sections, often literally with bricks and razor wire. In 2004, the town had grown into the perimeter of oil fields and infrastructures representing what the government perceived as a "zone of major risks." The town expansion, as well as the desire of multinational corporations to secure their operations in the Sahara, constituted the context for a 2004 government decree to relocate Hassi Messaoud away from the existing oil field-town grounds. The action plan froze the issuance of any building permit, public or private, for activities that were not necessary for oil operations. It also launched the planning and relocation of the population to the New Town of Hassi Messaoud some 70km away from the existing town. (Fig.4)

Although portrayed as a technological or engineering problem, the urban question of Hassi Messaoud is enmeshed in the State's territorial politics. Hassi Messaoud is a

---

18. Hydrocarbons play a crucial role in Algeria's economy, accounting for roughly 60% of budget revenues and over 98% of export earnings. See John Entelis, "Sonatrach: The Political Economy of an Algerian State Institution," *Middle East Journal* 53(1) (1999): 9–27.

space in which resource metabolism and population settlement have come into play, and in doing so they become "contradictions of space."[19] It is *in* space that different political-ecological realities come effectively into play, and in so doing they become contradictions embedded in forms and relations of the territory. On one hand, the space of resources favors metabolic analogies of circulation and energy flows. In this worldview, the territory is modeled as a network of industrial infrastructures – the oil field, pipeline, refinery – that extracts resources from the earth, transforming them into commodities that support the national economy. On the other hand, population settlement requires fixity in space. It deploys buildings and land programs by which people attach themselves to the earth's surface, come to occupy firmly or permanently one place, and establish themselves as residents with political representation. Both projects of state territory aim at reproducing social relations through space; however, as they project their contradictory interests in a place, they become contradictions of space. At moments when population growth is perceived to put the economy at risks of friction or clogs, their moment of density, the town in this case, is diagnosed as a pathological territorial organism that needs to be excised.

I. Saharan Industrial Center 1958-1984

The French conquest of the Sahara in the nineteenth century aimed to secure the empire's geostrategic interests in Africa and pacify internal revolts against colonial rule. The "poor" Sahara, or the Southern Territories as the region was referred to in relation to the Algerian North, did not represent an economic interest in itself and continued to be portrayed as a "miserable" and "quasi-sterile" space for the first half of the twentieth century.[20] The value of the Sahara shifted radically in the mid-1950s with the beginning of the armed Algerian revolution and the discovery of oil. For French officials, the Sahara represented the utopian optimism for the economic development of the *Métropole* (referring both to the Metropolis and the European Territory of France): "For the majority of French people, the Sahara and its 4 million km^2 represent the last chance for France to remain a major power," noted a French official, "It is the ultimate hope for the Franco-African whole, the panacea of all ills."[21]

The wealth of the hydrocarbon Saharan was predicated on the flow of material and labor into exploration fields and of the extracted resources out to markets. Hence, since the mid-twentieth century, the expansive hydrocarbon territory has been inscribed into circulatory networks. Prior to 1956, the Sahara had virtually no tarmac roads.[22]

---

19. Henri Lefebvre, *The Production of Space* (Oxford: Blackwell, 1991), 365.
20. For a history of the Algerian South 1830-1980, see Taoufik Souami, *Aménageurs de villes et territoires d'habitants. Un siècle dans le sud algérien* (Paris: Harmattan, 2003).
21. Daniel Strasser, *Le Sahara français en 1958*, quoted in Souami, *Aménageurs de villes et territoires d'habitants*, 289.
22. Louis Blin, *L'Algérie du Sahara au Sahel* (Paris: L'Harmattan, 1990).

So the first major work in 1956 was the construction of 2,000 km of roads and 7,000 km of tracks, funded by regional authorities and the oil companies. Exports soon began, first via a combination of a short pipeline and railway to the Mediterranean port of Philippeville (Skikda), to be replaced in December 1959 by a more efficient 400-mile-long, 25-inch-diameter pipeline to a new oil terminal at Bougie (Annaba). Oil-producing regions were also connected to the air network through a series of airports: Hassi Messaoud (1957), Ouargla (1960), In Amenas (1962) and Hassi R'Mel (1962).[23]

The revised administrative status of the Sahara established new logistical nodes. Long under military rule, the exceptional status of the Southern Territories and the associated civic status of its inhabitants were reformed in 1957 into a setup similar to that of the North, or the Métropole. In December 1959 and July 1960, two ordinances instituted the "industrial centers" of In Amenas and Hassi Messaoud and assigned their management to the newly established Organisation Commune des Régions Sahariennes (OCRS), for which the mission was the "development, economic growth and social advancement of the Saharan areas of the French Republic." Without being elected, the OCRS director had political and economic powers over the organization of the territory. The planning of the new centers posed a set of concerns. With the discovery of natural resources in its early days, the minister of the Sahara attested in 1958, "It is quite difficult to predict the future of these Saharan agglomerations. New explorations can still emerge in different places. The possibilities of expansion of a locality should not be followed up and the problem should be approached differently."[24]

Hence, the planning studies were conducted so the centers could receive a threefold increase in population or operate should it fall clearly below these numbers. "In other words," he concluded, "the planning projects in the Sahara should be conceived as living programs rather than fixed drawings, so as to anticipate new developments. The corresponding spatial organization was the zoning of the center into sectors, programmatically assigned and with a set population density.[25] The splitting of the oil field by the concession boundaries of the two operating French companies resulted in two camp settlements: the Maison Verte-CPFA in the north (currently known as Base February 24), and the Base Irara in the south. The industrial center had to compensate as well for the absence of agglomerations at short or medium distance and house the services and workers of the oil fields. "Algeria: The Miracle of the Sahara," *Time Magazine* had reported in 1957, promised to "cure France's chronic foreign-trade deficit."[26] Such miracle, however, faced the reality check of the Algerian War of Inde-

---

23. Hassi Messaoud is currently the Sahara's busiest airport in terms of flow – 590,000 passengers in 2002 – and the fourth Algerian airport with international direct connections.
24. Souami, *Aménageurs de villes et territoires d'habitants*, 369.
25. Ibid.
26. "Algeria: Miracle of the Sahara," *Time Magazine*, August 5, 1957.

pendence. Etienne Hirsch, head of the Fourth Republic's economic modernization program, warned that the war against Algerian independence had become a literal roadblock, whereas France's economic prosperity depended on Algerian roads and labor. "Moslem rebel gangs," *Time* reported, blocked vital routes to the Mediterranean, an implication that "without peace in Algeria, the Miracle of the Sahara could easily become a mirage."[27]

The long war of decolonization led to Algeria gaining its independence from France in 1962. Shortly after that, Sonatrach was established as the national hydrocarbon company. The role of Sonatrach was initially limited to the construction of a third export pipeline, from Hassi Messaoud to the Arzew oil terminal on the Mediterranean, and progressively expanded to include all aspects of hydrocarbon exploitation – research, production, transformation, and commercialization until the nationalization of the oil and gas sector in 1971. The nationalization of the hydrocarbon sector made the industry even more thoroughly bound up with national-level social and territorial agendas.[28] For the sovereign, the company and the hydrocarbon Sahara were the lynchpins of a self-contained heavily industrialized economy.

A series of administrative policies asserted the significance of the Sahara to the newly independent state. The Sahara was divided into nine provinces, as opposed to just two in 1962, and dotted with infrastructures such as hospitals, schools, universities, post offices, and banks. In 1965, the Algerian central authorities proclaimed Hassi Messaoud an "administrative center" to be governed by the central administration from the provincial capital in Ouargla; a status that Hassi Messaoud maintained after the nationalization of the industry.

II. Hassi Messaoud Commune 1984-2004

Owing to the tremendous growth of rents after the 1973 first oil embargo, Algeria had ambitious plans to use its rising income from the hydrocarbon sector for the socialist modernization of its society and economy. The heroic model of industrial modernization was laid bare with the precipitous decline in oil prices and the intensification of socio-economic hardships in the 1980s. The absolute power of the hydrocarbon sector was curtailed by the struggles amongst the state's power factions, leading to the decentralization of Sonatrach and the subdivision of many of its responsibilities into separate enterprises. Similarly to other oil-exporting economies that had engaged in

---

27. Ibid.
28. Konrad Schliephake, *Oil and Regional Development: Examples from Algeria and Tunisia* (New York: Praeger, 1977), 97.
29. Miriam Lowi, *Oil Wealth and the Poverty of Politics: Algeria Compared* (Cambridge: Cambridge University Press, 2009), 92.

heavy industrialization, Algeria faced problems with pronounced territorial distributional effects as well as an acute housing crisis and a high pace of urbanization.[29] The new slogan *Pour Une Meilleure Vie* (For a Better Life) aspired to reduce dependence on the hydrocarbon sector and to reorient development towards previously neglected sectors such as agriculture, consumer goods, and social infrastructure. In this respect, the government sponsored agrarian reform programs and investments in rural housing to improve the quality of farm life and the stability of rural population. Soon after, in the 1985 plan "The Sahara at Horizon 2000," the Ministry of Planning defined the fundamental objectives of relieving the acute pressure on urban housing and the Algerian coast by "redistributing population and activities" throughout the territory and making better use of the natural potential as well as the social advancement of the people and the country.

The potential economic opportunities of Hassi Messaoud incited the state to "develop" its productive hinterland and reinforce the presence of the population over the diffuse territory. The limitations of the administrative center model had already been the subject of discussions in the 1970s. Hassi Messaoud was mostly tied to Algiers and the European capitals and did not form a stable element in the future population of Hassi Messaoud. "The different nuclei are not the elements of a true urban ensemble," noted the geographers Marc Côte and Claude Castevert in 1970, "The urban fabric remains loose or even absent, not because of distances but because of the nature of the parts that forbids all centrality its raison d'être."[30] The Law of February 1984 on the territorial organization of national space lifted the exceptional status of Hassi Messaoud and zoned it as a municipality with an elected local assembly. The industrial oil zone was inscribed in national political representation. Following the change in its administrative status, Hassi Messaoud witnessed significant, if unplanned, growth. The political ascension of populist parties in the Sahara municipalities facilitated the acquisition of land at a nominal price and building permits in Hassi Messaoud. The town significantly grew in size and population during the 1990s, a decade when the highly secured city was one of the few secured sites in a country otherwise blasted with terrorism. Between 1987 and 1998, the population of Hassi Messaoud, not accounting for oil bases and informal settlements, grew thus from 11,428 to 40,368.

III. New Town of Hassi Messaoud 2004-

Following the 1990s "Black Decade" of terrorism, the state embarked on the double task of liberalizing the economy and building "social peace" throughout its territory. In negotiation with the IMF, the revised economic policies of the 1990s aimed to provide more competitive terms to attract foreign partners into oil and gas exploration in Algeria. The increased presence of multinational partnerships with the state oil

---

30. Marc Côte and Claude Castevert, "Hassi Messaoud," *Annales Algériennes de Géographie* 9 (1970): 107–116.

company, as well as the broader concerns of the settlement and security of the Sahara, brought forth the desire to dissociate the urban population of Hassi Messaoud from the industrial grounds. Hassi Messaoud's urbanization between 1984 and 2004 mostly led to the uncontrolled growth around the perimeter of the oil field, with some of its houses being built on pipelines and in proximity to oil infrastructures. In November 2004, Hassi Messaoud was proclaimed a "zone of major risks." Commissioned by the Ministry of Energy and Sonatrach, the experts' report defined risks of explosion, fire, contamination, and pollution that affected residents in areas adjacent to the petroleum installations. "These risks, should they advent, would cause the loss of human lives and the destruction of installations that have cost tens of millions of dollars." The Minister of Energy and Mines, Chakib Khelil, emphasized how important it was that Hassi became again what it had been originally, a zone of oil exploitation. "The logistics base should be separated from la base de vie."[31]

The latest iteration, the project of New Town of Hassi Messaoud can be conceptualized at the intersection of two main lines for the state's policies in the 2000s; the security of its strategic hydrocarbon interests, and the "Reconquest of the Sahara" within the national plan for the development of new towns. The desire to relocate the population joined the national desire to operationalize regional development as "peace balm." Although the incorporation of Hassi Messaoud ought to have brought it important industrial taxes from the oil operations, the town continued to be underinvested and presented few economic opportunities for its residents. Regional movements, such the Children of the South for Justice and the Movement of Citizens of Ouargla, protested against poverty, lack of provision of basic infrastructures, the non-transparent allocation of social housing, unemployment, and more broadly social exclusion from the state's territorial contract. State institutions painted a similar picture. The 2007 National Report on Human Development explicitly referred to regional disparities and the unequal distribution of the "fruits of development." National planning schemes sought to balance the development of the Coast, High Plains, and the Sahara by establishing the new towns of Sidi Abdallah, Bouinan, and Boughezoul in the semi-arid areas south of the fertile coastal zone.

Borne out of the concurrent desires of relocating Hassi Messaoud and the establishment of new towns, the Ville Nouvelle de Hassi Messaoud was promoted as a pole of innovation and productivity for renewable energy. The state has claimed the monopoly on the (violent) organization of space: the town was to be transferred out of the oil territory. The government declared Hassi Messaoud a matter of national interest, put in place a plan of action to secure the oil field of Hassi Messaoud, and froze all construction permits pertaining to activities that were not essential to the petroleum sector. A 2004 decree promulgated the delocalization of the population and the

---

31. "Pour Raison de Sécurité, Hassi Messaoud déménage," *Le Quotidien d'Oran*, January 10, 2005.

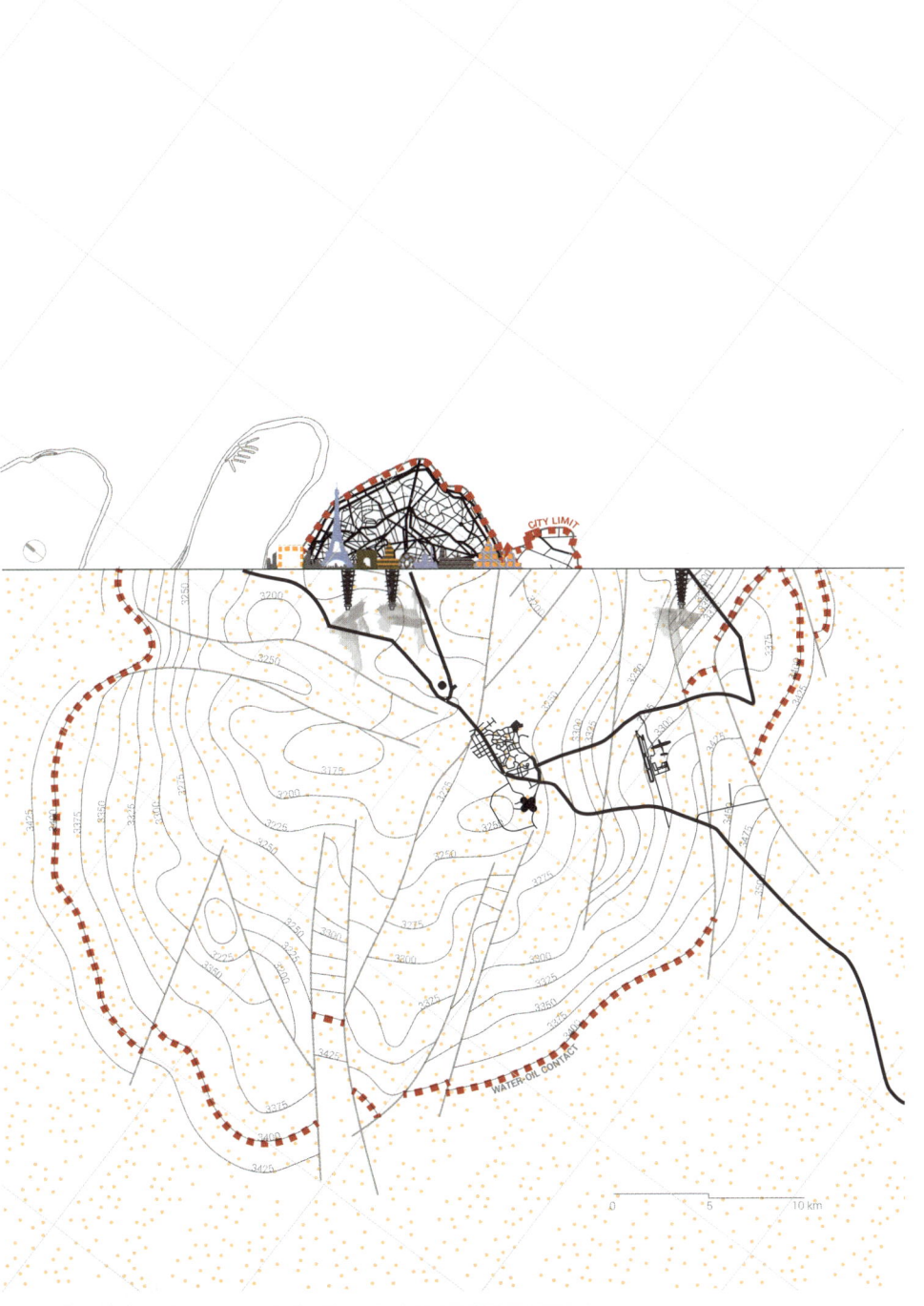

Fig.2 Scales of Energy_Juxtaposing Paris and Hassi Messaoud

establishment of a new town, at some 80km from the existing Hassi Messaoud, and equidistant to the other regional cities of Touggourt and Ouargla. The new city is projected to house around 80,000 inhabitants and occupy an area of 4,483 ha, divided into an urban perimeter and a logistics activities zone. The regional governor in Ouargla was instructed to carry out the destruction of slums and illegal buildings erected in the oil zone and in the town of Hassi Messaoud. The compensation and relocation of the residents of Hassi Messaoud remains, however, a pending matter.

Conclusion

"Closely following the oil," as Timothy Mitchell suggests, means "tracing the connections that were made between pipelines and pumping stations, refineries and shipping routes, road systems and automobile cultures, dollar flows and economic knowledge, weapons experts and militarism" – all of which, as Mitchell says, do not respect the boundaries between the material and the ideal, the political and the cultural, the natural and the social.[32] For the modern Algerian state, closely following the oil takes you to Hassi Messaoud. The genealogy of Hassi Messaoud's statuses embodies the different territorial agendas in which resource metabolism was enmeshed in the state's projects of population, economy, and security. The sociopolitical contradictions between the reproduction of resources (metabolism) and the reproduction of the population and workers (settlement) become negotiated in the space of resource urbanism. In the early years of oil development, the state favored a strategy of territorial exceptionalism to control the implementation of an idealized industrial site. From a de-territorialized site, Hassi Messaoud was gradually grounded in territorial population dynamics. Politically represented, the residents of the town of Hassi Messaoud represent a threat of potentially claiming a larger share of the resource pie, or at least constituting an undesirable nuisance in a region of high productive value for the state.

The project for the New Town of Hassi Messaoud is a displacement of the contradictions at stake on the ground by displacing the population, the dissociated attribute from the territory, as defined above. Through the case study of Hassi Messaoud, we interrogate whether it is possible to conceptualize the landscape of resources (or paysage) by recentralizing the country (pays) and the worker of the land (paysan) in the organization of nature's metabolism. Could we conceive of a Hassi Messaoud that negotiates the triad of pays-paysan-paysage? Otherwise, the cities of Hassi Messaoud might be continuously fleeing the shadows of a productive Hassi Messaoud. From this perspective, Hassi Messaoud becomes the ground zero of the metabolic conceptualization of the city-territory, in which urbanization is a process of contiguous de-territorialization and re-territorialization through metabolic circulatory flows.[33] The

---

32. Timothy Mitchell, "Carbon Democracy," *Economy and Society* 38(3) (2009): 399–432, 422.
33. Swyngedouw, "Circulations and Metabolisms: (Hybrid) Natures and (Cyborg) Cities," 22.

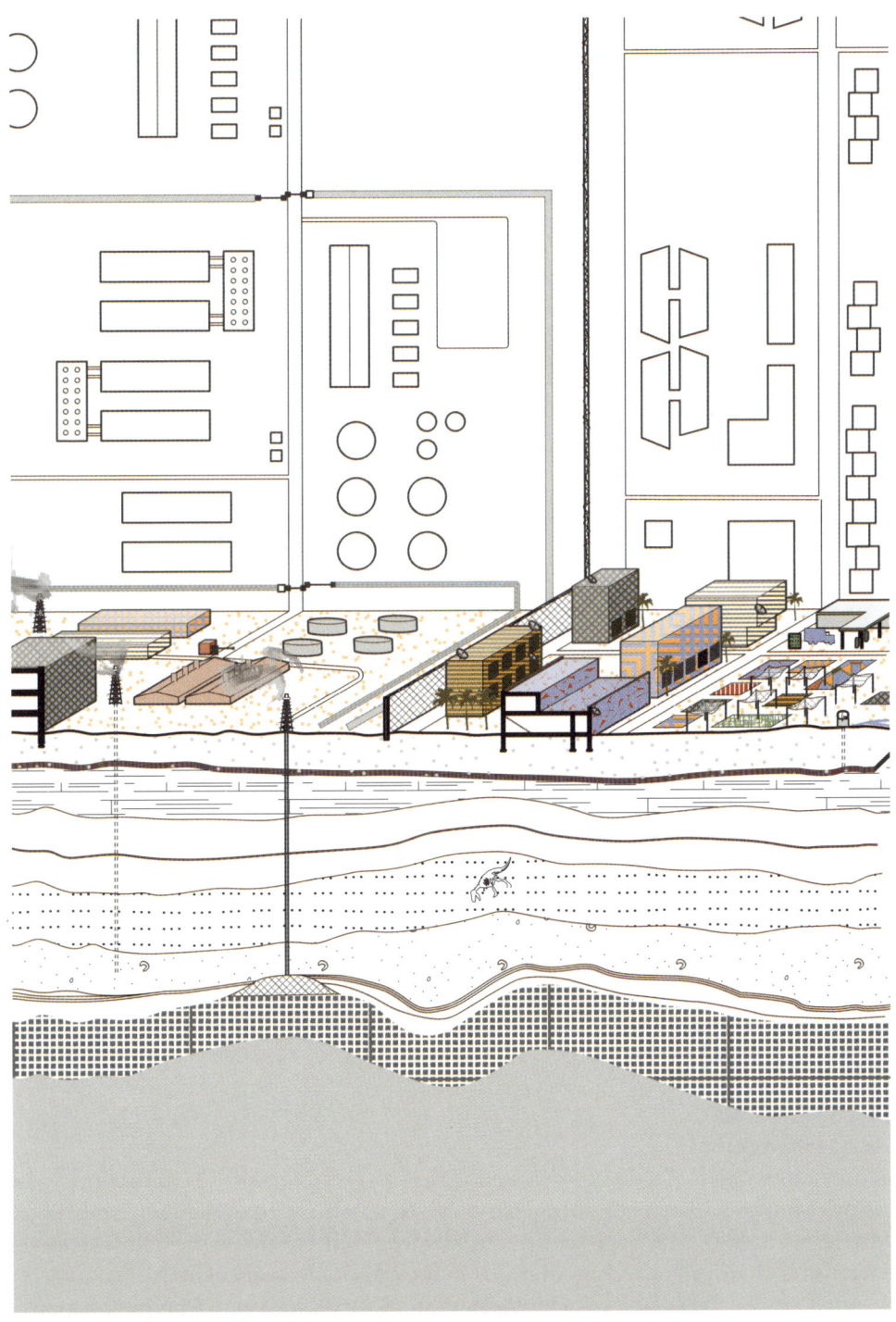

Fig.3 Hassi Messaoud Core Sample - A Geological Section through the Town

organization of space is always already provisional, where older and newer political orders overlay across multiple scalar frameworks. The forms of territorial ordering associated with industrial bases, so vividly embodied by Hassi Messaoud, appear less as a spatial exception and more as an integral dimension of urbanism, in the sense that the securitization of industrial ecologies, the containment of risks and clogs, and the externalization of undesired costs have been the cornerstones of the urban condition.

Acknowledgments
A previous version of this essay was published as Hassi Messaoud Oil Urbanism, in *New Geographies 6: Grounding Metabolism*, ed. N. Katsikis and D. Ibañez (Cambridge, MA: Harvard GSD, 2014), 144-153. The authors would like to thank the following individuals for their valuable contributions to the Hassi Messaoud visit: Ali Bouguerra, Mourad Zeriati, Salah Mekmouche, Yacine Laroui, Ouahiba Atoui, Hammoudi Moussa; as well as Alexandra Chen for her graphic collaboration on this essay.

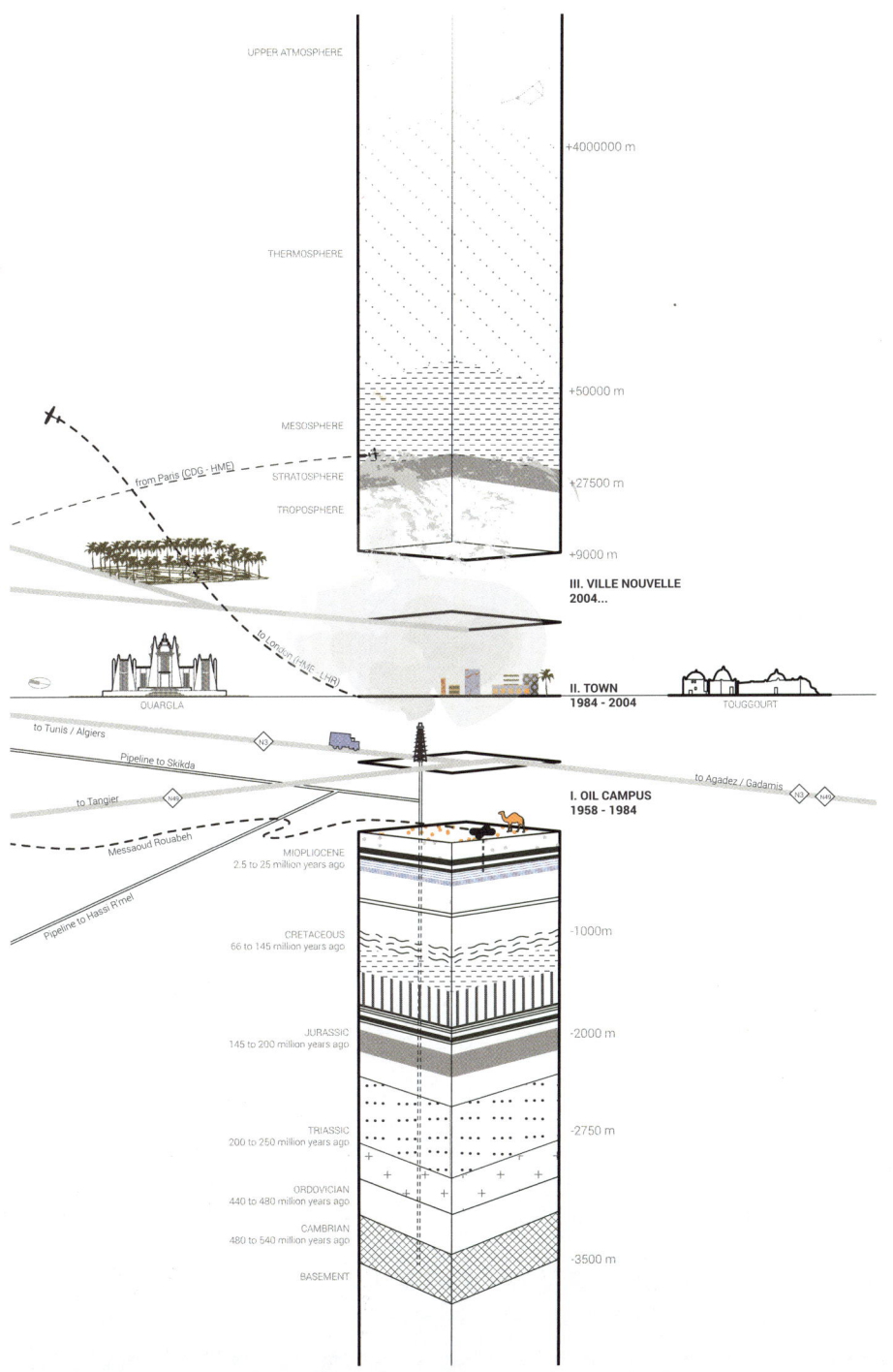

Fig.4 Spatial Genealogy of Hassi Messaoud- from Industrial Center, to Town, and Project for New Town

View of Hassi Messaoud_Bases-Vie

View of Camp Walls

Calama, Agustina Gonzaléz Cid, 2015

Resource-led New Towns and Challenges to Sovereignty
Diane E. Davis, Mariana Barrera

Back to the Future?

The current proliferation of new forms of urbanization that host the activities of private firms in the extractive and industrial sectors is a phenomenon worth exploring for a variety of reasons, including the fact that such experiments have a very long history. The industrial company town was relatively common during the industrial revolution in Europe and the United States, later being transplanted to Asia, Latin America and Africa.[1] Although by the late twentieth century support for company towns had declined somewhat,[2] owing to their negative social and environmental impacts, such practices are now back in vogue. Similar experiments in urbanization – some being built around temporary camps for rapid natural resource extraction and others appearing in the form of company towns with dedicated spaces for workers and production facilities – are becoming ever more common.[3] These company towns and their conceptually distant cousin, the charter city, have recently started to gain popularity in the global south because of a renewed interest in resource extraction and/or the need to site a new generation of high-tech factories in underutilized territories near transportation infrastructures capable of linking production outputs to global markets. In many instances, both public and private sector firms promote these developments, often by directly undertaking investments in infrastructure to sustain their own extractive or industrial enterprises, although some also rely on state support to turn as-yet-underdeveloped sites and territories into functioning new towns.

Whatever their origins, these new company towns frequently become sites where residents' daily activities exist under the sway of a company whose principal aims are extraction or production, in turn producing a direct social and spatial relationship between working and residential spaces. To be sure, the form, function, location, and character of a company town will differ depending on the nature of the industry it serves.[4] Extractive company towns are usually located in remote areas related to

---

1. In Latin America, some of the world's most renowned modernist planners and architects were hired to design entirely new towns to host new industrial manufacturing plants and their workers. One of the most known was Cidade de Motores in Brazil, designed by Jose Luis Sert's Town Planning Associates in 1945-1946, at the height of that country's industrial modernization.
2. Their decline also can be attributed to the preference for locating industrial activities within existent metropolitan areas, owing to the availability of low-wage labor and the likelihood that urban areas already hosted the necessary infrastructure needed by industrial firms.
3. Silicon Valley may be considered an extreme example of this. Some authors have gone so far as to describe this information technology "start-up" region of California as producing a community "where work penetrates and dominates the lives of its inhabitants," and as such consider it to be a reinvented company town; J.A. English-Lueck, "Silicon Valley reinvents the company town," *Futures* 32 (2000): 759-763, pp. 1.
4. Sydney Pollard, "The Factory Village in the Industrial Revolution," *The English Historical Review* 79 (1964): 513-531.

the exploitation of natural resources such as minerals, oil, fishing, and lumbering.[5] Their population is more homogeneous in terms of skill sets, and their land uses are often less diverse because they tend to emerge in isolated rural areas.[6] This also means they are more likely to have limited infrastructure, and thus may require more upfront investments in basic transportation, housing, and electricity services in order to accommodate town growth. In contrast, industrial new towns and charter cities tend to be located near populous areas, not just because their activities may require a more educated and diverse labor force, but also because the water, electricity, technology, and transport needs are slightly different than in resource-extraction towns. In industrial new towns and charter cities, the principal challenge may be to connect new infrastructural demands to existent urban and territorial infrastructures and networks. In both scenarios, however, these new urbanizations need to be situated within some form of existent governmental arrangement that allows them to function within the confines of existent constitutional arrangements and political expectations about who pays for infrastructure, provides social goods, and protects citizens from employers while also monitoring accountability on all fronts.

The Governance of Company Towns: Social, Political, or Economic Logic?
The question that concerns us here is how so-called company towns manage urban and governance challenges, particularly with respect to the distribution of infrastructure and services, with what implications for the willingness and capacity of private firms to stay put, and with what effect on the urban quality of life of its residents? With a specialized focus on extractive new towns (which are often referred to interchangeably as resource-led towns, boomtowns, or company towns), we consider whether the forms of town management that characterize new firm-led urbanizations are competing with or complementing current governance arrangements, and with what implications for both current and new residents as well as for the larger political geography and developmental gains of their host nations.

In the past, many company towns were economically dominated by local or national firms that understood town governance to be part of the infrastructure needed to make production possible. In the United States, Pullman, Illinois is a classic example.[7] Although the private developers who founded company towns often framed their investments under the rubric of philanthropy, they also sought to build cities that

---

5. J.Douglas Porteous, "The Nature of the Company Town," *Transactions of the Institute of British Geographers* 51 (1970): 127-142.
6. Richard Stedman, "Resource Dependence and Community Well-Being in Rural Canada," *Rural Sociology* 69 (2004): 213-234.
7. For more on Pullman, a new town outside Chicago built in the late 1880s and socially and spatially planned to host the production of railroad cars for Pullman Palace Car Company, see Stanley Buder, *Pullman: An Experiment in Industrial Order and Community Planning* (New York: Oxford University Press, 1967).

would make their labor force both productive and content so as to maintain a robust stream of economic revenue. They provided housing and a total urban infrastructure for their workers and managers, including streets, schools, churches, recreation spaces, hotels, stores, and public buildings that served all social classes. As noted by Porteous (1970), in those new company towns without direct railroad access (the equivalent to commuter transport in the industrial era), firms were often "obliged to provide many facilities including housing and public utilities in order to sustain the lives of (their) employees." In some cases, the influence of firms in town life was so extreme and universal that local place-names were those of company members.[8]

Yet in the contemporary era of globalization, there is some indication that new towns are being built by or in collaboration with foreign investors who may not have the same national loyalty to residents as provided by the company town "philanthropists" of the past. Many new industrial towns are in fact joint ventures with foreign manufacturing firms who have invested in these locations precisely because labor is cheap and exporting potential is high. In that sense, the particular firms involved in the appearance of new towns may have less loyalty to local residents, at least as compared to the past when industrial development was primarily a national project.[9] And with resource-led new towns, firms' willingness to take on the social responsibility for local conditions may be even less. The distant and isolated location of resource-led towns does not only require a larger investment in infrastructure, in order to territorially link these remote new urbanizations to global communication networks and regional modes of transportation connectivity, but it may also require greater investment in basic housing and other local services and infrastructures, primarily because these isolated areas have been poor and under-capitalized for decades. Such financial obligations may put limits on a firm's resources in ways that push them to cut corners with respect to social investments that enhance the urban quality of life. Complicating matters, the gap in the educational background and experiential realities of multinational firms and their executives or upper management, on one hand, and local authorities and residents on the other, may further limit firm willingness to take on responsibility for the wide range of social and economic needs required by town residents. Such discrepancies may be even greater in rural areas than in urban ones, thus directly affecting resource-led new town development in ways not seen in industrial new town development. In such environments, local authorities

---

8. David Frank, "Company Town/Labour Town: Local Government in the Cape Breton Coal Towns, 1917-1926," *Histoire Sociale/Social History* 27 (1981): 177-96.
9. To be sure, there are exceptions. In Mexico's newest experiments in new town development, both Audi City and Ciudad Model, there is a commitment to investing in local services for the population; and in the latter there are plans for a new water treatment plant and a language college.

may need to serve as mediators in facilitating new urbanization needs, thus further complicating the nature of town governance.

There is indeed some evidence that such political mediation was important even in the past. When mining firms in Australia began to lose control over town life, the government increased and transformed its involvement. "The traditional system of local government (was) replaced by a more complex set of governance arrangements comprising multiple levels of authorities, communities, non-profit organizations, private citizens, and corporate actors."[10] Firms were released from the duty of providing total urban infrastructure and fulfilling the guardian role. In exchange, they lost the formal control over those elements needed to make production possible, and were encouraged to develop new mechanisms to provide more efficient production. In this particular instance, the demands of good governance prevailed over the economic needs of the firm, and the firm was able to recuperate its losses nonetheless.

The question for us, however, is whether such pressures will always produce such positive outcomes? Were these relatively optimal gains specific to a country like Australia, where democratic governing arrangements prevail and state capacity is high? Some scholars have suggested that in poorer and less democratic countries where government capabilities are low, the "company state" develops by default and is understood as "an involuntary and hopefully temporary solution to problems posed by the prevailing social and physical environments."[11] Might the changes associated with the neoliberalization of governance arrangements and/or globalization of the resource-extraction industry also mediate such outcomes? All these concerns are particularly important to consider when thinking about new towns that are emerging in under-invested and minimally developed regions of the global south – where most extractive firms and many new industries are choosing to locate. Indeed, one must acknowledge that many modern "company towns" are developing in an historical context where the idea of governance itself has become more complex, and in which neoliberalization and globalization may have changed expectations about state-market collaboration.

With respect to the former, neoliberalization has formalized public-private partnerships while also devolving power down to the local level. This means that local "communities are often embedded within multi-scalar governance arrangements, wrapping together the interests and objectives of the state, private capital, and com-

---

10. Tiffany H. Morrison, Ceit Wilson, and M. Bell, "The Role of Private Corporations in Regional Planning and Development: Opportunities and Challenges for Governance of Housing and Land Use," *Journal of Rural Studies* 28 (2012): 478-489, pp. 480.
11. J. Douglas Porteous, "The Company State: a Chilean Case-study," *Canadian Geographer* 17 (1973): 113-126, pp. 115.

munities themselves."[12] With respect to the latter, globalization has multiplied the number of stakeholders involved in such conversations, bringing foreign and domestic firms into the mix in ways that do not always insure that they share priorities with each other, let alone with local authorities and residents. Such possibilities are particularly likely in extractive company towns, where local governance capacities are relatively underdeveloped. Many extractive sites are now being turned into new towns when only a few years earlier they were villages or temporary camps with limited infrastructure and very little institutional capacity. Indeed, this may be one of the reasons they were selected for resource exploitation in the first place. Most had underdeveloped political party structures and few governing agencies, and town leaders had limited experience dealing with large corporations or massive inflows of capital. Yet town leaders are now faced with transformative possibilities but possess little experience in making decisions about how to accommodate a wide range of new economic activities. In many of these towns, "invading" firms do not necessarily own land beyond their mining or industrial sites, if at all, thus arguing that they are not responsible for building housing or urban infrastructure for their employees. Yet because these new towns face the reality of high population growth directly linked to investment in work-generating activities, and because rapid urbanization patterns such as these often spur more capital-intensive activities, the demands for both infrastructural investment and land-use management continue to grow.[13] At the same time, shortages in housing and service provisions for lower-end workers tend to be a recurring phenomenon in booming places.[14] In this complex and unstable environment, local officials, citizens, and firms do not always see eye to eye on goals, with each frequently holding divergent priorities for accommodating, limiting, or managing town growth.

Our aim here is to develop a preliminary understanding of how resource-led new towns manage these challenges. We do so by focusing on two different "experiments in urbanization": Añelo in Argentina and Tete in Mozambique. Both were relatively isolated towns bypassed by previous decades of investment and national develop-

---

12. Misty Lawrie, Matthew Tonts, and Paul Plummer, "Boomtowns, Resource Dependence and Socioeconomic Well-being," *Australian Geographer* 42 (2011): 139-164, pp. 140. Lynda Cheshire, "A corporate responsibility? The constitution of fly-in, fly-out mining companies as governance partners in remote, mine-affected localities," *Journal of Rural Studies* 26 (2010): 12-20.
13. Changes in the built environment are spurred by the advent of new housing for extraction industry workers and mid-level management, as well as the development of supporting activities that often take the form of grocery stores, shopping malls, hotels, and even casinos, among other services.
14. Sara Beth Keough, "Planning for growth in a natural resource boomtown: Challenges for urban planners in Fort McMurray, Alberta," *Urban Geography* (2015). Accessed October 28, 2015. doi: 10.1080/02723638.2015.1049482.

ment, but which have recently been thrown into the limelight by the discovery of critical natural resources that are now considered critical for their countries' macro-economic growth: unconventional gas and oil (shale) extraction in Añelo and coal in Tete. In both cases, local and national authorities have tried to lure private firms with capital into investing in extractive production. Stakeholder "parachuting" into these villages on the part of global firms and regional as well as national authorities, together with huge flows of investment, are transforming the living experiences of the residents in these towns.[15] In both contexts, where foreign investors' capital accumulation are guiding extraction and urban development priorities, questions of sovereignty are also on the table. That the management of resource-led new towns raises concerns about sovereignty is due not only to the fact that the scale of decision-making involves domestic and foreign actors, both political and economic, who all seek the legitimate authority to make decisions for the town. It is also due to the fact that efforts to extract critical natural resources echo earlier historical struggles confronting the late-developing world during the colonial era, when struggles over sovereignty revolved around who had the right to control, monitor, and exploit a country's natural resources.

We begin with a discussion of the coal boom in Tete, Mozambique, and then turn to the shale boom in Añelo, Argentina. After exploring the emerging new relationships between the public and the private sectors in both towns, and discussing their effects on their long-term economic and social agendas, the chapter concludes with a discussion of the spillover effects of natural resource discovery on prosperity, governance, and citizenship, and how they affect stakeholder allegiances to the sovereign national state.

Coal Boom in Tete, Mozambique
The rush to exploit coal fields in Tete, Mozambique, less than a decade ago completely surprised the town's residents. A sleepy provincial capital dependent on agriculture and lacking state infrastructural investment, Tete was hardly prepared for its transformation after the discovery of huge coal reserves in 2008. Today, Mozambique is one of the world's top ten coal exporters, and coal extraction in Tete is expected to generate critical export earnings to support the future growth and development of the whole country.[16]

The national government, aware that this opportunity to modernize and develop the country was strongly dependent on foreign investment, offered incentives and

---

15. Mariana Barrera, "Long Live the Cow: Añelo, the Planning Opportunities of a Shale Boom Town Old," (MUP diss., University of Harvard, 2014).
16. "Republic of Mozambique MZ Governance Sharing Natural Resource Revenues with Affected Communities: Policy Options for Mozambique," *The World Bank*, Report No: ACS10342 (2014).

tax breaks to lure investors.[17] Investors' responses were swift and clear; the province had granted about 800 prospecting and mining licenses to 45 different national and international companies by 2013.[18] The first major stakeholder to settle in the area was the Brazilian company Vale, while the Anglo-Australian firm Rio Tinto was the second. Additional fortune seekers from around the world, such as "Chinese and Indian investors, South African hydraulics techs and geologists, Portuguese construction firms, Australian drillers, British crane operators, and American salespeople specializing in mammoth trucks and excavators,"[19] also arrived in Tete.

As the national government courted investors, local authorities became involved in fostering private investment in the area and reversed the historical absence of state at the locality. That said, they seemed to be directing their attention trans-nationally more than nationally or locally. Planning authorities likewise revised long-term development plans for the city in order to accommodate the interests of foreign mining corporations.[20] This has resulted in the resource boom fostering unprecedented urban changes in the area that "drastically changed the face of Tete's urban geographies with dramatic land use and demographic changes in the city center and its outskirts and considerable displacement and resettlement of local communities due to coal operations."[21] Population growth, along with the arrival of supporting services, developed previously non-existent areas in the nearby Matema and Matundo neighborhoods. The current existence of hotels, restaurants, bank branches, supermarkets, and gas stations proves that the resource boom has arrived, yet efforts to create a stable and viable economic base outside the mining sector are partial and inchoate.[22]

The dual economy in which non-mining residents struggle to afford living costs, the local protests led by dissatisfied relocated households, and makeshift dwellings and workplaces all reveal the lack of institutional capacity caused by years of a weak and neglected public sector.[23] This is the result of Mozambique's failure to successfully

---

17. Joshua Kirshner and Marcus Power, "Mining and Extractive Urbanism: Postdevelopment in a Mozambican Boomtown," *Geoforum* 61 (2015): 67–78, pp. 69.
18. João Mosca, and Tomás Selemane, *El Dorado Tete: Os Mega Projectos de Mineração* (Maputo: Centro de Integridade Pública, 2011), accessed October 28, 2015, http://pascal.iseg.utl.pt/~cesa/files/Comunicacoes/JMosca1.pdf
19. R. Moore Gerety, "Mozambique's Mining Boomtown," *Guernica: A Magazine of art and politics*, May 15, 2013. https://www.guernicamag.com/features/mozambiques-mining-boomtown/.
20. Kirshner, Power, "Mining and Extractive Urbanism: Postdevelopment in a Mozambican Boomtown," 67–78.
21. Ibid, 69. 22. Mosca, Selemane, *El Dorado Tete: Os Mega Projectos de Mineração*.
23. Joao Paulo Borges Coelho, "State resettlement policies in post-colonial rural Mozambique: The impact of the communal village programme on Tete province, 1977-1982," *Journal of Southern African Studies* 24 (1998): 61-91. M. Anne Pitcher, "Forgetting from Above and Memory from Below: Strategies of Legitimation and Struggle in Postsocialist Mozambique," *Africa* 76(1) (2006): 88-112.

implement the decentralization of government functions – the 1994 legislative reforms – and the provincial and local government's lack of human resources capable of dealing with powerful multinational companies and the new demands created by the resource boom. In addition, Tete's municipality faces financial constraints due to an unclear land titling system that undermines the collection of local property taxes.

Based on Gordon's (1991) idea that inactivity is a way of acting,[24] Tete's institutional void may be considered a deliberate strategy of shifting the economic and social agenda towards multinational companies' interests. In a context where most concessions are negotiated in Mozambique's capital city by national authorities, local representatives seem to have little influence on foreign investors.[25] However, they do represent a stumbling block that slows down firms' operations and encourages them to consider "filling the gaps." Unsurprisingly, these private stakeholders become engaged in the provision of goods and services in the mining area to increase production efficiency and build local support, which is an explicit form of risk management.[26] Such actions might address certain gaps, but "facing operational deadlines, mining corporations have often built new infrastructure without consulting affected populations or waiting for municipal approval."[27] Multinationals make huge sums of money that enable their ad-hoc investments. Vale, for example, has annual profits equivalent to nearly four times Mozambique's state budget.[28] "If they need a road, they build one, if they need a port, they build one. If they need lettuce in vast quantities, they import it from South Africa."[29]

Far from promoting a long-term development agenda, the coal boom in Tete has fostered a short-term dynamic of paternalism. Weak institutional arrangements enable powerful corporations to capture the regional development agenda, undermining Mozambique's prosperity. According to the United Nations (2014), Tete needs "urgent investments in social infrastructure [...] to respond to demographic pressures and

---

24. Colin Gordon, "Governmental Rationality: An Introduction," in *The Foucault Effect: Studies in Governmentality* (Hemel Hempstead: Harvester Wheatsheaf, 1991), 1-51.
25. Neissan Alessandro Besharati, "Raising Mozambique: Development through Coal," South African Institute for International Affairs (SAIIA), Governance of Africa's Resources Programme, Policy Briefing (2012) 56.
26. Lynda Cheshire, Jo-Anne Everingham, and Geoffrey Lawrence, "Governing the impacts of mining and the impacts of mining governance: Challenges for rural and regional local governments in Australia," *Journal of Rural Studies* 36 (2014): 330-339.
27. Kirshner, Power, "Mining and Extractive Urbanism: Postdevelopment in a Mozambican Boomtown," 76.
28. R. Moore Gerety, "Mozambique's Mining Boomtown."
29. Marta Barroso, "More coal for all in Mozambique?," *Deutsche Welle (DW), Ecomomy*, January 22, 2013, accessed October 28, 2010, http://www.dw.com/en/more-coal-for-all-in-mozambique/a-16430269.

other new challenges resulting from mining activities. Also, effective mechanisms are needed to monitor effects of such activities on the environment; on public health; and on the health and working conditions of miners and migrant workers."[30] Despite the current state of affairs, the national government fails to commit to long-term prosperity, as demonstrated by its response to population relocation conflicts. After decades of state absence in the region, the local protest against concessions to Vale was an opportunity for the government to cement local support at a relatively low cost by taking the role of regulator. The context and timing of electoral politics encouraged the government to promote a short-term "sustainable" solution.[31] In January 2012, 500 families relocated by Vale and dissatisfied with their new living standards protested by blocking the flows of coal exports for three days. A violent police repression ensured the preservation of revenue from the coal projects, and the maintenance of political order.[32]

Shale boom in Añelo, Argentina
The discovery of Vaca Muerta, the world's second largest shale gas reserve and fourth largest shale oil reserve, changed life in Añelo, a once forgotten Patagonian path through town whose main economic activity used to be agriculture. The local population increased from 2,689 residents in 2010 to 6,000 residents in 2014 – or 22% annual growth. Also, private and public stakeholders and entities from all over the country – and the world – arrived to pursue their own particular speculative goals. Given that Argentina became a net gas importer in 2007 and a net oil importer in 2011, Vaca Muerta represents an unexpected occasion for the provincial government to solve its budgetary constraints and for the national government to overcome a fiscal and energy crisis.

The provincial and national governments soon committed to the task of facilitating the expansion of the resource extraction industry in Vaca Muerta. They implemented financial and regulatory changes to lure International Oil Companies (IOCs) and to transform *Yacimientos Petrolíferos Fiscales* (YPF), Argentina's National Oil Company (NOC), into the most influential stakeholder at the site. They designed a structure of concessions and joint ventures that funnels the arrival of IOCs and filters their level of intervention. While the partnering firms provide funding and technology, YPF is responsible for the operations, including urban and infrastructure investment

---

30 "Natural Resource Management and Extractive Industries in Mozambique: A UN Mozambique Study," United Nations (2013).
31. Jessica Steinberg, "Strategic Sovereignty: Essays on goods provision, conflict, and governance in regions of natural resource extraction," (PhD diss., University of Michigan, 2014).
32. Kirshner, Power, "Mining and Extractive Urbanism: Postdevelopment in a Mozambican Boomtown," 76.

decision-making, making it a partnering stakeholder in local urban development. Although other companies from the oil sector remain relatively uninvolved with life in Añelo, they still have considerable influence at the local level through ad-hoc, isolated, reactive,[33] and pragmatic decision-making intended to avoid physical and institutional constraints. To overcome regulations that demand hiring local workers in a town devoid of adequate and well-prepared personnel for the industry, they contact people from other places and register them in Añelo hundreds at a time. Also, these firms do not build housing for their employees, but instead develop "creative" lodging ideas in a town with a nearly unchanged urban footprint despite the growing population. Oil companies not only book hotel rooms-via long-term leases- and rent the houses of local residents to host up to 10 to 15 workers at a time, they also allocate workers to temporary trailers in the industrial park. As pointed out by a real estate developer, "One company has brought 700 workers to live at the industrial park, and another one located its workers in a trailer at the entrance of the town, next to the road."

Local authorities also seem to be contributing to shifting the economic and social agenda towards resource extraction interests. For the first time in Añelo, planning regulation was approved in September 2013, but surprisingly, it was also amended six times within almost two years (September 2013-May 2015). Since the discovery of Vaca Muerta, Añelo's underfunded and understaffed local government, which is the primary administrator of zoning regulation in the territory, has used its administrative power and the lack of urban regulation and planning institutions to lure the private sector, concentrate power, and negotiate with external stakeholders. Land use legislation has been tailored to arising needs and one-off agreements, placing planning decisions in a short-term trap and undermining the town's long-term sustainability.

The resource boom didn't merely overwhelm the town's existing infrastructure; it surpassed the ability of both the private sector and the government to meet new demands. In particular, despite the existing shortage, housing projects are not planned with a comprehensive and long-term vision. La Forestada is a private urbanization located 5km away from Añelo's historic center. The project was started by both a developer and the owner of the land, the husband of a local legislator. When the project was initiated, the town had no zoning regulation nor was the Action Plan 2030 yet in place, but its characteristics were negotiated with the mayor and local council. Similarly, before the approval of local land use code, municipal authorities assigned selected hectares of fiscal land in the plateau for the development of social housing intended to reallocate families living in an informal settlement. A private real estate company that was looking for investment opportunities accepted to build the houses in exchange for land in the town's historic center to construct a shopping center,

---

33. Chris Skelcher, "Changing images of the state: overloaded, hollowed-out, congested," *Public Policy and Administration* 15 (2000): 3-19.

which was inaugurated in May 2015. The provincial housing authority enabled this development by providing funds to the local government. In none of these projects does it appear that the city's sustainability or future land use needs were considered.

In this context, the NOC took the lead in identifying the town's main needs by developing the Action Plan 2030, which was framed within the International Development Bank (IDB)'s Emerging and Sustainable Cities Initiative, published in December 2014. In doing so they worked with Fundación YPF, which manages corporate social responsibility. Although the mayor as well as representatives from COPADE (Provincial Council for Planning and Action for Development) were invited to join the working team for Añelo's Action Plan, the mayor has not used the action plan to guide his decisions. Local authorities still select projects to be developed based on land and funding availability from external stakeholders, thus undermining any attempt for local long-term planning. Resources are provided by capital transfers from the national and provincial governments, and the private sector is involved in selecting and developing projects. The industrial park, whose lots lacking urban services were completely allocated to oil companies, is a good example of firms "filling the gaps." Today, companies in the area are looking forward to creating a consortium intended to address the town's lack of infrastructure.

As it currently stands, the resource boom in Añelo is shaping and influencing the economic and social agenda without any apparent commitment to long-term prosperity at the scale of the city. Even so, it is shaping Añelo's built form, and not always in ways appropriate to the local topography. The municipal limit includes a geographic slope that divides the town into two unconnected areas where people live at different altitudes and very different urban conditions, with both experiencing different development paths. Two adjacent and complementary parks – an industrial park and an amusement park – have also emerged in Añelo, further dividing the landscape and the local economy. The focal area of the greatest urban transformation is the town's upland area, where the industrial park and 180 housing units are being developed. The historic center has also changed dramatically: two casinos, a shopping center, a hospital, and five hotels are some of the largest projects under construction. While the oil companies and service providers settle in the industrial park, the service-supporting industries of the shale boom settle in the historic center.

From Investment Gains to Sovereignty Losses?
The evidence presented here suggests that in resource-led towns where private companies operate as functional equivalents of local government and planning agencies by taking responsibility for basic infrastructure and prioritizing town needs, citizens are not equally served, urban spaces become divided, and larger developmental aims are easily compromised. Because weak and resource-poor local authorities have been unable to financially support the demands for housing and infrastructure, they have

allowed extractive companies to cover service provision gaps, although not uniformly. And while their efforts can be seen as a form of revenue transfer that reduces the burden on local authorities, it also comes with social, spatial, and political costs. In particular, by stepping up to the plate and absorbing responsibility for infrastructure, powerful corporate interests end up servicing only the part of the community that is directly linked to their extractive aims. Through these and other priorities, they also impact the local and regional planning agenda. Their extractive priorities not only reinforce short-term and territorially circumscribed thinking, favoring some town locations and specific workforce priorities, they also empower paternalistic relationships that undermine long-term development strategies that might produce sustainable gains for all citizens. Both developments can reduce the state's abilities to govern local and regional territories in accordance with a longer-term, more inclusive development agenda.

Such dynamics can have implications for sovereignty – at least if we define it as the state's willingness and capacity to build and preserve long-term governance aims that are inwardly directed and that accommodate the social, political, and economic needs of citizens rather than foreign firms. To the extent that town infrastructure investment decisions are focused only on the sites and regions of extraction, and to the extent that they are guided by the knowledge, power, and interests of global firms, they hold the potential to undermine sovereign capacities and relegate residents' priorities to the back burner in ways that make it difficult for residents to assert their rights to full citizenship.[34] To be sure, some scholars have argued that, "The vacillations toward liberalization and encouragement of foreign capital do not necessarily contradict the national mode of state sovereignty, as they can be constructed as regrettable but necessary local 'sacrifices' for a greater nation, public good."[35] However, in historical terms sovereignty always been measured by regulatory control and self-determination of natural resource uses within a nation's territorial bounds, whether land or capital assets, so as to deploy them for national development. If foreign capital investments facilitate national resource outflows while also undermining a local or national agenda of territorially inclusive citizenship, sovereignty and the capacity to govern in the service of national progress may be in jeopardy. Although the long-term results of the

---

34. For a further discussion of definitions of sovereignty, see John Agnew, "Sovereignty regimes: territoriality and state authority in contemporary world politics," *Annals of the Association of American Geographers* 95 (2005): 437–461. Doi: 10.1111/j.1467-8306.2005.00468.x, and John Agnew, *Globalization and Sovereignty* (New York: Rowman & Littlefield Publishers, 2009).
35. Jody Emel, Matthew T. Huber, and Madoshi H. Makene, "Extracting Sovereignty: Capital, Territory, and Gold Mining in Tanzania," *Political Geography* 30 (2011): 70-79, pp. 77; Tundu Antiphas Lissu, "In gold we trust: The political economy of law, human rights and the environment in Tanzania's mining industry," *Law, Social Justice and Global Development Journal* (2001), accessed October 28, 2015, http://www2.warwick.ac.uk/fac/soc/law/elj/lgd/2001_2/lissu1

public-private arrangements in Añelo and Tete still remain to be seen, the preliminary evidence suggests that oil companies in Añelo and mining multinationals in Tete have invested in infrastructure and urban services not because of any larger concern with local citizens or domestic prosperity, but to facilitate their extractive efforts while also reducing their risks. In Añelo, they have achieved the latter aims by finding local allies and increasing the efficiency of their operations. Yet because these are ad-hoc, isolated, reactive, and pragmatic responses to the institutional voids characteristic of state and planning capacity in these communities, these private sector actions have not served all local residents equally. In Tete, the situation is even more disturbing. Long-term local development plans were actually revised to accommodate foreign mining companies, representing an extreme case of local sovereignty arrangements being challenged by the arrival of external stakeholders. These actions have also produced greater social and spatial segregation, most clearly seen in tensions between those households more and less connected to the extraction industry. The development of a dual economy, characterized by circuits of investment and exchange that differentiate between resource and non-resource households, has been reflected in the physical distribution of housing and infrastructure. The case of Añelo is particularly striking because the socio-spatial fragmentation that has ensued is reinforcing a geographic landscape that divides the town into two areas at different topographical altitudes with different service demands. This geographic divide further complicates the capacity of elected officials to create strong relationships with both parts of town; and in the absence of institutional decision-making processes that bring all citizens together, public and private stakeholders rely on one-off agreement in ways that undermine town cohesion, thus limiting local authorities' political capacity to push back against foreign firms. This is in some ways a classic case of threatened sovereignty, at least at the local level, one that results from fragmentation of the body politic. Yet more than merely affecting urban form and town social cohesion, foreign actors' desires to set the local infrastructural agenda have also impacted the regional planning agenda and relations between regional and national authorities. This is due to the fact that the larger region which hosts these natural resources is often as poor as the small village where extraction occurs, making regional politicians and authorities are just as eager to reap the large gains emanating from foreign investments. In such a context, regional elites have lobbied national authorities to allow foreign investors to operate without extensive controls and with limited transparency or oversight, in ways that themselves may defy national norms. And the sheer distance of these regions from the capital city has made it easier for national authorities to willingly accommodate concessions to private firms without facing national public outcry about the challenges to national sovereignty or the lack of transparency. Yet this situation often means that local authorities themselves have even less willingness or capacity to address the concerns of their residents, particularly if they question or push back against the economic priorities of regional and national authorities. Again, local sovereignty is compromised, and on the national scale fragmentation of sovereignty is the result.

To be sure, some of this is due to limited state capacity to protect citizens, or even lack of political will, for which foreign firms cannot be held responsible. Indeed, in Mozambique negotiations and contracts signed by government authorities and mining companies are not subject to a formal political process. Most concessions are assigned by the national government on a first-come first-served basis, with no need to prove real capacity or previous experience.[36] Yet in some cases, the national administration also lacks qualified staff and faces poor coordination among its ministries, leaving it unable to monitor the activity of extractive companies even if it wanted to. In the particular case of Tete, not even the Provincial Directorate was aware of the content of the contracts in their area.[37] As a result, there are growing concerns about natural resources management and the capacity for re-distribution of income generated from some operations. "Standards were initially set low to avoid putting off investors, but the state introduced a new Mining Tax Law in September 2014, which established that that all capital gains arising from the direct or indirect transfer of mining rights by nonresident entities, with or without permanent establishment in Mozambique, will be taxable at a fixed rate of 32%."[38] But it is often the limited state capacity that explains why foreign firms are in these countries in the first place.

Although state capacity is more institutionalized in Argentina than in Mozambique, a lack of political transparency has reinforced the capacity of foreign firms to prevail in local extractive activities, despite initial national government insistence on maintaining sovereign control of national resources. In early 2014, the country's main oil company and key decision-maker in the Vaca Muerta site, the YPF, was charged with signing an agreement with the American multinational oil firm Chevron containing confidential terms of reference. Such duplicity was set in motion by prior national and provincial government collaboration to introduce new regulations fostering joint ventures between YPF and IOCs. These regulations, which were intended to enable the exploitation of non-conventional resources, came less than two years after Argentina's President had publicly announced YPF's *nationalization* in April 2012, a move touted as a way to achieve "*self-sufficiency* in the supply of hydrocarbons, as well

---

36. Thomas Selemane, "Mozambique to become one of biggest coal & gas producers: From aid dependence to mineral dependence?," *Mozambique Political Process Bulletin* 53 (2013): 1-12, accessed October 28, 2015, http://www.open.ac.uk/technology/mozambique/sites/www.open.ac.uk.technology.mozambique/files/files/Mozambique_Bulletin_53_coal-gas.pdf
37. Mosca, Selemane, *El Dorado Tete: Os Mega Projectos de Mineração*.
38. Power, Kirshner, "Mining and Extractive Urbanism: Postdevelopment in a Mozambican Boomtown," 69.
39. This decree was formally approved approved by Argentina's Congress on May 3, 2012. See Form 20-F: YPF Sociedad Anónima, for the fiscal year ending December 31, 2013. United States Securities and Exchange Commission. Washington, D.C., 2013.

as in the exploitation, industrialization, transportation and sale of hydrocarbons, *a national public interest and a priority for Argentina.*"[39] Yet by October 2014, the national hydrocarbons law was amended to lure foreign oil companies to invest in Argentina, accompanied by measures adopted by the Ministry of Economy to reduce tariffs applicable to oil exports.

The Resource "Curse" and Fragmented Sovereignty: Concluding Remarks
History has shown that without appropriate long-term planning and management, resource abundance can be a double-edged sword, particularly when it becomes fodder for foreign firms' global strategies of resource extraction. Not only does it hold the potential to engage local, regional, and national authorities in bargains that may undermine national sovereignty aims, but it also generates demand for new town development in areas that are ill-prepared for urbanization. To the extent that the town investments required by the extraction of resources are relegated to sub-national levels of management, such pressures can lead to "poor quality public expenditure and the waste of much of the new resource revenue."[40] All this suggests that in situations of finite and irreplaceable natural resources, stakeholders should concentrate their efforts on developing long-term agendas structured around local infrastructure and planning goals that might help insure the purposeful reinvestment of local and national revenues associated with resource extraction. All this is easier said than done. Dependency on global flows of capital to help provide infrastructure provisions for short-term gains can threaten such lofty goals.[41] The fluctuation of international commodity prices creates a boom and bust cycle within resource-dependent communities and countries and discourages extractive firms from committing to long-term development goals. In this context, "Only the state can provide coordination, constitutional protections and mechanisms of accountability to a broader public."[42]

For precisely this reason, stronger institutional arrangements need to be developed to reinforce the capacity of local, regional, and national authorities to coordinate the urban and developmental dynamics in new towns that "are primarily created to enhance the progressive accumulation of capital."[43] One key justification for

---

40. Javier Arellano-Yanguas, "A thoroughly modern resource curse? The new natural resource policy agenda and the mining revival in Peru," Institute of Development Studies, Working paper series 300 (2008), pp. 3.
41. Sara Beth Keough, "Planning for growth in a natural resource boomtown: challenges for urban planners in Fort McMurray, Alberta."
42. Tiffany H. Morrison, Ceit Wilson, and M. Bell, "The Role of Private Corporations in Regional Planning and Development: Opportunities and Challenges for Governance of Housing and Land Use," 487.
43. John Bradbury, "Towards an Alternative Theory of Resource-Based Town Development in Canada," *Economic Geography* 55 (1979): 147-166, pp. 155.

demanding such action is its potential to help reverse the fragmentation of sovereignty, while citizenship is another related concern. Without oversight and shared responsibility for managing the infrastructural requisites that enable and emerge with resource-led new towns, extractive activities can eat away at governance norms, planning capacities, and the rights of citizens to demand accountability with respect to the transformation of their immediate physical environment. To be sure, neither fragmented sovereignty nor citizenship challenges are produced by resource discoveries, the arrival of multinational investors, or the success of oil and mining companies alone. Sovereignty and citizenship are threatened when foreign firms operate in a context of weak state capacity, limited accountability, and divided institutions of governance, because these are the conditions that enable extractive companies to develop paternalistic agendas, short-term goals, and a minimal commitment to the long-term future of their host towns and their residents. So be forewarned: natural resource discoveries may encourage developing countries to loosen up sovereignty mandates in return for the promise of future prosperity. But this promise may remain nothing more than an unfulfilled dream, one that is likely to be accompanied by the stark reality of life in the company town, where socio-spatial inequality and limited civic accountability produce less-than-desirable sites where quotidian livability and long-term progress may remain elusive.

View of Chuquicamata's mining site from Calama, Jeannette Sordi, 2015.

Coping with Complexity: Experiences in Post-Disaster Recovery for Extractive Towns in Chile
Pablo Allard, Maria Ignacia Arrasate

One of the main challenges for urban regeneration in extractive settlements is the difficulty of adapting to change, particularly when change is prompted by natural disasters that severely affect the main economic drivers of those communities. In order to review the challenges and lessons learned in post-disaster planning and implementation, the following essay will depict the recovery efforts of three Chilean towns related to different extractive industries. The cases will be the town of Chaitén (salmon industry) destroyed by a volcano eruption in 2008, and the towns of Dichato (fishing and tourism) and Constitución (forestry) severely affected by the 2010 earthquake and tsunami. The experience of these three cases will help to understand how to overcome difficulties to develop resilient urban recovery master plans given the complexity of post-disaster recovery, fragmented sectorial agendas, the time-consuming processes imbedded in the public investment system and centralized decision making practices in Chile. Building on evidence from the cases, the objective of this chapter is to showcase the lessons, innovations and design-based strategies implemented to cope with such challenges.

1. Planning for Resilience in Extractive Territories

Chile is exposed to different types of natural events, such as earthquakes, tsunamis, volcanic eruptions, landslides and flooding. Some of these events throughout the history of the country have been extremely severe with catastrophic social and economic costs. The most powerful earthquake ever recorded in modern history occurred in the city of Valdivia, located in the south of Chile, in 1960, rating 9.5 on the Moment Magnitude Scale (MMS), triggering a tsunami with high levels of destruction.[1] Other notable disasters are the 2008 eruption of the Chaitén volcano, which left the town of Chaitén, with a population of 5,000, partially buried by ashes and led to the complete evacuation of the city and temporary relocation of its inhabitants for more than two years. The 8.3 magnitude earthquake in Tarapacá and the great fire of 2014 in Valparaíso destroyed neighborhoods and left thousands homeless. One of the most recent ones, the 8.4 MMS earthquake and following tsunami in September 2015 affected the area of Illapel causing severe damages in the towns of Tongoy and Coquimbo. All these events are reminders that risk and resilience are part of life of Chilean towns.

In this context, the succession of post-disaster recovery processes that have taken place in Chilean settlements include the continuous improvement of building codes, implemented for the first time after the 7.8 magnitude earthquake in the town of Chillán in 1939, with the sad record of a death toll of around 28,000 according to the newspapers of the time. The advancements in this area were validated 70 years later during the 8.8 magnitude earthquake on the morning of February 27, 2010, known to many as the "27F disaster". Despite the earthquake's magnitude and extend, only

---

1. The death toll and monetary losses arising from such a widespread disaster are not certain. Official estimates vary greatly from 2,231 to 6,000 victims.

few structures collapsed, and most of the buildings with damages were the ones built before the existence of the codes or exceptional cases in which they did not comply with the regulations in force. Buildings subject to the new building codes and standards for infrastructure operability suffered much less damage and lives were saved. Despite this long tradition of seismic building codes and enforcement, in Chile there is still a pending debt toward a more holistic approach to planning for resilience in order to minimize damages and facilitate a faster recovery. The impacts of recent disasters demonstrate that in Chile most of the focus has been placed in individual building codes and regulations and basic conditions for town planning rather than planning for risk mitigation and resilience.

2. Main Challenges for Integrated Master Planning in Chile

Chilean planning regulation requires that every town must comply with a local municipal zoning plan, named "Plano Regulador Comunal (PRC)." This plan defines land uses, densities, and building conditions, along with the street network and public space. Even though it's mandatory for every municipality and its towns to comply with an up-to-date PRC, in many cases the plans are drafted after most urbanization has taken place, and in other cases the plans have limited-not binding considerations to local risk conditions. This issue became critical during the "27 F" disaster, since risk assessment studies such as geological maps or tsunami charts were necessary but not mandatory nor binding inputs for the approval of PRCs in Chile. This regulatory gap gave way to one of the weakest points in Chilean planning, since most of the casualties from the "27 F" were not related to collapsed buildings; instead they were in the wrong place when the tsunami and the landslides hit their towns. This regulatory shortcoming led to the inclusion of risk zones by tsunami flooding in 2011.[2]

In order to consider the importance of planning and design for risk mitigation and resilience, we must understand the different approaches to Urban Disaster Mitigation. In most cases these approaches can be classified in two groups, Structural and Non-Structural Measures:

STRUCTURAL MEASURES
By structural measures we understand the land use definitions or the necessary infrastructure for risk mitigation, constructing physical barriers in order to reduce or minimize the impact and damage of a determined risk in order to achieve hazard-resistance and resilience in structures or systems. Structural measures can be classified in two major groups:
- Location measures: These refer to the possibility of conditioning building codes and land use planning laws and their enforcement in order to avoid the threat or minimize risk. This approach requires having enough information on geological

---

2. OGUC, DS 09 year 2011. Modification to article 2.1.17.

or other natural hazards related to a specific territory, as well as the existence of alternative locations. It is important to note that location measures are much more effective when planning new towns, or when the economic driver of such town is not directly related to its location. In the case of existing towns or settlements directly related to extractive industries such as fishery, mining, or agriculture, in many cases the location and land uses are directly related to the place where resources are available. For example, a fishermen's cove must be next to the seashore, a mining town next to the mine, and a farmer´s village along a water stream. One of the main difficulties in implementing land use location measures relates to the strong attachment to land that many communities demonstrate in case of extreme solutions such as relocation or limitation of certain activities in risk zones are applied.

- Risk Mitigation Infrastructure: The second structural approach is to evaluate, design and implement the necessary infrastructure aimed to resist or minimize the damage of a potential threat. In this case, the high cost of building mega structures such as dams, flood levies, wave breakers, tsunami walls, storm water energy dissipation works, and volcanic lahar retention structures known as SABO, makes this approach difficult to implement. In most cases, this kind of investment is developed when risk can't be avoided and the costs of relocating are higher than investing in mitigation. The main design approach for this kind of infrastructure is the feedback and historic record of previous disasters, as well as the recurrence period for each event that allow decision-makers to foresee future risk scenarios.

NON-STRUCTURAL MEASURES

By non-structural measures we understand the operational and management measures aimed to reduce the exposure to risks and impacts or to transfer the economic cost of the damage. In this group we can find:

- Operational measures: Related to public awareness raising, training and education or other non-physical actions taken by a specific community related to their preparedness for a specific event or risk, and to timely react to avoid any potential damage. The most common approach to this is the existence of monitoring and early warning technologies, evacuation protocols and emergency response capacities. In most cases this approach is aimed to save lives and critical goods, but not necessarily reduce the physical and economic damage.

- Transfer of Risk: By transferring of risk to others, we must understand the use of insurance and other economic instruments to transfer the monetary cost of an eventual damage to a third party. Despite the fact that this is one of the most used measures, it is limited in its scope since it does neither transfer nor reduce the physical damage or loss. Other limitations include the extension of the disaster, in order to guarantee timely coverage to all the ones affected, the terms of the insurance policy, and the coverage level among private homeowners.[3] Besides, in developing countries, flooding or earthquake insurance coverage might be limited, and therefore losses are just partially mitigated by this type or measure.[4]

As can be seen from the different approaches to planning, design for risk mitigation and resilience, there is no specific or clear recipe or preferred solution. In most cases, a combination of all of the above is necessary, but it requires the existence of a series of conditions to allow the deployment of several scales of planning and design solutions. Unfortunately, in the case of Chile, despite the fact that most towns comply or are updating their PRCs, there are several gaps that remain obstacles to a holistic solution. Some of the main difficulties can be found in the following weaknesses:

- Master Plans do not exist in Chilean regulation: Chilean laws define regional, municipal and town planning instruments and then jump into site-specific ordinances. In other words, a city-wide or district-wide Master Plan that guides development and integrates land uses with zoning, massing, built form, landscape, infrastructure, and other physical aspects of a specific town has no legal support or value.

- Fragmented sectorial agendas and decision-making: Despite the highly centralized structure of Chilean government, the executive power of the state is distributed in several ministries. Each ministry manages its own budget and capacities to plan and implement policies and projects, and each minister is evaluated by his or her capacity to comply with the government's plan and agenda. This structure allows for efficiency and accountability in the way the government agencies make use of public funds, but creates disincentives for collaboration among agencies. In other words, the possibility of coordinating and leveraging the capacities of the Ministry of Public Works with the Ministry of Housing and Urbanization in order to promote integrated urban infrastructure solutions is not fostered by this institutional design.

- The National Public Investment System is too slow: For almost forty years, Chile has developed a straightforward public investment policy, oriented towards the efficient use of scarce public funds. In the case of infrastructure or any social plan or project that requires funding for implementation, each plan or project has to go through a rigorous economic and social evaluation process, where it competes for funding based on its social rate of return. Once the project is selected and prioritized, every stage of it – Conceptual Design, Basic Engineering, Design, Construction and Operation – must be evaluated again by the system, and funding is granted on a yearly basis. This system is one of the pillars of Chile's

---

3. The total amount of damages from Hurricane Katrina was US$135 billion. Private insurance claims covered less than US$30 billion of the losses.
4. In 2012, the Chilean Insurance Association (AACH) estimated that in Chile from the total of US$30 billion loss of the 27F disaster, only US$7-8 billion was paid by insurance companies.

development, since it has helped to focus most public funding in projects and plans with high social benefits, and has also helped to detect and avoid high-cost pork barrel projects that can dilapidate public funds. The problem is that despite the economic efficiency of the system, it tends to deter and make the development of any urban project excessively slow, particularly when it is required as part of an emergency recovery plan.

- <u>Centralized structures and limited local capacities:</u> The highly centralized structure of Chile´s national government, with most decision-making concentrated in the office of the President and its ministers, and with non elected regional governors, called "Intendentes," which are personally appointed by the President, results in a detachment from local needs and expertise that in some cases can make rapid and effective response to emergency recovery difficult. This detachment and lack of reliance on local capacities have also led to the use of a "Presidential Delegate" for recovery or reconstruction in some cases,[5] creating a superstructure beyond the regional or local authorities with uneven results. On the other hand, given the dispersed and complicated nature of Chile´s territory, there are still many regions with poor human capital or weak local capacities for coping with complex planning and implementation challenges such as recovery from urban disasters.

- <u>Lack of experience in community participation:</u> Another critical aspect of planning and design for urban recovery is the increasing demand for community participation in every stage of the process. Current regulations in Chile have stated the need to incorporate active participation in urban planning and design, but there is still a lack of clear procedures and experience in the depth and breath of this matter that works against co-creative and participatory planning strategies to be effectively implemented.

- <u>Increased mistrust in public–private partnerships (PPP):</u> Upon the return to democracy in the early nineties, Chile based most of its successful economic development on an open market economy model with strong public–private partnerships. This was made possible by the privatization of most government-owned companies and public utilities during the final years of Pinochet´s dictatorship and continued with one of the most successful private provisions of public services model with the implementation of the public infrastructure concessions program for ports, roads and airports.[6] Unfortunately, as the model provided more than 15 billion dollars of private investment in public infrastructure, the evidence

---

5. In July of 2011, Felipe Kast, assumed the role of "Reconstruction Presidential Delegate," with the main task of speeding up the reconstruction process for the families living emergency houses villages created after the 27F disaster.

6. Ministerio de Obras Públicas, Coordinación de Concesiones, accessed February 2015. http://www.concesiones.cl/quienes_somos/Paginas/default.aspx

of mismanagement and regulatory capture began to damage the trust in the system. This weakening of public and private partnerships has increased in recent years as several scandals related to corruption and campaign finance emerged in both the political and the private sector.

- <u>Difficulties of communicating the complexity of the plan and managing expectations:</u> As a disaster-prone country, Chile has developed great emergency response capacities by means of the National Emergency Office, ONEMI.[7] The problem is that there is still no national policy or guidelines on mid and long-term planning for recovery. This lack of a National Reconstruction Policy derives in a case-by-case response that depends on the scope and nature of the event, as well as the specific agenda of the authorities. In this sense, there are no explicit guidelines on how to approach the communities and stakeholders involved in a disaster, in terms of the timeframes and stages of the process, thus increasing anxiety and expectations in the affected communities as well as the burden on those officials and agencies in charge of the recovery efforts.

All of the difficulties framed above are common to any urban regeneration or disaster recovery project, but become more complex in towns and communities that are highly dependent on one main economic driver, as in the case of extractive territories. The next section will depict the main challenges, failures, and lessons learned in three different cases. The first, the town of Chaitén, a small and isolated geopolitical outpost in Chilean Patagonia – where one-third of its population were public servants, one-third farmers, and one-third dedicated to services for both tourism and salmon industries – refers to one of the first comprehensive resilient planning efforts ever driven in Chile after the eruption Chaitén volcano, which unfortunately fell prey to the painstaking time-consuming nature of the Chilean Public Investment System and the ever-changing nature of political will. The other two cases, Dichato and Constitución, depict two of the most successful Strategic Recovery Master Plans PRES-PRBC[8] developed in the aftermath of the "27F" and show different approaches and results. The first one derived from government-led planning, for the fishing and tourism town of Dichato, and public–private partnership in the case of the forestry and cellulose town of Constitución.

3. The Case of Chaitén

On May 3, 2008, the 5,000 people living in the small but thriving town of Chaitén were awakened by the fierce eruption of its homonymous neighboring volcano. Neglected by geologists and dormant for more than 250 years, the small volcano sits just three

---

7. Oficina Nacional de Emergencias del Ministerio del Interior (ONEMI).
8. PRES: Planes de Reconstrucción Estratégico Sustentable / PRBC: Planes de Reconstrucción de Borde Costero.

Aerial view of the town of Chaitén buried by volcanic ashes carried by the Blanco River on its way from the Chaitén volcano (on the left). In the center of the town, the new course of the river divided the city into two; the alluvial cone of debris filled the bay and destroyed the airfield (on the right). Chaitén, Palena Province, Chile, February 2009. Source: Allard and Rojas OCUC.

miles from the then capital of the Palena Province, and the town was a keystone in terms of connectivity and services for the isolated communities of Chilean Patagonia. The danger of massive pyroclastic flows or the collapse of the dome forced authorities to evacuate the area, and despite the difficulties to access the town, more than 7,000 people were evacuated in less than 48 hours with no fatalities to lament.

In the meantime, the column of incandescent ashes reached more than 12 kilometers high, covering most of the region with tons of volcanic dust. At some point the cloud was so large that it even reached the city of Buenos Aires in Argentina, thousands of miles away, forcing the cancellation of commercial flights in the area. During the early days of the eruption, the town and its surrounding hills were covered with more than two feet of ashes, but the disaster came not directly from the volcano as it was feared, but from the towns´ own River Blanco. Despite the fact that Chaitén is characterized by its intense rains, it had not rained in ten days, so when it happened, most of the ashes were washed out, clogging the river and forcing it to find its way through the city, destroying more than two-thirds of its properties and most of its infrastructure, including the regional hospital, the hospital, the courthouse, and two schools, and severely limiting the port operations.

The Chilean government responded rapidly, by assigning the Minister of Defense to be in charge of coordinating crisis management until a special authority was appointed for disaster relief and reconstruction. The "Presidential Delegate for Chaitén" was named in June, with the powers and budget to help displaced families with temporary accommodation and a monthly displacement subsidy of about US$1,000 per family to cope with the loss. Along with the Presidential Delegate, the regional government and several agencies began to implement plans and projects to improve communications and connectivity to the smaller towns and remote communities that depended on Chaitén for their daily life and development. The temporary loss of Chaitén revealed the strategic importance of the town and the fragility of the transportation network, which meant that many small communities and a complete region would have to depend on Argentina to maintain their communications and connectivity, access to hospitals and services, literally dividing Chile in two and posing a complex geopolitical dilemma for Chile's sovereignty in a territory that was highly contested twenty-five years ago.

The impact of the volcanic eruption worsened over time, as it became clear it would last longer than expected. By late July, the river had destroyed most of the town. Small groups of Chaiteninos were allowed to return to the town only to recover whatever was left after the catastrophe, and a few decided to stay, defying the volcano and the government´s call for complete evacuation. At that point, a series of civil organizations and community groups from the region and the town contacted the Cities Observatory (OCUC) – an urban and territorial intelligence unit based at the Catholic

University in Santiago – to respond to their apprehensions on the effects that short-term emergency planning could have in such a fragile and environmentally sensitive region. Chilean Patagonia is one of the least populated areas in Latin America; it is considered a worldwide reserve of the biosphere, and its economic and social future is closely related to eco-tourism, conservation, and sustainable development.

Acknowledging the great response from the government in terms of evacuation and support for the displaced, there were no plans of action in terms of reconstruction, since most of Chaitén's urban area was still under high volcanic risk. In response to the call, the OCUC offered regional and national authorities its services for the creation of a special Task Force that could rapidly analyze strategic scenarios for reconstruction or relocation of the town, depending on the evolution of the volcano activity.

The Task Force incorporated more than 30 professionals, aimed at the development of a comprehensive set of recommendations that could orient critical decision-making for national authorities while helping the displaced communities to understand the scope of the disaster and reduce their uncertainty regarding the prospects of return. Among the specialists congregated for the team were Venezuela's former Vice-Minister of Infrastructure, David Gouverneur, and urban planner Oscar Grauer, who led the special planning task force in the aftermath of 1999´s landslides disaster in the coastal state of Vargas – a massive catastrophe that took more than 15,000 lives, changed the geography, and completely destroyed historic towns. They combined their experience with the Integrated Sustainable Urbanism Unit team from the UK-based engineering firm ARUP,[9] who brought to Chaitén their "Sustainable Projects Appraisal Routine" (SPeAR©), and developed a new methodology (MeAL©) that allowed the group to objectively evaluate and compare different relocation scenarios from a cost-benefit standpoint. The Task Force also included the award-winning design team of ELEMENTAL,[10] and a group of geologists and geographers from the local Universidad Austral, who had long-term experience in Patagonia. The Task Force was completed with experts in planning and environmental law, sociologists, infrastructure and transportation engineers, and economists who covered most aspects of such a complex situation.

The Task Force worked along with a technical counterpart, comprised by professionals from the regional government, the National Geological Service, the Presidential

---

9. ARUP is a UK-based design and engineering team specialized in carbon neutral urban design, known for their groundbreaking eco-cities projects in China and the Middle East.
10. ELEMENTAL is a "Do Tank," founded in 2000 and led by Chilean architect Alejandro Aravena, which develops state-of-the-art low-cost housing and innovative approaches to incremental urban design and planning. Aravena has recently been recognized with the 2016 Pritzker Award for his achievements in architecture and planning.

Delegation in Chaitén, the Ministry of Public Works, Housing and Urbanization, and several specialists from governmental agencies and the Armed Forces. The best capacities available were congregated to cope with the complexity of evaluating and defining the future of Chaitén.

The eventual reconstruction or relocation of Chaitén posed a great challenge and an opportunity for a country like Chile to develop a response policy for its many natural disasters. Instead of understanding emergency short-term response as a cost, the idea was to consider its planning as an investment to guide future development. The continuous volcanic activity provided time to evaluate and consider mid- and long-term scenarios while responding to disaster relief. This simultaneous vision was key if we consider Patagonia as one of the most sensitive and isolated areas in Chile, as well as a unique biosphere reserve.

This new vision could be materialized in a sustainable low-impact development that could prioritize the efficient use of economic and natural resources. This issue was particularly important in the Palena Region, where most human settlements are still dependent on Chile´s mainland for most of its services and provisions. On the other hand, the small scale of Chaitén allowed for innovation in terms of sustainable urban planning and design. A small town of 5,000 is comparable to any Master Planned Community, it has the right scale and components for self-sufficiency and low dependency on external services such as energy, water waste management and goods. Its potential for replication was high, not only as a sustainable urban model, but in terms of opening the way for new tools and capabilities that could allow developing countries to elaborate appropriate policies and contemporary approaches to small and remote town planning in the future.

By the time the OCUC implemented the Task Force, preliminary information showed that the level of destruction was so high that any potential scenario meant starting from zero, in terms of urbanization, infrastructure, energy provision, and services. In this sense, starting from scratch made it possible to liberate restrictions and think of a settlement for the future. The potential for exploring new infrastructure paradigms was supported by the fact that Chaitén is located next to the six priority hotspots for geothermal generation in Chile, allowing the new town to reduce its current dependence on a 60-mile high-voltage line and a diesel plant.

Considering the geopolitical importance of the city within the region, and the visibility of its natural features, the future of Chaitén and the Chilean Patagonia relies strongly on the development of an eco-tourism industry, conservation, high-end services and sustainable production. In this sense, the new city should capitalize on the high value of the landscape, its biodiversity, and natural environment with an equivalent in the built environment. Converting Chaitén in a model town, attractive, competitive, carbon-neutral, and self-sufficient, with memorable architecture that is in harmony with nature in aesthetic, functional, and environmental terms.

In summary, uncertainty over the future of the volcano provided a window of opportunity to define an adequate strategy, aligned with a clear development vision. And Chaitén presented an opportunity to align four key issues defined by Chilean Government as priorities for the future development of the country: Territorial Equality, Sustainability, Innovation, and Country Branding.

The main priorities of the work of the Chaitén Task Force were people and the territorial integrity of the region in the following order:
- Keep people's lives safe from natural risks (volcanic, flooding, earthquakes), urban hazards (fires, short-circuits and structural collapse) and sanitary dangers (plagues, infectious diseases, and lung-related problems associated to exposure to silica from ashes)
- Preserve, if possible, public and private property, particularly those of the displaced families, considering tangible and intangible values such as their history, culture and traditions.
- Procure the sustainable future development of the town and the region by maintaining a simultaneous vision of emergency and long-term planning, understanding the process as the transition from catastrophe to opportunity.

The work of the Chaitén Task Force was comprised of four phases, during a period of five months:
- Phase 1: Compilation of all geographical, geological, demographic, social and territorial information available in order to establish a comprehensive GIS database to run the analysis. Along with it, the group met with community leaders and displaced groups in order to define a development vision. This Phase lasted four weeks, and was presented in November 2008.
- Phase 2: Evaluation of the viability of reconstruction on the original site and preliminary analysis of potential sites for relocation. These studies were performed using the MeAL© matrix, considering aspects such as natural and geological risk, mitigation measures, infrastructure, accessibility, economic potential, sustainability and urban character. This process allowed reducing potential scenarios from five to two locations, privileging those with the most positive attributes and development potential. This phase was developed over the course of six weeks, and brought up enough evidence to allow the Vice President and Minister of Interior to announce by late December 2008 that the town was not a feasible site for reconstruction and new locations needed to be evaluated.
- Phase 3: Comprised an advanced evaluation of the two alternative sites for relocation, Development of a Conceptual Master Plan and Recommendations for Implementation. This phase was developed over the course of six weeks and led to the decision for relocation in Santa Barbara, a site seven miles north of Chaitén

Aerial view of the city of Constitución from the mouth of the Maule river, two weeks after the tsunami. The presence of the Orrego Island increased the speed and height of the waves, destroying all the buildings and fisherman's wharf located in the south banks of the river.
Constitución, Maule Region, Chile. Source: Pablo Allard, March 2010.

and safe from any volcanic hazard. This decision was announced in February 2009 by the Minister of Interior and the Mayor of Chaitén, just days after the partial collapse of the volcano's dome towards the town.

- Phase 4: Socialization and communication of the results of the Task Force to main players, community leaders and displaced groups. This phase ended on April 2009, with the announcement by President Michelle Bachelet that by May 21st a police station and some municipal services would be operating in temporary buildings in Santa Barbara, as the initial stage of reconstruction. The Government also announced a compensation plan for all properties located within the danger zone, the end of the Presidential Delegation in Chaitén in June, the end of the displacement fund and a series of special subsidies and funding for entrepreneurs.

Upon the end of the Task Force work, the Ministry of Housing and Urbanism, along with the Regional Government, took over the Planning and Construction process, developing a series of studies and works aimed to ensure the rebirth of Chaitén as a competitive, sustainable, and thriving gateway to Patagonia. Studies for a new port and construction of a new airfield in Santa Barbara were submitted to the National Public Investment System and more than 100 million dollars were approved by congress for the implementation of the new town in the 2010 national budget. By the end of 2009, the road between Chaitén and Santa Barbara was paved, a temporary airfield was put into operation in Santa Barbara, and electricity lines were set up in the new location. In February 2010, the Ministry of Housing and Urbanization unveiled a complete master plan for the town of "Nueva Chaitén" in Santa Barbara, and ran a design competition for the new city hall, hospital, and schools. Most of the families displaced by the volcano joined several housing committees and were working on the housing schemes available at the new town. It was expected that at least one-third of the original Chaiteninos would return to their homeland by 2011, and once the public buildings were set in place, most public employees would return to the then provincial capital.

The complete plan for the new town of Chaitén was meant to be announced by President Bachelet at a ceremony in the city of Puerto Montt by the end of February 2010, as one of the legacies at the end of her administration, but another natural disaster redefined the national priorities and changed the course of the events. The night before the ceremony, Chile was struck by one of the most devastating earthquakes and tsunamis ever recorded in its history. The ceremony never took place, and the new administration of President Sebastián Piñera moved into office with the difficult task of the recoveries of not only the small town of Chaitén, but more than 20,000 villages, towns, and cities severely damaged by the "27F." With the new priorities, the government struggled to evaluate the viability of investing more than 100 million dollars in a small town while there were more urgent issues.

Despite the efforts to include Chaitén in the National Reconstruction Plan, almost three years after the volcano eruption, most of the projects for the new town were still stalled at the National Public Investment System, and only the new airport in Santa Barbara continued to be developed; the rest of the projects were postponed or cancelled. When the people of Chaitén realized that the return to their land would take longer than expected, and given the reduction of the volcanic activity, the Major and City Council began pressuring authorities to allow them to return to the partially destroyed town. While the Ministry of Interior Affairs debated the best scenarios available, several Chaiteninos began to return and demand utilities and basic services in the abandoned town. By October 2010, the Minister of Interior Affairs authorized the partial return of the original settlers to the northern part of Chaitén at their own risk and cancelled any plans for the new town, given the national emergency after the "27F" earthquake.

Nowadays Chaitén is back from the ashes, about one-third of the population has returned and the new regional airport has begun operations in Chana, next to Santa Barbara. This situation led to the sprawling development of the town along the 7-mile road between Chaitén and Santa Barbara, a disperse and informal urbanization pattern completely opposed to the original vision for the reconstruction of a compact and sustainable town, while the southern areas of the city remain as a ghost-town of partially destroyed buildings covered by ashes. There is still uncertainty on how much of the vision and opportunities detected during the process could be implemented, while most of the population and services are operating in an active volcanic hazard zone. Chaitén failed to overcome the painstakingly time-consuming nature of the Chilean Public Investment System in order to ensure the sound and timely implementation of a comprehensive plan. The lesson was clear: in order to effectively respond to planning for an urban disaster, we must accelerate all the tools and means available for disaster recovery before priorities change.

4. The cases of Dichato and Constitución

The "27 F" earthquake ranks as the sixth-largest earthquake ever recorded by a seismograph. It was felt strongly in six Chilean regions, affecting about 75 percent of the country's population, equivalent to over 12 million people. Subsequent blackouts affected around 93 percent of the country. Over 530 people died with around 25 missing. The earthquake and tsunami partially devastated a broad range of urban settlements, comprising five cities of more than 100,000 inhabitants, 45 towns of over 5,000 inhabitants, and more than 900 villages and communities distributed across more than 600 km from coastal areas to rural settlements (MINVU, 2010). The total cost of the damage was estimated at US$30 billion, equivalent to 18% of Gross National Product, composed of US$21 billion in physical assets (including buildings, housing, roads, and schools) and US$9 billion in business and indirect losses.[11]

---

12. The law is still pending for approval in the Chilean Congress.

The extent and diversity of the damage across the Chilean territory highlighted the need to integrate disaster risk management into the recovery process focused on more broad-based solutions in order to pursue more sustainable future development. This was an enormous challenge for governmental agencies and officers, since the earthquake happened two weeks before the elected President Sebastián Piñera moved into office as the first center-right administration in two decades. Therefore, the recovery process started with the complexity of a new administration. This, however, also served as an opportunity to incorporate important changes and adjustments into the government's development agenda to strengthen both the emergency response and recovery policies nationwide. Governors and secretaries were appointed, considering post-disaster recovery as their main task, and a series of reforms and special programs were drafted to fund and coordinate the process. Among these were a Special Reconstruction Tax Reform and the creation of a network of seismographs (managed by the National Seismological Center), implemented for the primary impact assessment when an earthquake event occurs.

Redundancy was added to the telecommunication system to avoid the cessation of service in such an event, and a law was proposed to reformulate the National Emergency Office regarding emergency management response, disaster prevention, and other procedures to better address future risks.[12] The new law also incorporated a National Fund for Civil Protection to prepare people for risk events at the local and regional levels and to increase the responsiveness of public institutions and private entities. Finally, other regulatory updates included strategies addressing hazard and risk assessment, improvement of early warning systems, upgrades to building codes and other regulations, risk reduction policies integrated into land use planning, and the development of regional and local capacity through decentralization.

In a scenario in which Chile is poised to become a developed country, the earthquake exposed the fragility and neglect existing in many localities, but also the opportunities presented by reconstruction and recovery plans to improve the current and future situation of the communities affected. The dilemma was moving quickly to resolve the emergency without compromising the long-term vision extended beyond rebuilding homes, on the understanding that urban planning contributes to rethinking the cities from a holistic view, where the concepts of sustainability, quality of urban life, and resilience will be key to the future. To guarantee a comprehensive holistic approach to reconstruction and to ensure a resilient approach to inhabiting the coast, the Ministry of Housing and Urbanization (MINVU) with the collaboration of a series of public and private entities prepared 27 master plans for the main urban centers located in the coastal area affected by the tsunami and more than 150 reconstruction plans for intermediate towns.

---

12. The law is still pending for approval in the Chilean Congress.

This double challenge of rebuilding fast enough to meet the urgent needs of the victims while ensuring their future was not compromised, presented all kinds of dilemmas. As the case of those families of the coastline towns like Dichato or Constitución, which were expropriated to build tsunami mitigation works in order to reduce risk and facilitate the safe reconstruction of the rest of the city, the enforced expropriation of those few families to clear way for mitigation infrastructure made possible the collective benefit of the whole city and, although they were expropriated at market value, for them it was not worth the displacement from the site they had always lived in and enjoyed. Such dilemmas are constantly experienced, not only in coastal towns, but also in urban centers, historic districts, and other areas of high heritage value.

Organizing urban reconstruction was not easy for the Chilean government, so it appealed to local initiative and self-determination of the communities to decentralize the process. In order to do so, the central government developed a series of programs aimed at recognizing the capacity of the communities along with support from private companies, institutions, and civil society, to contribute to the recovery by means of a public and private collaboration scheme to fund and develop studies and master plans for local reconstruction which would be then evaluated, prioritized, and implemented by the central and regional government.

Given the magnitude of the task, it was necessary not only to recognize the ability of the self-determination of communities, but also open new grounds for community participation and public–private partnerships. To do so, it was necessary to rebuild bonds of trust, which resulted in a series of joint planning efforts led by mayors and municipal councils with the support of private companies, social organizations, or institutions, who made their capabilities and resources available to municipalities in order to develop Strategic Plans for Sustainable Reconstruction, called PRES, in locations such as Constitución, Juan Fernández, Pelluhue-Curanipe-La Pesca, Curicó, and Talca. On the other hand, in the case of the coastal edge of the Biobío region, the regional government decided to form an ad-hoc agency to coordinate the reconstruction of 18 coastal towns, named PRBC18,[13] with proper multi-sectorial coordination and participatory bodies.

Dichato
One of the 18 towns within the work of PRBC18 was Dichato, a small coastal town reliant on fishing and tourism, located north of Concepción, in the Biobío region with around 4,000 residents,[14] which was severely damaged by the disaster, with 80% of the town destroyed.

---

13. PRBC18: Reconstruction Plan of 18 coastal settlements - Planes de Reconstrucción de Borde Costero de 18 localidades.
14. According to the 2002 census.

Aerial view of the town of Dichato completely destroyed after the earthquake and tsunami of February 27, 2010. The configuration of the bay increased the hight and speed of the tsunami that frontally hit the structures located on the first line of the beach and later entered through the estuary devastating 80% of the town's building and infrastructure. Dichato, Biobio Region, Chile. Source: Pablo Allard, march 2010.

The aftermath of the earthquake and tsunami in Dichato presented a unique situation compared to other affected urban areas in terms of the scale of the destruction and the resulting scale of the needed aid. There were significant political, organizational, environmental, logistical, and capacity issues. The reconstruction master plan of Dichato sought to promote resilience through zoning, the construction of mitigation infrastructure, a coastline park with contention walls, and updates to construction codes for tsunami flooding areas supported by housing subsidies. The plan included different mechanisms of participation such as assemblies and meetings across communities. Between May and November 2010, the Dichato recovery planning process included 23 meetings, focus groups, and workshop discussions. Between 10 and 400 people participated in these meetings (Cartes, 2010).

For the Dichato reconstruction master plan and 17 other cities located in the coast of the Biobío Region, the regional government took a proactive role and led the development of all the region's master plans, creating a special local team consisting of urban planners and architects. This case was an unprecedented experience at a regional level, demonstrating that a regional platform with a level of autonomy from national government could respond adequately to a local problem, facilitating coordination, monitoring and implementation of all decisions and projects – all essential conditions for realizing public investment initiatives.

The criteria utilized to inhabit the flooding area defined by the conducted tsunami risk modeling studies was a mixed strategy combining mitigation works to reduce the energy of the waves and avoid future damages, zoning according to tsunami exposure conditions, and constructing tsunami-resilient housing with special subsidies to cover the extra costs of construction. The purpose was to respect the attachment of coastal communities to the land without hindering reconstruction. For a middle-income country such as Chile this was especially relevant because if reconstruction in coastal areas were completely forbidden, communities would build back anyway, resulting in informality and low-quality construction.

Besides the efforts related to the master plan of Dichato, several initiatives were undertaken by non-governmental organizations with governmental support, such as Desafío Levantemos Chile,[15] providing new boats for fishermen to resume their jobs, Harvard Recupera Chile,[16] helping communities through livelihood-restoration and economic development-oriented projects (Ahlers, 2013), and Viva Dichato, a music

---

15. NGO created after the 27F disaster to help communities go back to normal by repairing boats and reconstructing schools. http://www.desafiolevantemoschile.cl
16. Recupera Chile offers a range of services for the economic, social, health, and sociological recovery that focus on three Chilean communities: Cobquecura, Perales and Dichato. http://www.recuperachile.com

festival with the aim of attracting people to foster tourism in the town. These initiatives were key to fostering the community's economic recovery and contributed to restoring their livelihoods during the period of reconstruction.

Five years after the disaster, Dichato's reconstruction shows high levels of completion both in housing and urban projects accompanied by the social and economic recovery of the community. The tsunami mitigation sea wall and promenade was built in less than two years; the hydraulic works to avoid flooding of the Dichato creek have been undertaken, and the tsunami mitigation forest and park are in the works. Daniel Vera Boulevard – Dichato's main commercial street – has been redesigned and implemented with ample sidewalks and shading elements that have helped the recovery of local businesses and restaurants. In terms of housing, all the affected families eligible for reconstruction subsidies repaired or received a new home in the town, and those fishermen and families who needed to remain living in potential hazard areas were granted special subsidies for the acquisition or construction of innovative tsunami-resilient homes and apartments. At least in terms of these results, the recovery of this town should be considered a good example of Chilean recovery, validating strategic and sustainable urban planning and citizen participation during all stages of the process. Moreover, the strategy utilized in Dichato highlights the importance of strengthening local capacities, fostering partnerships among stakeholders, and promoting decentralization to ensure the implementation of the plan.

Constitución
Constitución is a city of 46,081 residents located in the south margin of the Maule River estuary.[17] It is known as one of the main wood production hubs of the country and it is characterized by the industrial activity related to the Arauco cellulose plant, which produces paper and pulp.[18]

Located few miles north of the earthquake's epicenter, Constitución became one of the most severely affected coastal towns after the 27F earthquake and tsunami, with 172 deaths and more than 50% of the city destroyed. Despite the structural damage produced by the seismic shock, the effects of the tsunami produced most of the deaths and destruction as it entered the Maule river estuary by the time the town was celebrating a traditional river festival in the Orrego Island at the mouth of the estuary. It is considered that more than 90 people were killed by the tsunami as it wiped out the island. Not only most of the basic services located in the center of the city collapsed after the disaster, damages also included the cellulose plant, which was devastated by the waves.

---

17. According to the 2002 census of the National Statistics Institute (INE).
18. Forestal Arauco is one of the largest timber and cellulose companies in Chile; it is part of the COPEC conglomerate.

Aerial view of the town of Dichato completely recovered four years after the earthquake and tsunami. In the foreground left, the new housing projects in upland areas above the risk zone. On the coastal edge, the new tsunami mitigation wall and park, flanked by tsunami-resilient high rise buildings, and hydraulic work in the estuary on the right. Dichato, Biobio Region, Chile. Source: Pablo Allard, 2014

The cellulose plant and the piles of wood stacked on the coastline acted as a dam that mitigated the strength and speed of the tsunami, preventing the destruction of the western part of the city but disabling key sections of the mill, affecting the main economic driver of Constitución.

After this tragic event, a public and private partnership was formed between multiple stakeholders to create a sustainable reconstruction plan for the city, known as Plan de Reconstrucción Sustentable or PRES Constitución.[19] The purpose of this plan was to serve as a driver for recovery and articulate the interests of the community, the public sector, and the private sector to pursue an equitable recovery with a long-term perspective to promote sustainable development.

The main partners of this collaborative effort included the Arauco Timber Company as the main sponsor, providing the funding for the plan. The Ministry of Housing and Urban Planning, the mayor and city council of Constitución represented the public sector (including both the national and local levels of government). The idea was to organize a task force capable for delivering a comprehensive recovery master plan that could orient the reconstruction of the town. Following its participation in Chaitén, and its relation to Arauco, ELEMENTAL[20] was this time in charge of the design and coordination of the plan. The planning team also included members of diverse sectors that joined this partnership like ARUP, the University of Talca, Fundación Chile, Tironi, and Marketek Consulting.

The dispersal and complexity of the damage after the earthquake, affecting six regions and more than 150 cities and towns, explains why governmental authorities accepted and relied on the help from private corporations, non-governmental agencies, and institutions to provide expertise and funding for several recovery master plans. In order to avoid any chance of corruption, speculation, or conflicts of interest, MINVU established a series of conditions for the development of these plans called PRES, or Planes de Reconstrucción Estratégico Sustentable. Some of these conditions were:
- Each PRES should develop a vision and preliminary master plan within a 90-day period, in order to provide a comprehensive approach to the recovery of the city that could orient the implementation of coordinated short and long-term investments.
- The involvement of private organizations in the planning would not replace the role of government. Each PRES established a public and private development committee, and leadership was established at the local level. The mayor would chair

---

19. See: www.presconstitucion.cl.
20. Since 2005, ELEMENTAL has been sponsored by COPEC, one of Chile's main energy and industrial conglomerates that is the main shareholder of Arauco.

the committee and the plan needed to be approved by the city council in order to be endorsed by MINVU.[21]

- Each plan must try to articulate several multi-sectorial investments in order to provide an integrated recovery plan that could leverage public and private investment. The goal is not only to reconstruct the pre-existing infrastructure and city fabric, but also to take the process as an opportunity for the future development of the town. Each plan must provide a prioritized list of projects and programs, which could be evaluated in the National Public Investment Program in order to be funded and implemented.

- Each PRES must incorporate open public community participation and representative decision-making processes such as polls, focus groups and plebiscites. The PRES were not binding, they did not replace the official Zoning Plans or recovery policy, but were key to orienting the role of the central government in the process.

- Each PRES will deliver a final master plan and a set of projects along with the institutional local capacity to persevere in its long-term implementation.

The citizens of Constitución were included from the beginning as the drivers of the urban recovery proposal. In this Public-Private Partnership the power of everyone involved was carefully balanced to achieve symmetric value. The PRES Constitución was the first out of seven of such privately funded plans. The other six were the Island of Juan Fernández (sponsored by the British Embassy, Honda Motors, and the National Architectural Offices Association), PRES Curicó (sponsored by the local chamber of commerce), PRES Pelluhue and Curanipe (sponsored by the Catholic University and the NGO Techo), PRES Talca (sponsored by the Consorcio Group), and PRES Duao-Iloca-La Pesca (sponsored by Hatch and Universidad Mayor). PRES Constitución was developed under the premise that the master plan is an instrument with the power of synthesis, developed with citizen participation with a sense of reality.[22] Therefore, the approach utilized consisted in designing an effective participatory plan, but above all, a plan that understood participation as an open space for the construction of joint solutions, without distributing beforehand the expertise and roles, and with the real implication of citizens in decision-making processes.

---

21. In the case of the city of Talca, city councilors did not agree on the sponsorship of PRE Talca by the Consorcio financial group, arguing they had real estate operations that could result in conflict of interests. Despite the group not having any operations in the region, and the fact that they signed an MOU stating they would not invest in real estate operations in the following five years, political differences between city councilors and the Mayor acted against consensus. MINVU did not endorse the PRE Talca, and the Mayor persevered in its development without the participation of the central government.
22. Interview with Alejandro Aravena by Asad Syrkett, "Alejandro Aravena." *Architectural Record* 201(3) (2013): 36. Academic Search Premier, EBSCOhost, accessed May 1, 2014.

The participatory approach promoted by the PRES Constitución was materialized in the construction of the Open House or "Casa Abierta," located in the core of the city beside the main foundational plaza. This was the center of operations of the participatory work. All the assemblies and activities to gather the community were held in this place. The Open House was not only a building but also it constituted a symbol of the importance of the participatory approach utilized in this process.

The participation methodology included "hybrid forums," composed of different stakeholders with diverse interests in order to address the opinions of everyone. These forums were the main instance for co-designing the initiatives in close collaboration with the technical teams. This three-month process implied modifications and updates to the designs developed by the team in accordance with the feedback received from citizens. An example of the successive changes was the case of the river park. The function of this park was to protect the city from future flooding and at the same time compensate for the lack of public space, reconnecting the city with the riverside. However this intervention required the use of public domain to expropriate the land. After a controversial process over the need to expropriate riverside owners to build the park, the same citizens decided for this alternative instead of others presented by the technical team.

With the double purpose of ensuring participation and prioritizing the co-designed proposals, the Open House registered more than 10,000 visits, an estimated 1,200 written opinions were received in the "ideas mailbox," 9 hybrid forums were celebrated, in addition to 45 sectorial meetings and 50 thematic gatherings.[23] The community emphasized the need to reconstruct public buildings and housing that were destroyed by the tsunami and also the construction of mitigation infrastructure to reduce damage in case of future tsunamis. In addition, several pre-disaster urban problems were addressed, such as the need for transportation infrastructure improvements, the reactivation of commerce and the diversification of economy for long-term development, addressing the lack of public spaces, improving accessibility to the river shore, and controlling bad smells generated by the cellulose plant.

Considering the needs raised by the citizens, the PRES Constitución team developed multiple initiatives grouped in five lines of work: infrastructure, open space and social facilities, housing, economic development, and sustainable energy. The infrastructure line included a mobility plan, a water management plan, and a mitigation plan composed by tsunami mitigation infrastructure and an evacuation system of routes and safe areas. The main proposal related to the line of public space and social facilities was the river park to recover and upgrade the city's green space and also serve

---

23. Eugenio Tironi. "Modelo participativo para el diseno de planes maestros," Recontrucción Urbana Post 27F (MINVU, 2012). Santiago, Chile: Government of Chile.

as tsunami mitigation infrastructure. The housing plan included several typologies of condominiums distributed in the urban area; among them, the incremental housing project of Villa Verde designed by ELEMENTAL. The economic development plan sought to diversify the economic base, combining industrial activities with tourism. To do so, tourist-related infrastructure and open facilities related to wood production were proposed. Finally, the sustainable energy plan attempted to promote a shift to the use of renewable energy sources by reusing the heat produced in the cellulose plant, producing biogas from waste management and recycling, and the inclusion of solar panels in housing projects.

The PRES Constitución was proposed with a sense of opportunity and as a long-term vision for the sustainable development of the city, grounded in reality by the strong participatory process conducted. Six years after the disaster, however, the implementation of the plan shows high levels of completion on the housing projects and some public facilities such as the public library and cultural center, and low levels of completion regarding the bigger urban projects, delaying the expected social and economic recovery. Despite the criticism, given the participatory nature of the process, the community understands that major urban infrastructure projects affect larger areas and require more resources, so anxiety has been reduced as they are aware that such projects tend to take longer to plan and implement compared to individual buildings and other construction. This fact illustrates the challenge of how to manage community expectations in a plan, which included different types of initiatives, defined by a highly participatory process that will take a long period of time to be implemented.

Furthermore, the complexity of the multiple urban proposals contained in the PRES, are a good example of the need of extended multi-sectorial coordination necessary for their successful and timely implementation, which extends from the phase of design to their construction and completion. Without an execution team with a decision-making capacity and funding that can bridge the existent gaps among governmental sectors and can perform continuous monitoring of the overall progress of the works beyond political cycles, it's hard to affirm when and if the implementation of many of the urban proposals included in the plan will be achieved.

One of the main innovations at the central government in order to coordinate all PRES and PRBC plans was the creation of the Reconstruction Executive Committee. This committee was hosted by the Secretary of Regional Development of the Ministry of Interior Affairs, and had the mandate to seat at the same table the reconstruction coordinators from all of the different ministries and agencies, along with the reconstruction coordinators from every region and town. This committee had weekly meetings, dedicated to reviewing the progress of the Plans for every region and town, reporting and generating indicators to follow and accelerating the design, approval, and funding at the National Public Investment System. Some of the benefits of the Reconstruction Executive Committee came via its capacity to break traditional sectorial silos and agendas, leveraging multi-sectorial investments and forcing the sharing of critical information among agencies. On the other hand, it did not contest the capacity and power held in the different agencies, ministries, or territories – as happened in the case of the Presidential Delegate to Chaitén that overlapped the existing local capacities – so instead of changing or improvising institutional or governmental super-structures, it innovated within the existing bureaucratic structure and emphasized that it should work efficiently and in a coordinative manner. In other words, the lessons from the slow and complex reconstruction efforts that derived from the failure of Chaitén had now been learned and integrated into key innovations at the planning, participation, and institutional levels.

5. Key Issues, Innovations, and Lessons Learned

The experience of these three cases help to understand how to overcome difficulties of developing resilient urban recovery master plans given the complexity of post-disaster recovery. Among the key issues to be addressed in any recovery effort we must consider:

- Creating a management and execution capacity that builds upon and stresses the existing bureaucratic structures;
- Strengthening opportunities for community involvement;
- Designing a realistic and technically grounded plan;
- Incorporating, empowering, and strengthening local capacities;
- Reconciling transparency with efficiency;
- Building common indicators and defining goals to move forward;
- Maintaining leadership and achieving political consensus.

Once those issues have been identified and taken into consideration, it is important to have the capacity to adapt to change, particularly when change is prompted by natural disasters that severely affect the main economic drivers of those communities. In that sense, it is key to innovate and challenge pre-existing institutional frameworks in order to move as rapidly as possible from planning to implementation. Among the main innovations in implementation developed from the 27F recovery we can find:

- Design-based master plans as integrators: PRES, PRBC and PRU;[24]
- Promotion of inter-sectorial coordination: the Reconstruction Executive Committee;
- Enhancement of local and national collaboration;
- Definitions of the role and limitations of private-sector involvement and integrating of the community;
- The providing of an adequate financial model to succeed.

---

24. **PRU: Planes de Renovación Urbana.**

In terms of the lessons learned, most of the difficulties, failures, and complexities of any urban recovery plan are related to the underestimation of the importance of the following issues:

- Communicating the complexity of the task in order to better manage community expectations;
- Involving and obtaining commitment from local leaders, by integrating them from the earlier phases of the process;
- Avoiding displacement if possible, and always incorporating participation to define alternative solutions when possible;
- Promoting strategies for urban resilience and regeneration for a sustainable development;
- Incorporating risk mitigation works that can also serve as social infrastructure to improve livelihoods (e.g. mitigation parks);
- Integrating actions for social and economical recovery going beyond just physical rebuilding;
- Balancing the vision of the disaster as an opportunity for improvements and what can be implemented;
- Diversifying the economical activities in mono-industrial towns is seen as highly recommended, using reconstruction as a driver for new businesses and services that could add value to the community and make it more sustainable in the long-term.

6. Conclusions

One of the biggest innovations of the recovery process following "27 F" was the incorporation of the Master Plans for Reconstruction, called PRES and PRBC18 for large urban and coastal areas, and PRU urban regeneration plans for intermediate locations. These plans allow coordination and acceleration of the reconstruction of critical infrastructure, facilities, and public spaces with a comprehensive, participatory vision and understanding the recovery as an opportunity to improve quality of life and community resilience. While master plans still do not exist as a planning tool in Chilean legislation, its implementation in over 150 towns made it possible to generate a portfolio of projects prioritized by each community that is now up and running. In the case of the coastal towns, by 2014 more than 27 urban infrastructure recovery projects had been completed with more than 120 million dollars invested, with examples as successful as Dichato, Coliumo, or Talcahuano; and there are still about 46 projects in progress with an expected investment of 200 million dollars. Unlike what some critics believe, the level of progress of the main urban proposals comprised in the PRES, PRBC and PRU is within the expected timeframe, as stated in the MINVU Reconstruction Plan published in 2010,[25] where it is estimated that the

---

25. Ministry Housing and Urban Planning (MINVU) (2010). Reconstruction Plan: Chile United for Better Reconstruction, 1st edn. Santiago, Chile: Government of Chile. 12.

execution of the majority of the projects considered will run until 2018, as it comprises highly complex projects such as the river and tsunami mitigation park currently being built in Constitución.

The effectiveness of the PRES and PRBC, and their decentralized nature, as in the case of Biobío where the Agency for Reconstruction coordinated 18 plans and was awarded the National Urban Prize in 2013, account for the value of urban design for building resilient communities. This experience has been collected into the New National Urban Development Policy enacted by President Piñera in 2013 and ratified by President Bachelet, and hopefully will soon allow incorporating the Master Plans as tools that can provide the necessary guidelines for the development of the best possible cities in times of disaster and peacetime alike.

References

Doug Ahlers, *Genesis of Recupera Chile* (Cambridge, MA: Belfer Center for Science and International Affairs, Harvard Kennedy School, 2013).

Iván Cartes, "Plan Maestro de Reconstrucción de Dichato: del sitio cero a las plataformas de futuro," *Arquitecturas Del Sur* 38 (December 2010).

Ministry Housing and Urban Planning (MINVU), *Reconstruction Plan: Chile United for Better Reconstruction*, 1st edn. (Santiago, Chile: Government of Chile, 2010).

Ministry Housing and Urban Planning (MINVU), *Reconstrucción Urbana Post 27F* (Santiago, Chile: Government of Chile, 2013).

05

Mina de Chuquicamata, Agustina González Cid, 2015

1. Introduction: Territorial Complexity of Extraction

Throughout its history, Chile has developed an economic model based mainly on mining activities, and mining appears as the main activity nationwide, alone providing almost 20% of the gross domestic product. The great Chilean mining produces a third of global copper production and expects a significant increase in production in the coming decade. This is an increase in both positive and negative impacts for regions and communities living around the mining sites. The mining industry, along with internalizing the requirements of new technologies, greater efficiency, and productivity, are now required to integrate sustainability and, most recently, long-term planning in consensus with the communities they affect.

While there is broad consensus on these demands and needs, little progress has been made specifically in terms of how initiatives and projects should be part of a solution, much less provide types of solution to solve the problem. In part, attempts to address such demands were formulated on the basis of incomplete assumptions that considered only the intra-urban dimensions, regardless of the mining production systems in the area. Moreover, solutions have been based on prevailing trends of urban and architectural projects of the moment without considering the territorial realities of the place. This is a case study of the mining cluster of Calama, where mining centers extend over more than 100 kilometers from its urban and logistics center. While this logic of an extended mining district has created new opportunities and benefits, it has also had significant costs for the city of Calama, such as the significant increase in congestion, strong demand for public services, intense impact of the floating population by multiple processes of segregation, permanent damage to the archaeological heritage, and imminent danger to the conservation of the Oasis of Calama, among many others.

It is from this perspective that this chapter of the book arises from an analytical focus through the development and uses of methodologies of analysis, management, and modeling of spatial data that intends to measure the extension of the mining cluster. Thus, the main objective is to generate through this process the evidence of a reported spatial calculation in determining the territorial characteristics of a complex mining cluster. Attempting to understand a new territorial dimension produced by unconventional processes such as mining development, it also includes a new range of new understandings to address new scales and territorial dynamics, different from those used in city environments. These scales involve at least three categories. First, determining the dimensions of the spaces territorialized by mining. Second, characterizing levels of functional dependence of the cluster between operational centers of mining and the city that operates as a logistics center in the production process. And third, analyzing the intense infrastructure linking flows of inputs and outputs that are made in relation to mining in different degrees of urbanization over its notion of territorial extension.

Overall, the challenge is how to stop the isolation of problems only focused inside the head city, or only on mining extraction locations, or only dedicated to the natural environment as unconnected elements, and to advance an articulation of a territorial vision that can explain areas of intense productivity; in this case extraction. Establishing these functional correlations in the territory may establish a foundation for the discussion of developing possible scenarios to inform correlations in territories of production as they can be made at early stage decisions.

Incorporating a notion of a productive functional area in a mining cluster like Calama implies an advance response from a territorial perspective to the most fundamental questions related to the exploitation of natural resources on a large scale,[1] namely: how to answer the "contentious" effect of mining in terms of their adverse social, environmental, and economic impact for many but with significant gains only for a few, and how to respond to the ambiguous status between communities and local populations with extraction sites, toward which perhaps mining could contribute much more? In this sense, the existence of so much conflict over mining should not be surprising, since despite the arguments of potential or actual mining profits, there are enough reasons for the territorial socio-economic situation of mining to continue adding to the differences and inequalities.

Therefore, from a territorial perspective, spatial data modeling will be addressed through tools specifically designed for sizing and relating these new scales, as well as establishing connections that exist between the components of these productive landscapes. One of these tools are related to routing capability, also recognized as network analysis, which establishes which system components will be included within the cluster. These are called the functional areas of a mining cluster, and are determined by the road structure between components, and the connectivity and travel times between them. Another of these tools, and used thenceforth, is the consideration of the relative weights of the different system components – these being camps, towns, or villages that have equipment and services used for any purpose in the process of mineral extraction – in order to establish the likelihood of functional dependencies.

2. The Notion of Functional Dependence

So it is necessary to contrast information from resident and floating populations in the cluster, production and waste removal, workers, contractors and mining service companies, and other factors such as resources related to the dependency between mining and their villages and above with its cities that function as system headers.

---

1. Anthony Bebbington, Leonith Hinojosa, Denise Humphreys Bebbington, Maria Luisa Burneo, Ximena Warnaars, "Contention and Ambiguity: Mining and the Possibilities of Development," *Development and Change*, 39(6) (2008): 887-914.

With the modeled spatial data, it is possible to establish a cluster of urbanization created by the complex mining activity, based on gravitational or territorial attractiveness models.[2]

In the case of the mining cluster of Calama, like other cases in the Andean mining region, the territorial overlap of mining activities with cities and their regions has created a profound transformation. The concession areas have been gradually extended to form a near continuous domain of exploration and exploitation rights over the territory, along with future implications for water resources, land value, and employment opportunities, among others. These cases illustrate how an economic activity of sufficient intensity and scale in a territory can generate risks and increase uncertainty about the implications for existing life and sustainability. Indeed, a radically extended exploitation right of territorial coverage has been understood as "mapping geographies of risk and uncertainty."[3]

But in turn, areas of concessions point to where extractive activities can potentially occur without necessarily happening, and even, as shown in Figure 1, the mining concessions can cover larger areas than they actually are effectively exploring. That is, the superimposed display of the territory with the concession areas of exploration and mining are the administrative definition of the public authorization to operate in a spatial domain, which does not reflect the spatial correlation between extraction and territory, but rather is a potential interpretation of productive intensity in the territory.

Therefore, to understand the spatial correlation it is also possible to be more solicitous in the spatial understanding of the territorial behavior of extraction. In practice, although the mines are a singular point in space, from the spatial perspective they are in turn more intense. It is necessary to explore methodologies based on territorial evidence that enable spatially delimiting the territorial reality of competencies and conflicts arising from the extraction.

If, on the one hand, the role of cities in the economic and social performance of countries and regions has increased awareness of the importance of urban areas, on the other hand, and in many cases, these same urban areas experience intense territorial relations strategically related to its production system. Therefore, it is significant to not only look in detail at the traditional conceptions of economics and urban planning within cities, but also the relationships of these with their environmental re-

---

2. J.R. Ritsema van Eck and T. de Jong, "Accessibility Analysis and Spatial Competition Effects in the Context of GIS-supported Service Location Planning," *Computers, Environment and Urban Systems*, 23(2) (1999): 75-89.
3. Anthony Bebbington, N. Cuba, and John Rogan, "Visualizing Competing Claims on Resources: Approaches from Extractive Industries Research," *Applied Geography* 52 (Aug. 2014): 55-56.

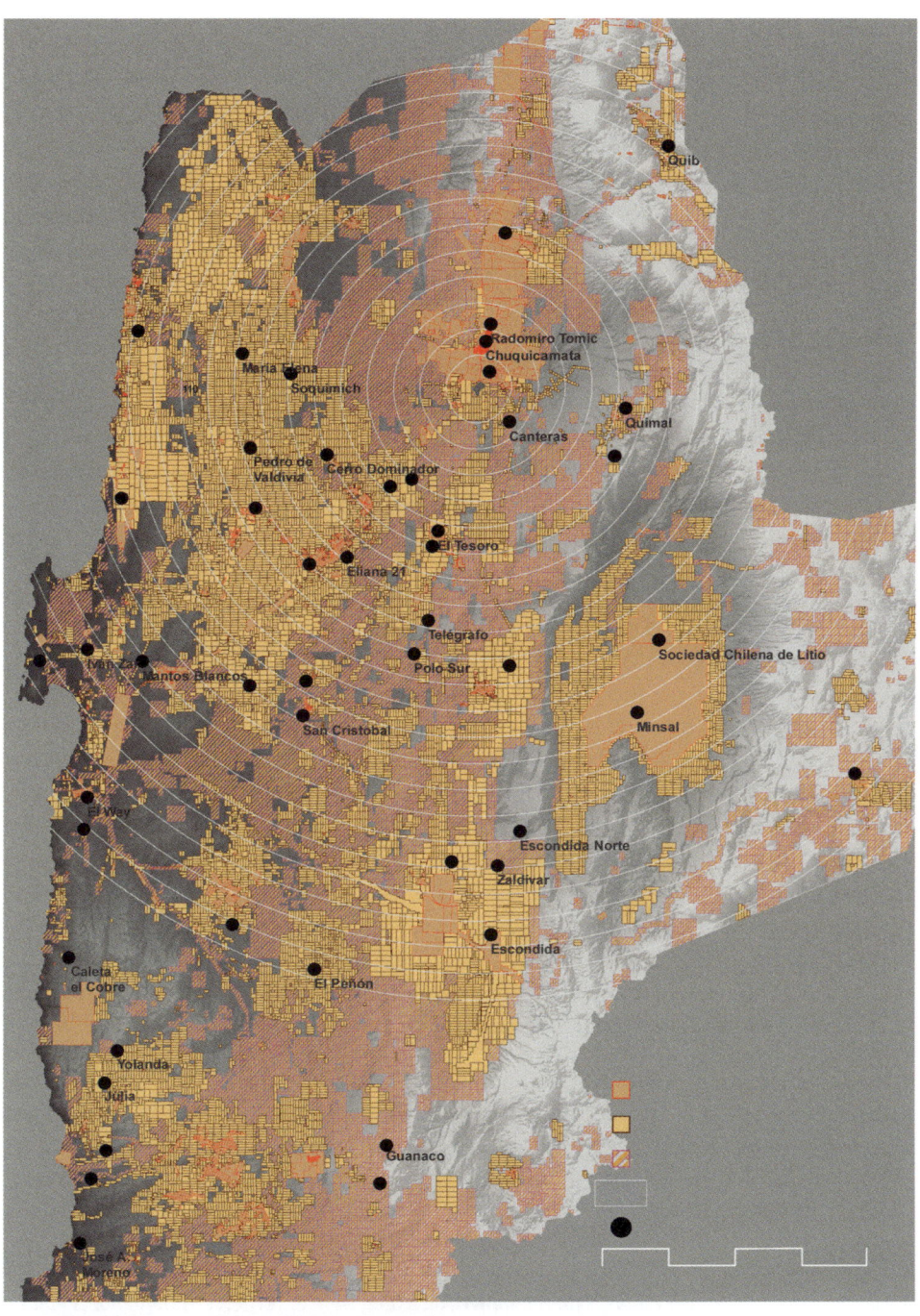

Figure 1: Mining Concessions at the Region of Antofagasta, Chile.
Source: Center for Territorial Intelligence, using IDE from Ministry of Mining.

sources in relation to production in order to understand and eventually adopt models that incorporate territorial relations between natural resources and mining.[4]

In this sense, the mining cluster of Calama is a form of widespread urbanization in the territory. There is evidence of how the magnitude and complexity of producing an economic sector is able to impact the developmental conditions and quality of life in a territory.[5] The main objectives of the development of the region, such as increasing social cohesion, critically depend on how cities grow and how they interact with each other and with their zones of territorial influence.

However, it is not only development in the classical sense in which urbanization is what fits the definition of urban and city, but also a broader definition and more ambiguous than the duality of urban and rural time. It takes more understanding of the fact that this development is not new, but just trying to register and properly link it to spatial systems, because it can take many forms and in turn can have an impact on the social and economic development and even within the same city. Therefore, public policies require good modeling of spatial and functional relationships on the use of resources. Currently, little is known about the diversity of the dynamics of extensive urbanization in a mining cluster that has an important impact on public policy.

The territories in which mining intervened over centuries through explorations, excavations, camps, roads, energy infrastructure, water use, transportation of supplies, waste, and more, eventually generated the successive intervention of urbanization. This has two distinct natural conditions and unexplored territories. First, they have modifications and interventions that respond to the business model system for which compliance functions. Second, it is a production system with a series of activities that mobilize resources, inputs, waste, and products throughout the territory. So for both conditions, the occupation of space is understood as a result of the physical environment, population, production, property, infrastructure, buildings, equipment, regulatory frameworks, both institutionally and socially. Of all of them, the territorial model is an effort to synthesize the correlation and spatial organization of all the elements: an area of functional dependence.

To establish an area of functional dependency on a cluster of extraction, it is compulsory to understand the territorial framework in which these relations are located. Therefore it is necessary to explain the way in which the various stakeholders, communities, and society relate, occupy, and transform the territorial space of mineral production.[6] Within this criterion are considered growth processes of relations in

---

4. Neil Brenner and Stuart Elden, "Henri Lefebvre on State, Space, Territory," *International Political Sociology*, Vol.3(4) (2009): 353-377.
5. Patricio Aroca and Nathaly Rivera, "Escalas de producción en economías mineras: El caso de Chile en su dimensión regional," *EURE* (Santiago) 40(121) (2014): 247-270.

space, decreased activity, correlations between the spatial elements of the territory and activities happening in it. From this perspective, space is considered both a structure and an infrastructure. Structure to the extent that its intrinsic characteristics are the support to various activities along with social and economic development. Infrastructure to the extent that the activities transform the territory, creating different spaces and different capacities. Thus, the space has a dual role:[7]

> ...[F]irst, it is the framework in which all social processes (economic production, social relations, etc.) to the extent that all human activities are performed in a specific space and time are developed; secondly, space is an integral part of these social processes, because it is a 'resource' which is transformed (infrastructure, buildings, etc.) or preserved in these processes to facilitate reproduction and perpetuation of the same.[8]

A methodology for a territorial model establishes a spatial correlation of strategic components for the purpose of defining a relative notion of dimensions of functions between them, and therefore a sense of hierarchy and the degree of functional relationships of the various mining settlements, towns, and cities in the space of the territory. It is important to characterize the relationships between these entities produced in the territory, ranging from aspects of physical infrastructure, employment, and services to the mining industry. In this regard it may be mentioned beforehand the following functional relationships:[9]

> - The territorial model of a production system:
> The structure of the settlement system and its demographics.
> The structure of the productive system.
> The infrastructure, levels of connectivity, centrality, and urbanization.
> Areas of service facilities and homes.
> Administrative and institutional organization of the territory.
> The land uses, concessions for exploration and exploitation.
>
> - The basic territorial relations of the territorial system:
> Movements of origin and destination labor work.
> Economic relations of production flows.
> Movements to and from access to equipment.
> Decision centers and cultural, political, and social control over the area.

---

6. Antonio Serrano, "El modelo territorial europeo: tendencias para el siglo XXI y sus implicaciones para el modelo territorial español," *Urban* 8 (2003): 35-54.
7. Ibid.
8. Ibid., 36.
9. Ibid.

As the delimitation of the territorial area is functionally related to the extractive industry, the limits of a functional area do not correspond to conventional characterizations of the urban and the rural, or other similar territorial categorization; the limits tend to be vague and diverse in their definitions of criteria according to the variables considered above. In the case of urban functional areas, their borders and boundaries have spread to distances as great as 100 km, but they most likely correspond to a spatial continuity of the built city surface. Instead, in the case of productive functional areas, the economic model of those consistent with profitability, the zone's extensions can be more than four times greater when connected by the intense flow while deprived of any continuity in the infrastructure of constructed buildings.

Extrapolated from the methodology for defining functional urban areas as functional economic areas developed by the OECD,[10] comparing their size, form of development, density, and population growth, a definition of productive functional areas was found in order to better analyze the relationships between urbanization and economic growth of complex sites as a mining cluster, where development can occur through the diversity of links between one or more urban areas and one or more extraction sites. This is intended to take an initial step towards developing a new understanding of the ways productive territories grow, and specifically dedicated to the extraction of natural resources.

In its methodology, the OECD identifies the following three steps to redefine urban areas. These are the same steps taken for this investigation and subsequently explained in detail in the methodology. The steps are as follows:
 1. Areas of continuous urbanization or highly inter-connected urban centers are identified.
 2. Urbanized areas are identified with a functional relationship.
 3. Mobility area or functional area is a defined territory.

In the case of a productive functional area, such as the case of the Calama Mining Cluster, these steps have been adapted as follows:
 1. Areas of urbanization, hereinafter "collection centers" and the city center, in this case the city of Calama, are identified. The result is the definition of which mining centers, located by geological conditions of natural resources, have a link to the city center and city headboard understood as those without the condition according to the efficiency of travel time from one to other.
 2. Extraction centers highly interconnected with the city of Calama, one of the two capital cities in the Region of Antofagasta and Calama Antofagasta, are identified. Extraction centers are considered integrated because they use services and trans-

---

10. M. Brezzi, "Redefining urban areas in OECD countries", in OECD, *Redefining "Urban": A New Way to Measure Metropolitan Areas* (Paris: OECD Publishing, 2012).

portation infrastructure of the city center. In addition, all the mining centers are differentiated by travel time accessibility to the city center.

3. In identifying mining centers related to the city center by way of a polycentric system, the last step is to define the territorial form of this system or hinterland. The dimension of this area will be a dimension in the case of using the demographic amount of workers.

The outcome is a new territorial definition of the limits generated by the functional relationship of a production process and not the administrative political character such as communes. In addition, you can subsequently add other variables of territorial domains such as transport and export ports of mining products, the location of waste, capturing water resources, origin and transport of labor and productive inputs, services and specialized outsourcing, among other dimensions.

3. Methodology: Unit Determination and Cluster Modeling

The methodology is approached from two perspectives in the case of the mining cluster of Calama: on the one hand, the displacements generated in the territory and the consequent generation of their areas of influence, also known as hinterlands; and secondly, the establishment of functional groupings clustered between the mining sector and territorial dependent urban areas. The first analysis was developed through the use of routing tools, making a modeling of the time for establishing the hinterland or area of influence of the primary cities in the Region of Antofagasta and Calama Antofagasta. The aim is to verify from the perspective of time and the corresponding composition of mining for the header cities to which they relate. The second approach corresponds to the use of spatial interaction models (accessibility) based on the offer of a territorial center (regional or provincial capital city), known as gravitational models.

3.1 Network Model Displacement

The displacement model network uses private transport impedance to discriminate based on the shortest time, and which are the optimal routes. From this calculation, service areas are the spatial concatenation of optimal routes of equal time, in other words the generation of isochronous curves. This methodology is usually occupied for calculating market areas in urban environments[11] and the definition of adequacy of equipment in areas of urban development.[12] This will define the limit where the choice of a city as an urban header for the group of mines in the region of Antofagasta is determined between the cities of Calama or Antofagasta. Note that this calculation

---

11. Galetovich, Poduje & Sanhueza, "Malles en Santiago, de centros comerciales a centros urbanos," *Estudios Públicos* 114 (2009).
12. K. Oh and S. Jeong, "Assessing the spatial distribution of urban parks using GIS," *Landscape and Urban Planning* 82 (2007): 25–32.

is based solely on the connectivity provided by the network (number of existing roads between origins and destinations of trips) and travel speeds on it (and thus time) for the main roads.[13] The result is then verified with the modeling of optimal routes, in order to confirm the appropriate use of the interurban road structure in the choice of destination. While this method assesses the territorial status of connectivity and access times as a condition that is not random, but responds to a phenomenon of localization of a sequence of productive activities in the territory, it avoids parameters of spatial interaction of interest to analyze where a territorial system presents a significant density of dispersed production activities in the territories and two regional head cities that can serve as places to facilitate the habitability of these productive activities. Depending on this, the use of a gravitational model is proposed.

3.2 Gravitational or Spatial Interaction Model

The application of the gravitational model[14] should consider a variable supply or destination, and displacement. The variable displacement can be given by the impedance measured across the network or private transportation's actual distance, or also by the Euclidean distance.[15] The mathematical formalization of the gravity model, adapted from the model proposed by Ullman (1980) is as follows:

$$T_{ij} = k \frac{P_i P_j}{d_{ij}}$$

---

13. The road system is calibrated according to the road hierarchy with assigned average speeds for urban areas and maximum speeds for intercity roads.
14. Gravitational models come from the empirical adaptation of the traditional model of Law of Universal Gravitation, published by Newton in the seventeenth century. Adaptation and corresponding application was particularly attractive in territorial spatial interaction models, specifically addressed through the models of location theory developed by Von Thünen, Weber, and Christaller, among other contributions of economic geography (A: Precedo, *Ciudad y Desarrollo urbano* (Madrid: Editorial Síntesis, S.A.,1996); L. M. Ruiz and C. Marmolejo Duarte, "Hacia una metodología para la detección de subcentros comerciales: un análisis para Barcelona y su Área Metropolitana," *Arquitectura, Ciudad y Entorno* 8 (2008): 199-217). Applications of this type of model subsequently varied for use in transport models (Edward Ullman, "Geography as Spatial Interaction," in *Geography as Spatial Interaction by Edward Ullman*, ed. Ronald R. Boyce (Seattle: University of Washington Press, 1980), 13-27) and intercity or regional territorial contexts, as well in the territorial development of urban polycentricity work (J. Parr, "The Polycentric Urban Region: A Closer Inspection," *Regional Studies* 38(3): 231-240).
15. Euclidean distance corresponds to the calculation of a straight line between the origin and destination; this measure is usually replaced by the actual travel throughout urban environments; however, for regional measurements this is less sensitive.

Where:
T_{ij} is the spatial interaction between origin i (mining) and destination j (head city).
P_i and P_j correspond to the population of origin and destination. In the case of origin, for calculating mining centers working as a unit.[16]
d_{ij} impedance understood as distance or travel time between origin and destination.

The result of the method is applied in a dual manner, always referred to the situation of origins. On the one hand, the location of the origin with respect to the chosen destination is evaluated – in this case for Calama or Antofagasta; a second indicator corresponds to the probability of belonging to the destination, thus the higher the probability, the more likely the connection and therefore less likely to be unelected. In the particular case of application of Calama's cluster, as potential destinations there are two values of weights that can take a trip between 0.5 and 1. The interpretation, and then the result, will be the definition of the cluster according to which variable weight is applied; in this case it is demographic. Notwithstanding that in this case, this definition will be established in discrete form, evaluated in reference to the points (in this case mining), and therefore it is necessary to define a continuous spatial definition from these points.

3.3 A Cluster Definition

To build the territorial definition of the mining cluster, specifically corresponding to Calama, the network analysis methodologies for the generation of service areas is again used. The formation of the service areas should follow the logic of market areas,[17] that is to say, mutually exclusive in terms of the regional head cities. The complexity and adaptation is such that the cluster must be created from mining, and the duality of choice between the head cities of Calama or Antofagasta requires the establishment of an area of overlap that must be prioritized from the shortest time from the communal head. In practical terms, the methodology for identifying the cluster process can be defined in the following scheme.

4. Calama's Mining Cluster Territorial Definition

4.1 Modeling Displacement Times

The first form of analysis addressed has to do with the direct modeling of time travel to the cities that act as headers within the region of Antofagasta. For this, it is set directly based on calibration shifts with average speeds in urban areas and displacement with maximum speeds in interurban areas.

---

16. Later the dimensions of each of the mines, testing variables of production, and number of workers added.
17. Galetovich, Poduje & Sanhueza, "Malles en Santiago, de centros comerciales a centros urbanos," *Estudios Públicos* (2009): 114.

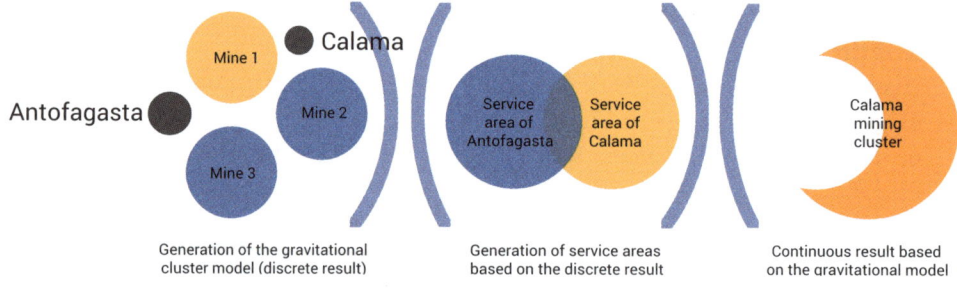

Scheme 1: Methodological Framework for Defining Cluster
Source: Center for Territorial Intelligence, 2015

The result presented on the map in Figure 2 shows the territorial status of accessibility understood as the simple measurement of time. Such modeling is not isometric, but is subject to the speed limit for the road infrastructure and the presence of the same road connectivity, which in this case is directly linked to the location of cities, but also to the productive mining activity in the region. This activity in many cases is the only explanation for the siting and development of roads, highways, and freeways to territories clearly isolated from the demographic perspective. This then allows a first approach based on territorial modeling of the area of influence generated from the cities, but grounded in the mining industry, in which, in the case of this model, its road infrastructure is mainly supposed to serve production and connect with other chains in the territorial process.

In order to check travel times between the head cities of Calama and Antofagasta through optimal routes, these are defined in more detail according to the road infrastructure situation and their respective network, as shown in Figure 3. This confirms that the situation of the service areas as functional territory exceeds the conventional hinterland of an intermediate-sized city and seeks criteria that go beyond long-distance connectivity between Calama and Antofagasta, or situations between these two cities and the port of Mejillones. The density of the road system is explained by the locations of multiple secondary activities related to mining, situated in a territory with unusual features for generating the infrastructure, such as low density localities, high territorial concentration, and difficulties in the desert-type of habitability, among others.

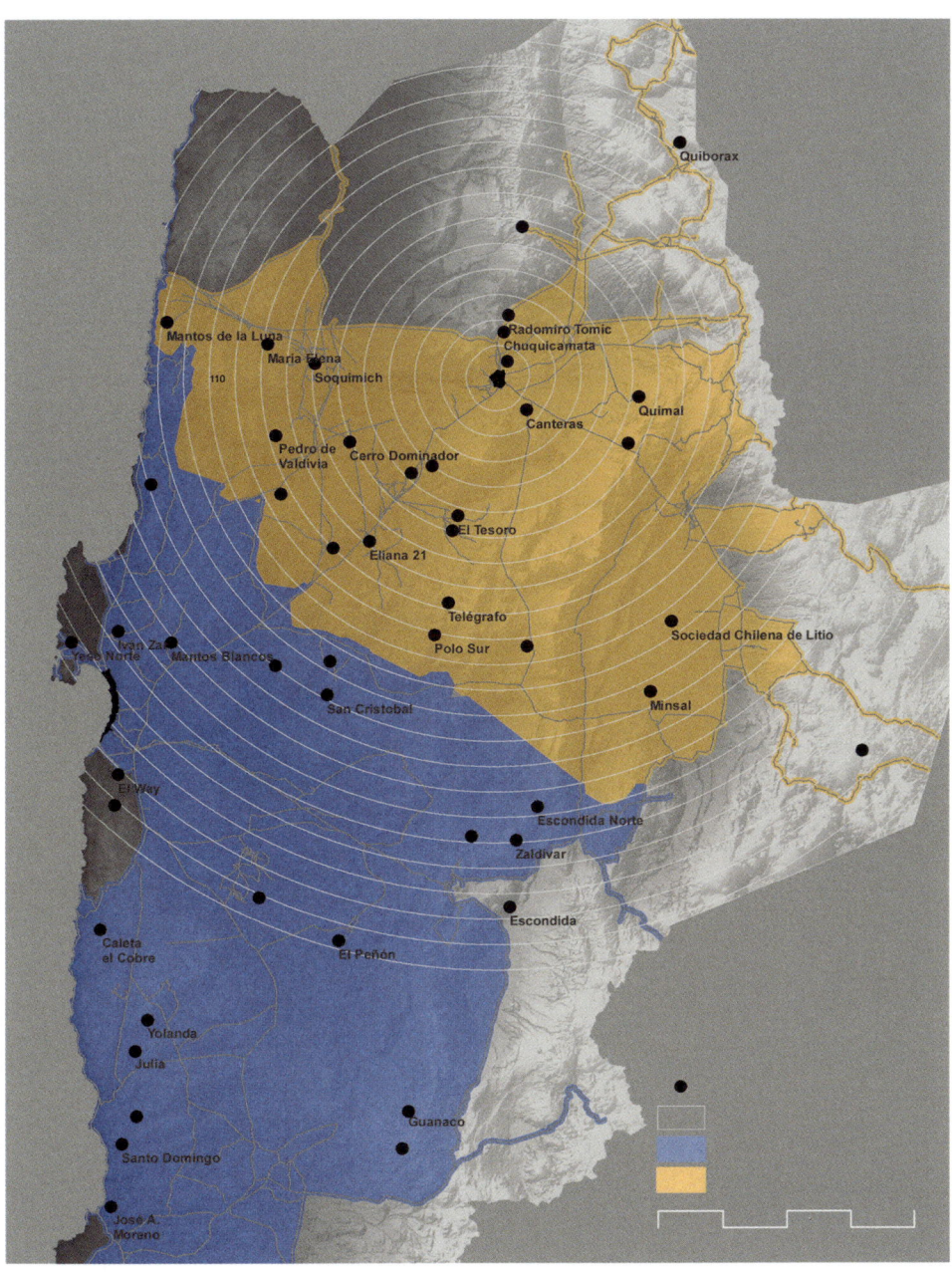

Figure 2: Catchment Areas by Travel Times
Source: Center for Territorial Intelligence, 2015

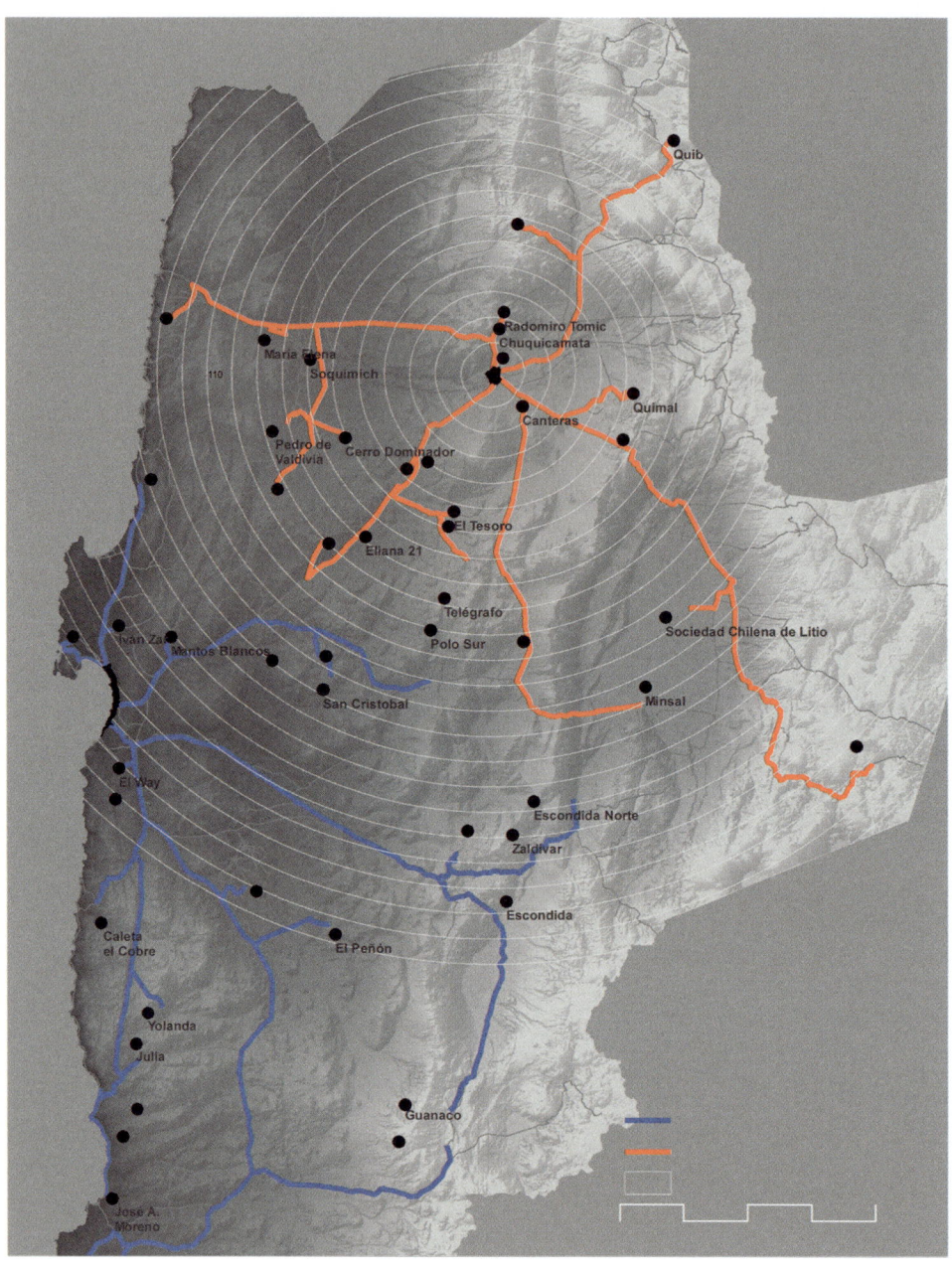

Figure 3: Territorial Map of Time Displacement
Source: Center for Territorial Intelligence, 2015

Notwithstanding the foregoing, the definition purely explained through time and connectivity does not allow for a more complex understanding of spatial relations, and it is the reason why it is necessary to deepen the interaction between the urban and productive activities in the territory. The specific weight values of the respective head cities as presented in this methodology – which are understood as fundamental functional units for the mining activity throughout a territory – do not grasp low-quality living conditions among the diverse components of the mining cluster. All this requires having a large amount of information to find those links and to seize them.

4.2 Gravitational Models Based on Demographic Weight

Previously, in order to establish a functional area in a territory not only through mobility, a model for evaluating the potential attractiveness of the header cities in the Region of Antofagasta was applied. A first variable in this line is the demographic weight of these cities, for which it is evaluated with the population data extracted and projected from the Pre-Census 2011 (Source: Prepared on the basis INE, 2011). Upon applying the variable gravity model adapted from Ullman,[18] the following results, which can be seen in Figure 4, are obtained:

- Of the 52 mining sites considered in the regional analysis (with medium and large mining) 28 are within the area of likely preference of Antofagasta as a cluster and 24 of Calama as a cluster.
- Antofagasta cluster's 28 sites are at an average distance of 162 kilometers; Calama cluster's 24 sites are at 106 kilometers.
- Overall, the average probability of belonging to mining sites in Calama is 92.4%; for Antofagasta 93.89%.
- The functional limit of the model is given for Calama as being between 95-130 kilometers linear distance, while for Antofagasta it is between 65-105 kilometers.

Importantly, the gravitational model establishes a functional limit, which although Antofagasta has more than twice the population of Calama, its capture area is smaller, as shown in Figure 4. This is possible to explain through two reasons: the first being that Antofagasta has a area of greater dispersion of mines, a more linear emphasis toward the southern part of the region, and the reason why it loses some strength against Calama; the second has to do with the higher road density of Calama, as noted above, a situation that allows you to have more alternatives to reach destinations, with lower average actual distance.

---

18. Edward Ullman, "Geography as Spatial Interaction," 13-27.

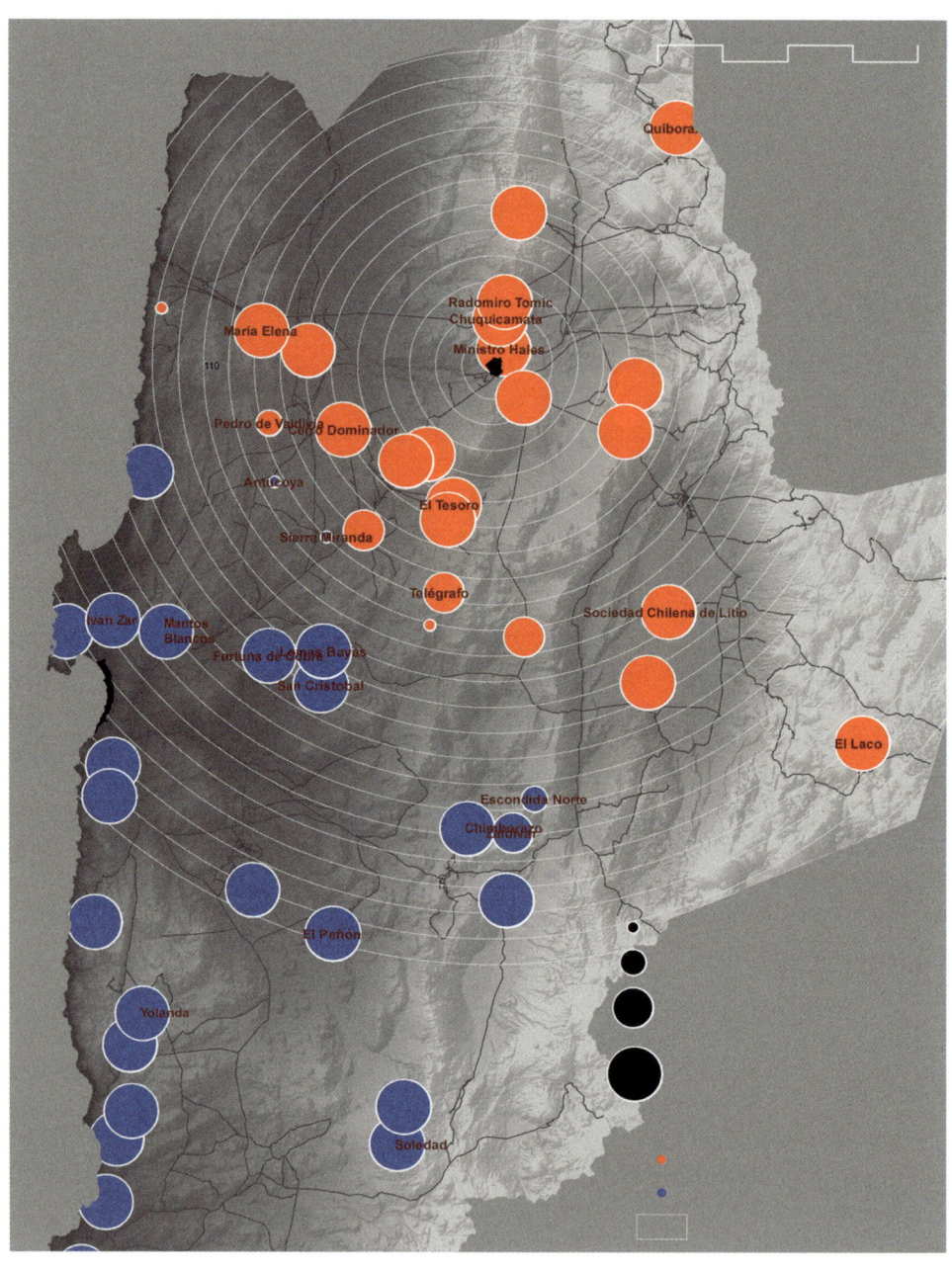

Figure 4: Gravitational Model, based on demographic weight
Source: Center for Territorial Intelligence, 2015

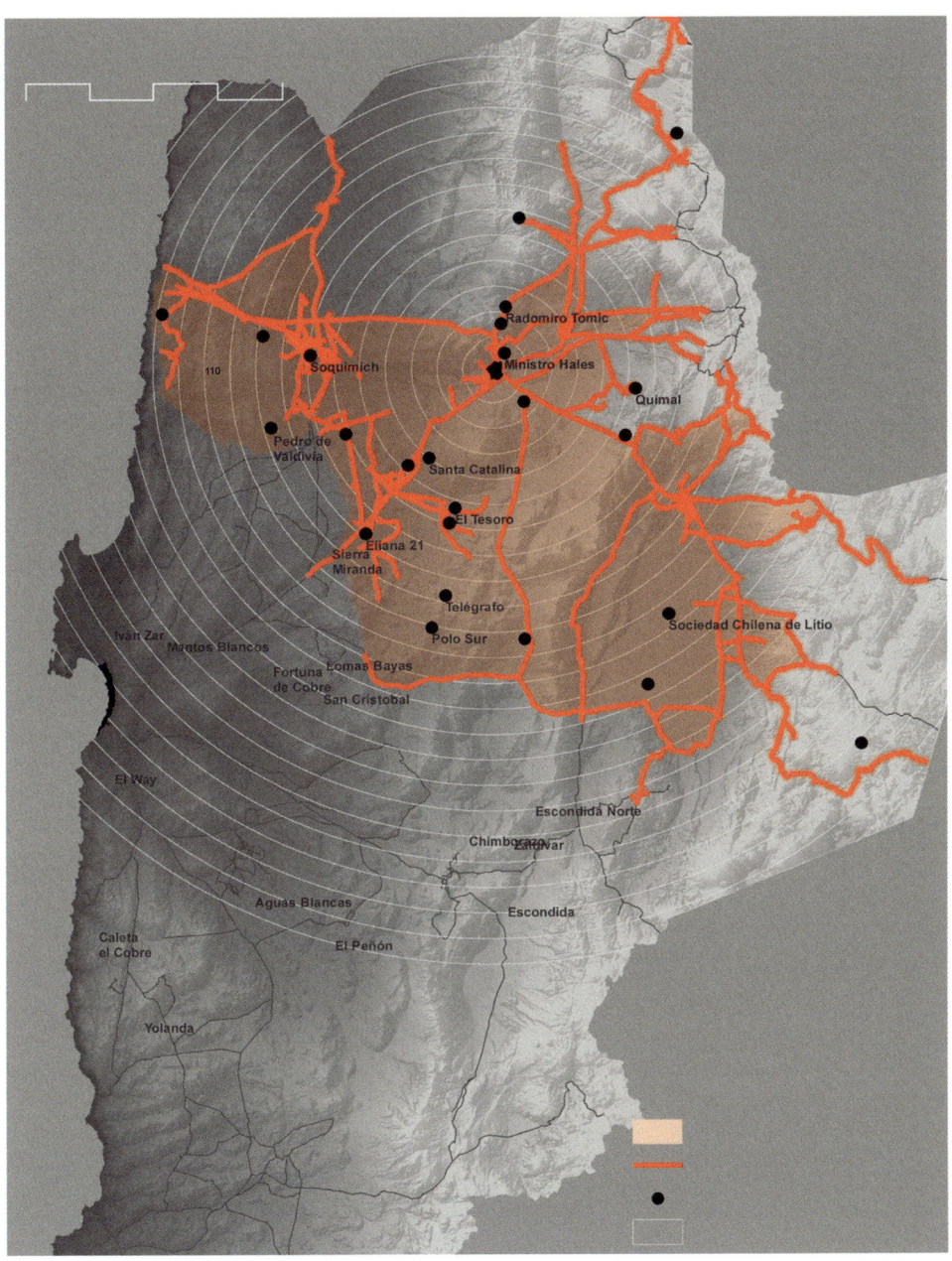

Figure 5: Mining Cluster
Source: Center for Territorial Intelligence, 2015

4.3 Mining Cluster

The developed model builds the hypothetical territorial extension of the mining cluster to Calama, which means from discrete to continuous modeling information; the method used is the creation of service areas, this time from the production areas. The definition of the mining cluster is then constructed from the functional perspective through overlapping service areas of satellite mines in Calama and their respective routes. This sets a territory or hinterland around Calama's productive sector that determines the interaction logic of the city understood as providing head city livability to the rest of the productive territory.

Challenges Facing Complex Functionality

One of the conclusions is that mining has a very high capacity for transforming the territory, and the construction of the functional area related to the mining cluster of Calama proves it. Indeed, as a result of the methodology applied to the definition of functional areas of production, it is possible to produce a spatial representation that covers the production system based on territorial evidence and is to be confirmed by operational decisions in extraction centers. The single display of the extended territory of Calama's Mining Cluster allows us to understand the depth of the territorial impact as a result of the dynamics of economic sector. From this, it is possible draw conclusions related to the extent of urbanization in areas of extraction, the dynamics of the various movements of flows, the complexity of services and outsourcing in mining, and other territorial dimensions related to resources and waste. Subsequently, these characteristics are detailed as follows.

5.1 The City and the Extension of its Urbanization

As initially discussed, a city in a mining cluster, such as the case of the city of Calama, consists not only of the urban but also of the system generated from it up to the locations of extraction points. In that sense, the territorial definition of the cluster is more extensive than the logic of any existing political or administrative boundaries. The map of Calama's Mining Cluster, shown in the figure above, defines the direct and functional relationship between the two types based on the direct link made through road infrastructure centers. First, the association was generated by a strong logic cluster in terms of corridors. For the specific case of Calama, we can count up to six corridors. Second, cluster management logic is constituted by thresholds measuring accessibility from the city center. Thus, both measurements establish the criteria for the definition of the extent of urbanization in the cluster. Remarkably, the cluster of Calama is widely extended territorially, as evidenced by comparing its situation with that of Antofagasta (according to the extracted results of the gravity model). From this, it follows that the same productive activity around the city provided a denser road infrastructure in a territory with less dispersion than in the case of Antofagasta's mining cluster.

5.2 Flows of Movement

Mining, and certainly also the case of the mining cluster of Calama, in time, has significantly increased its expansion in every scope of its activity. Environmental issues, concerns about pollution and health, altered landscape impact, and the rights of indigenous cultures have added dimensions to the complexity of mining. In this scenario, a logical observation certainly lies in increasing mining productivity in recent years in Chile. But it is also a plausible reason that the mining productivity and business model has changed to a more complex model with more actors, and is more efficient and more globalized. In other words, to extract a mineral unit many inputs and workers should be mobilized, and this flow of movements has strong repercussions in the territory. Mining is no longer about an isolated extraction camp in a distant territory; new mining extraction has resulted in a complex and extended territorial system configuration. Then, the final definition, if ever possible, of the mining cluster will depend on variables of flows of movement that are linked to mining centers. The territorial definition of the cluster based on linking road infrastructure and the demographic weight of the presented cities and mines are open to other dimensions that generate an even more complex cluster definition.

5.3 Services and Outsourcing

Indeed one of the most noticeable changes in the mining industry since the 1980s has been the increasing incorporation of contract workers, service companies, and outsourcing. Today, on average, for each worker of a mining company, there are three other employees of contractors working on various tasks in the mining center. This proportion of direct and indirect workers reflects the exponential growth of companies dedicated to outsourcing services and mining. As part of that reality, outsourcing services firms operating with one or more mining companies have also been developed. These companies' competition for services and outsourcing realities have had significant spatial implications. On the one hand, the requirements for a service company have increased requirements in terms of security protocols, quality of materials, as well as experience. This has resulted in a tendency to attract global mining services companies, which unlike local companies, are operating in head cities and extraction centers. Moreover, outsourcing companies also have specialized by increasingly taking larger roles in mining companies, such as mining transportation and exploration logistics, housing and food provisions, and even waste removal. As a result, these companies' outsourcing services operate in more than one mine – making the mining cluster an increasingly complex system – intensive among the extraction and infrastructure of the city of Calama as a hub.

Calama, Mailys Meyer, 2015

5.4 Resources and Waste

The origin of the resources needed for mining production is very diverse. Beyond pieces of machinery and highly specialized computer systems, there is another area of resources such as chemicals, fuel, and building materials (mainly concrete and steel) that also have their spatial effects in the final determination of the territory linked to a mining cluster. Likewise, waste from mining production tends to be massive, substantially more massive than the same production of the mineral extracted. As it is shown in the figure below,[19] the waste from the production of copper is 450 times greater than what is produced. Placement and disposal of waste is not only extensive and pollutant, but also has met with stiff public opposition. Therefore, these locations are not only strategic, but also highly sensitive within the territorial definition of the mining cluster.

This research approach takes steps to determine a notion of the territorial extension of the extractive mining activity and thus to establish the territorial areas it involves from a functional perspective. It is also a step toward building an ecosystem approach that is inclusive of processes corresponding to geographical scales. Although mining production occupies a small area of the territory considering the points of extraction, labor, waste disposal, processing and export, compared to other productive activities such as forestry or agriculture, their effects have a high impact and are also spatialized in the territory. However, the discrete location of the procurement system is more extensive given the necessary resources and mobilizes inputs continuously for a certain territory. Consequently, the dominant perspective of the social impacts of mining only based on physical relationships directly related to the industrial process and waste ought to become an integral territorial perspective where different community, government, and mining sector actors are understood.

---

19. Gavin Bridge, "Contested Terrain: Mining and the Environment," *Annual Review of Environment and Resources* 29 (2004): 205-259; Ian Douglas and Nigel Lawson, "Material Flows Due to Mining and Urbanization," in *A Handbook of Industrial Ecology* (Cheltenham, UK: Edward Elgar Publishing, 2002).

Oasis of Calama, Jeannette Sordi, 2015

A Landscape Approach for Calama's Oasis:
Negotiating Landscape Conservation, Agricultural Livelihoods, and Mining
Flavio Sciaraffia, Sourav Kumar Biswas

Part of this paper includes research conducted as part of the project funded by Surdna Foundation on "Next Generation Infrastructure for Sustainable Environments on Water Systems," at the Zofnass Program for Sustainable Infrastructure, Harvard University Graduate School of Design. Summer 2015. Project PI Prof. Spiro N. Pollalis. Research supervised by Richa S. Vuppuluri, Researchers: Sourav Biswas & Flavio Sciaraffia.

1. Introduction

"The operational scale of planning and management today grows inexorably towards the landscape."[1]

Calama's Oasis plays a pivotal role in the historical development of the city, both as a driver of early human settlement and subsequent urbanization, and as a cultural and environmental asset. Water withdrawals for mining activities and urban development have led to a steady retreat of the Oasis over the years. Urban encroachment and speculation endanger agricultural and indigenous livelihoods, the fading cultural-historical heritage, and the untapped opportunities of the Oasis as a landscape element for an extreme-desert urban environment. The lack of planning and policy instruments to deal with the conservation of landscapes embedded in urban systems prevents the proper management of the Oasis in conjunction with urban, extraction, and production processes. From a decision maker's standpoint, harnessing the ecological attributes of the Oasis to improve the quality of the urban environment and bringing certainty to the stakeholders with stakes in its many resources might become a priority if these are unveiled and understood in spatial terms. Considering the need for innovative and actionable approaches for the sustainable management and planning of the Oasis, this research aims to present an alternative planning approach, providing a methodological framework that incorporates Landscape Planning and Landscape Ecology as suitable disciplines to address complex socio-ecological systems involving multiple stakeholders and interests, such as Calama's Oasis.

First, the paper introduces the Landscape Approach as a spatial methodology that could be applied to the Oasis of Calama, and to other landscapes in Chile. Second, it delves into the main spatial questions that need to be considered in order to initiate a Landscape Planning process, and to develop the proposed planning phases in the context of Calama's Oasis. Third, it delves into the theories, methods, and principles stemming from Landscape Ecology and how these inform recent frameworks for Landscape Planning. Fourth, it introduces a set of landscape management and policy strategies that could be applied on site to secure a sustainable transition of the Oasis as urban and regional processes evolve. The paper concludes with a summary of the core attributes of a Landscape Approach, and a discussion regarding the

---

1. Richard Forman, foreword to *Applying Ecological Principles to Land Management*, by Virginia H. Dale and Richard A. Haeuber (New York: Springer-Verlag, 2001), v-vii.

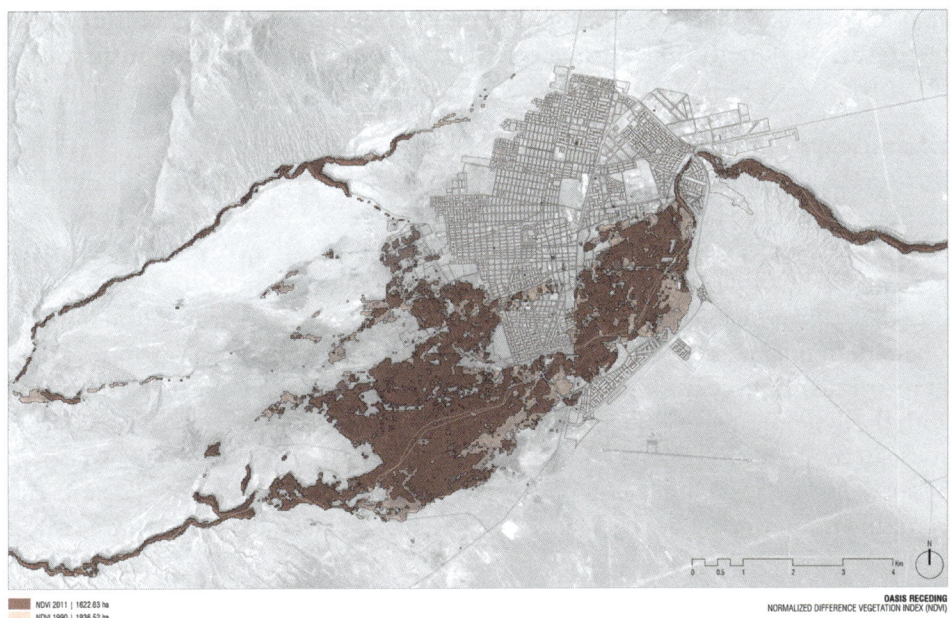

Map 1. Oasis Receding 1990-2011

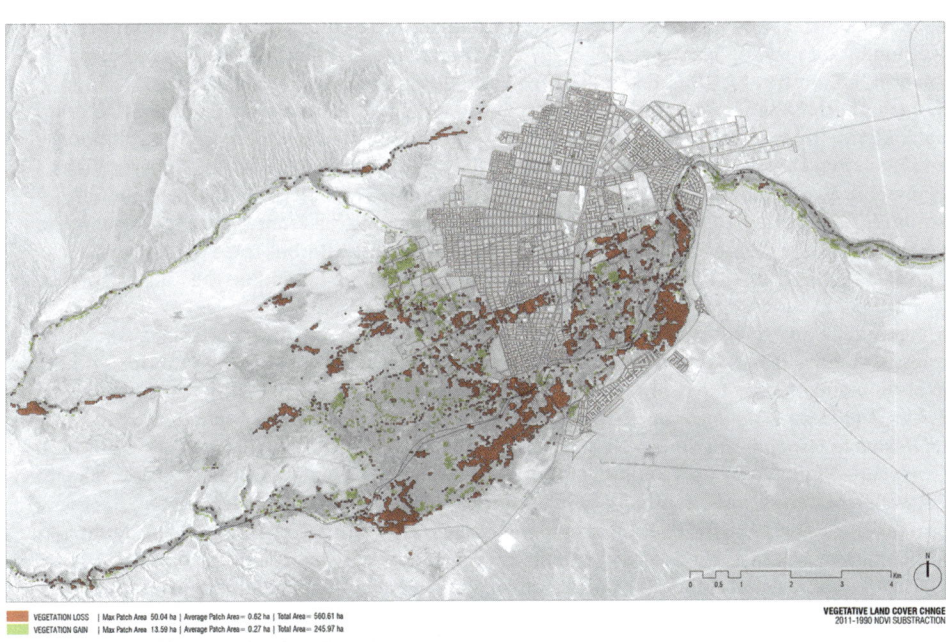

Map 2. Vegetative Land Cover Change 1990-2011

A Landscape Approach for Calama's Oasis | **165**

challenges of developing and implementing such approach, in light of the current regulatory and institutional framework for land development and administration in Chile.

2. Landscape Planning

During the last thirty years, Landscape Planning has re-emerged with the development of Landscape Ecology.[2] As another branch of ecological sciences, Landscape Ecology developed the theoretical and analytical basis to incorporate the spatial dimension into ecology. Eventually, this allowed ecological principles to permeate into disciplines such as spatial planning, design, policy, and decision-making.[3] J. Ahern defines Landscape Planning as the spatial dimension of sustainability aimed to integrate resource conservation and development.[4] Landscape Planning works with the dynamic quality of landscapes, therefore it is never considered complete or static in time. On the contrary, it takes on a strategic and adaptive approach driven by spatial scenarios that act as hypotheses of ecological theories.[5] Several Landscape Planning frameworks have been developed as operational tools in the United States and Europe.[6]

---

2. André Botequilha and Jack Ahern, "Applying Ecological Concepts and Metrics in Sustainable Landscape Planning," *Landscape and Urban Planning* 59 (2002): 65-93.
3. Ibid, 65-93.
4. Jack Ahern, "Spatial Concepts, Planning Strategies, and Future Scenarios: A Framework Method for Integrating Landscape Ecology and Landscape Planning," in *Landscape Ecological Analysis*, ed. Jeffrey M. Klopatek et al. (New York: Springer-Verlag, 1999), 175-201.
5. Jack Ahern, "Spatial Concepts," 175-201; Ahern, Botequilha, "Applying Ecological", 65-93; Jack Ahern, "Integration of Landscape Ecology and Landscape Architecture: An Evolutionary and Reciprocal Process," in *Issues and Perspectives in Landscape Ecology*, ed. John A. Wiens, Michael R. Moss (Cambridge: Cambridge U. Press, 2005), 311-319; Jack Ahern, "Theories, Methods and Strategies for Sustainable Landscape Planning," in *From Landscape Research to Planning: Aspects of Integration, Education and Application,* eds. Bärbel Tress et al. (Dordretch: Springer, 2006), 199-131: and Paul Opdam, "Design in Science: Extending the Landscape Ecology Paradigm," *Landscape Ecology* 23 (2008): 633-644.
6. Botequilha and Ahern [Ahern, Botequilha, "Applying Ecological", 65-93 and Jack Ahern, "Theories, Methods," 199-131] provide a summary of the main frameworks in the American tradition; in chronological order these are: (1) Landscape Planning by Julius G. Fabos (1985): Julius Fabos, *Land-Use Planning. From Global to Local Challenge. A Dowden and Culver Book. Environmental Resource Management Series* (New York: Chapman & Hall, 1985); (2) Framework Method for Landscape Planning by Carl Steinitz (1990): Carl Steinitz, "A Framework for Theory Applicable to Education of Landscape Architects (and other environmental design professionals)," *Landscape Journal* 9 (1990):136-143; (3) Landscape Ecology by Richard T.T. Forman (1995): Richard Forman, *Land Mosaics. The Ecology of Landscapes and Regions* (Cambridge: Cambridge U. Press, 1995); (4) Framework Method for Sustainable Landscape Ecological Planning by Jack Ahern, (1999): Ahern, "Spatial Concepts," 175-201; (5) Ecological Planning Model by Frederick Steiner (2000): Frederick Steiner, *The Living Landscape: An Ecological Approach to a Landscape Planning* (New York: McGraw-Hill, 2000); (6) Sustainable Land Planning by André Botequilha and J. Ahern (2002): Botequilha and Ahern "Applying Ecological", 65-93.

Botequilha *et al.*[7] highlights R.T.T. Forman's framework[8] as being influential in the American context. Forman proposes identifying the landscape elements in a patch-corridor-matrix model, followed by the identification of landscape functions and disturbances, and finally using the correlation between patterns and processes to inform a decision support system.

2.1 A Spatial Methodology

According to J. Ahern,[9] Landscape Planning Frameworks can be categorized according to their theoretical orientation (substantive or procedural), their resource or goal orientation, inter- or trans-disciplinarity, strategic orientation (protective, defensive, offensive, and opportunistic), and the use of spatial concepts. Botequilha and Ahern[10] find that there are commonalities within the different frameworks that have been developed. All of them aim toward sustainability goals and use Landscape Ecology concepts, theories, methods, principles, and guidelines. Drawing from several authors, five phases that are common to most Landscape Planning Frameworks can be recognized.

Phase 1 frames the problem and context, and extracts the main goals and objectives by engaging directly with stakeholders. This phase is deemed critical since the success and sustainability of the planning process will depend on how stakeholders' goals and aspirations are negotiated by understanding the trade-offs and synergies. Phase 2 focuses on background research, data gathering, and characterizing the general

PHASES	DESCRIPTION	SECTIONS	ATTRIBUTES
Phase 1	Problem Framing and Goals	Descriptive / Evaluative	Landscape scale as broad spatial unit and landscape pattern-process-change dynamics as analysis, assessment and projective tools
			Integrated goals and hypothesis (for ecosystem goods or resources; for ecosystem services and functions; and for multiple stakeholders' socio-economic and cultural goals: land use, infrastructure, recreation, preservation, etc.).
Phase 2	Perliminary Analysis		Identification of stakeholders, and integration of local knowledge and values.
			Planning process is replicable, spatially and methodologically explicit.
Phase 3	Landscape Diagnosis		Strategic approach focusing equally in both the drivers of change, and the effects of change
			Related with the above: inter and transdisciplinary
Phase 4	Scenario Modeling	Prescriptive / Planning	Use of spatial scenarios, concepts and iterations
			Scenarios are based on sound landscape ecological theory, concepts, methods, and principles
			It is inherently spatial, design oriented and proactive. Plans and projects are adaptive hypothesis of the effects of pattern over processes
Phase 5	Implementation and Monitoring		Address uncertainty and lack of information through a combination of empirical and intuitive thinking, as well as adaptive management
			It integrates science and planning/design in a feedback loop that allows the creation of new knowledge for adaptive management

Figure 1. Landscape Planning Phases

---

7. Ahern, Botequilha, "Applying Ecological", 65-93.
8. Richard T.T. Forman, *Land Mosaics*.
9. Ahern, "Theories, Methods," 199-131.
10. Ahern, Botequilha, "Applying Ecological", 65-93.

socio-ecological attributes of the landscape. Phase 3 uses the data gathered in the previous phase to perform a landscape diagnosis. This phase precipitates a systemic understanding of how the landscape is functioning, in order to screen for the potential of different management and policy strategies, and to prioritize goals in subsequent phases.

Phase 4 proposes landscape management and policy strategies to be deployed in the landscape context. The strategies are considered best practices and innovative in nature, and are expected to meet the goals as defined by the stakeholders throughout the engagement process. Weaving through the trends highlighted in the problem framing and analysis phases, and the opportunities and constraints detailed in the diagnosis phase, the strategies are combined and modeled into several possible scenarios. The scenarios are incremental, providing a set of landscape transitions that start from a base situation in which nothing is done by decision makers, to scenarios in which a set of strategies are implemented. Phase 5 considers scenario evaluation and monitoring. It engages in quantitative and modeling methodologies to assess and confront the response of each spatial scenario with the goals defined in the initial phase. Ultimately the landscape management and policy strategies, together with the scenarios, and its evaluation, co-create a decision support system for the stakeholders. The evaluation methodologies are applied throughout the planning and implementation phases to further inform practice and theory in Landscape Ecology and Landscape Planning.[11]

The phases can also be categorized in two sections: descriptive-evaluative and prescriptive-planning.[12] The first part is concerned with the theories and methods that allow for characterizing, surveying, and assessing a landscape in its abiotic, biotic, socio-economic, and cultural attributes. Goals, objectives, stakeholders, areas of spatial conflicts, and measures of success are also defined. The prescriptive/planning part comprises spatial scenarios, strategic approaches, and means of implementation in a collaborative fashion with the different stakeholders. A decision support system is developed so that each scenario is revised and evaluated according to the goals and baseline analysis. Monitoring and adaptive management tools are set in place to re-assess and update plans by feeding information back into ecological theory and the planning process.

3. A Landscape Planning Framework for Calama's Oasis

In the following section, the paper delves into Calama's context, and the spatial questions that need to be considered to initiate a Landscape Planning process. A summary of the process is presented for Phases 1 through 3 of the Planning Framework in the

---

11. Nassauer, "Design in Science," 633-644.
12. Ahern, "Spatial Concepts," 175-201; Steinitz, "A Framework," 136-143.

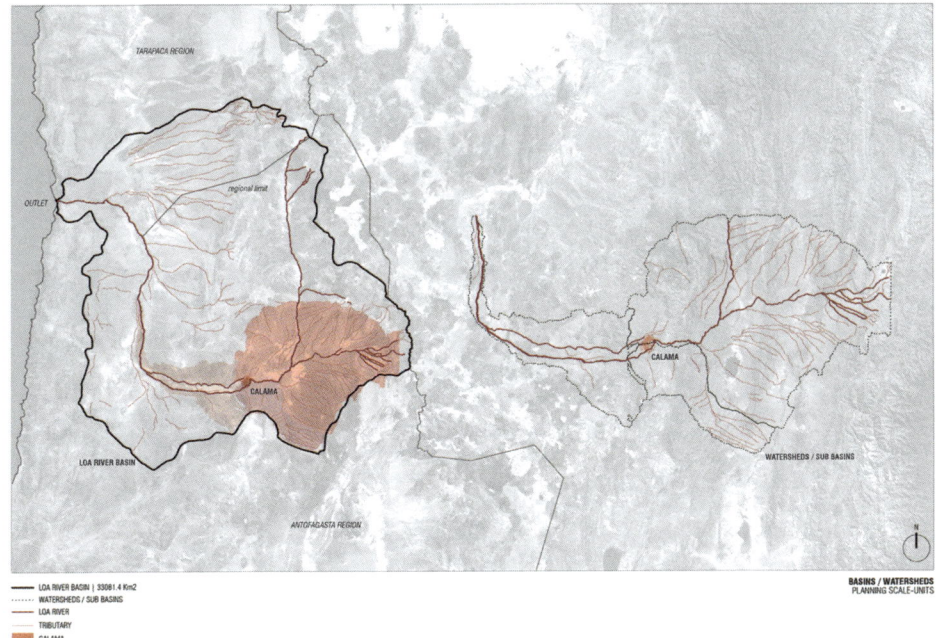

Map 3. Basins / Watersheds

context of Calama's Oasis. A set of landscape and agricultural conservation strategies that could be applied on-site to secure a sustainable transition and conservation of the Oasis are displayed as part of Phase 4.[13]

3.1 Phase 1 - Problem Framing and Goals

The Oasis landscape in Calama has been in steady retreat due to the compound effects of water withdrawal for mining activities in different reaches of the Loa River basin, urban expansion, land use changes within the Oasis that support the mining industry or other urban functions, and the absence of irrigation or long periods of fallowed agricultural land leading to extended tracts of dried-up land. Even if water withdrawals and water supply in the Loa River basin are balanced at a high level of environmental policy – and sufficient water is secured for the survival of several oases along the river including Calama – other processes such as development pressures, land use changes, and agricultural fallowing could contribute equally to its fragmentation. Therefore, while framing the problem, the focus should be on the latter factors and their func-

---

13. Phase 5 is not addressed in this paper, since the choice of evaluation methodologies is case-specific, going hand in hand with set goals. Such methodologies are borrowed from fields ranging from economic and social sciences to environmental assessment, etc. A suitable approach to address the final phase would involve a case study revision to gauge the level of success of a range of evaluation methodologies.

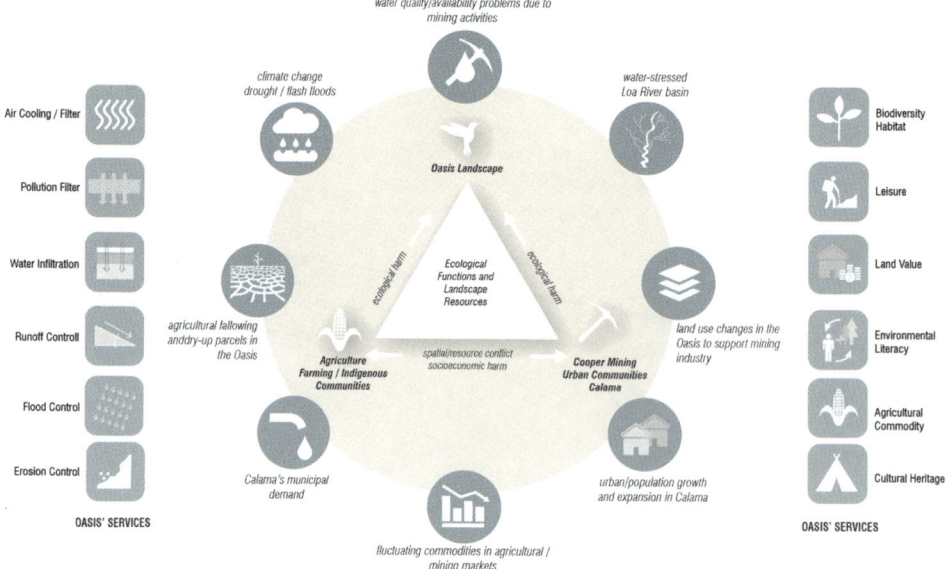

Figure 2. Problem Framing and Goals

tional interaction at the watershed scale. Watersheds are landscape aggregations with clear boundaries in terms of material and energy flows; they are commonly used as a scale-unit for ecologically oriented planning frameworks.

A specific set of questions for the watershed scale are presented in the analysis phase. The variety of stakeholders on the watershed can be categorized in the three sets according to the main land uses in Calama. First, there is copper mining, which has an extended spatial footprint from the mine pits of Chuquicamata to the city of Calama, where a great percentage of the population is involved directly or indirectly with mining. Second, there is agriculture, including farming and indigenous communities. Finally, there is the oasis landscape, with constituencies and advocates in both urban and agricultural/indigenous communities.

The development of goals requires a direct engagement with stakeholders. Nevertheless, some assumptions can be made in order to delineate general directions. The first assumption is that all the stakeholders have a stake in the resources provided by the Oasis, and they need certainty over those resources. In the case of mining, the scale is larger because water for mining depends on the water balance of the entire Loa River basin, and the underground aquifer dynamics. For agriculture and the Oasis, the scale is local and defined by the extent of the riparian and flood plain landscape patterns. The second assumption is that the Oasis landscape is transitioning and fragmenting due to the processes mentioned earlier; therefore, certainty cannot be secured by

LOA RIVER BASIN SYSTEM

GENERAL QUESTIONS	Scale	CALAMA'S CONTEXT
Pattern		
What are the watersheds contributing to the competing patterns?		Competing patterns are the land uses with stakes on the Oasis' resources. In this case is the Loa River basin and smaller tributary basins. At the Oasis scale, these are small watersheds conforming the riparian landscape.
What are the hydrological features in the watershed?		Such as rivers, tributaries, aquifer recharge areas, and underground aquifers.
Process		
What is the functional connectivity between hydrologic features?		How much of the Oasis and the riparian landscape along the river is depending on the underground hydrology, superficial hydrology (river) or farm irrigation.
What are the patterns and location of water extraction, storage and diversion processes?		This helps to understand if the Loa River flow is depending on reservoirs, or augmentations from other rivers or reservoirs. It also unveils the infrastructure set in place for mining, urban and agricultural uses.
What are the patterns of land-use, land cover, urban limit, roads, road crossings, and artificial drainage?		This applies for watersheds with higher pluvial regimes. How much is urbanized affects water quality and hydrological functions.
What are the patterns of filtering buffer zones, such as grasslands, forests and wetlands, and the patterns of interception, aquifer recharge, runoff and erosion processes?		These patterns hold key ecological functions like flood protection in summer rains in the Andes, habitat for different species, and recreation. The extent of the Oasis is in itself a filter for aquifer recharge.
Are there any other areas of ecological significance for hydrologic processes?		Such as small wetlands or natural embankments along the Loa River. These can act as a filter for water pollutants, and as aquatic habitat.
What is the pattern and percentage of impervious surface cover (ISC)?		This applies for watersheds with higher pluvial regimes, in which ISC can affect the transport of pollutants and produce peak-flows and foods.
What is the erodibility/drainage capacity of the soils?		Flash floods from summer rains are fairly frequent in the Loa River, therefore, maintaining soil structure and plant cover in riparian and flood plain landscape is desirable.
How the soil's drainage capacity is related with slope and aspect?		This matters in case runoff is a pervasive process, which is not the case for Calama.

ECOLOGICAL ATTRIBUTES

	Scale	
Process		
What are the patterns of ownership and water management boundaries at the different scales?		This helps to understand what are the constituencies dealing with water management and gives an idea of the feasibility of action over the land considering the number of ownerships that need to be engaged.
What are the land values across the patterns of ownership?		Attribute information that unveils the development pressures, helping to prioritize action and allocate investment in land-management strategies.
What are the population density and socio-economic characteristics?		The socioeconomic make-up reveals equity issues as compared to the city, as well as the use value that communities are giving to the Oasis. Also it helps detecting internal process of migration.
Change		
What is the stream regime and flow?		Patterns of floods, and flow-volume cycles can help to phase consumptive use, assess risk of flooding for agriculture or other uses within the Oasis, and prepare mitigation strategies.
What are the natural/anthropogenic disturbances, such as droughts, fires, floods, peak water demand, and its patterns in the landscape?		Similar to the above, temporal patterns set up an adaptive approach when it comes to plan the Oasis. Spatial extent of floods and draught periods are critical for systemic management of the Oasis.
What is the level of water stress of the contributing watersheds?		It creates boundaries for action when water is the critical resource holding uses and cultural practices. The Loa River Basin water stress should be addressed at a higher policy level considering other land uses in Calama.
What are the patterns and cycles of urban growth over the landscape?		Land use changes in the Oasis are not necessarily a measure of urban growth, but highlight expansion trends that could fragment the Oasis to a point in which it will continue to shrink. Metrics of fragmentation are critical.

SOCIOCULTURAL / ECONOMIC ATTRIBUTES

Figure 3. Preliminary Analysis: Loa River Basin

OASIS AGRICULTURAL SYSTEM

GENERAL QUESTIONS		CALAMA'S CONTEXT
What is the position in the landscape of the agricultural system: floodplain, piedmont, stream corridor, etc.?	Pattern	In Calama agriculture locates is mostly flood plain. Flood plain have different ecological functions and landscape structure. Also, in Calama the flood plain landscape depends on underground aquifer fluctuations.
What are the patterns of grasslands and forest covers around the agricultural system?	Process	This is a measure of landscape connectivity and structure. As much of Calama's Oasis is farmland, plant cover connectivity across plots performs key functions that need to me enhanced.
What are the patterns of filtering buffer zones, such as grasslands, forests and wetlands, and the patterns of interception, aquifer recharge, runoff and erosion processes?		These patterns hold key ecological functions like flood protection in summer rains in the Andes, habitat for different species, and recreation. The extent of the Oasis is in itself a filter for aquifer recharge.
Are there any other areas of ecological significance for hydrologic processes?		Such as small wetlands or natural/artificial embankments along the Loa River. These can act as a filter for water pollutants, and as aquatic habitat.

ECOLOGICAL ATTRIBUTES

What are the patterns of irrigation infrastructures set in place?	Scale	The amount of irrigation/canal companies set up a neat unit for land-management and policy straggles. Nevertheless, cross-boundary strategies need to be considered to account for ecological processes.
What is the pattern and scale of the agricultural system managed by the irrigation/canal company?		Similar to the above, this allows to quantify the amount of land being irrigated, and water consumptive use for different crops and cycles.
How is the parcel-ownership structure for farms?	Change	Multiple ownerships makes landscape planning more challenging. Ownership structure overlap with landscape functions can help to prioritize planning actions: Indigenous communities v/s single private owners.
What is the boundary condition between farms (cultivated land v/s non-cultivated land; crop v/s non-crop)?		This also helps to quantify the spaces in which landscape conservation strategies, and management regimes could be combined with farming in the Oasis.
What is the structure, hierarchy and management of the water-rights holdings?		Water right holdings is yet another factor for prioritization in planning actions. How to weight larger rights v/s multiple smaller rights, combined with active and fallowed land becomes a priority.
What are the soil properties?	Process	This could help to target the best land for agricultural uses and allocate incentives for agricultural conservation, whereas les valuable soil could be negotiated with multiple uses with conservation features.
What types of crops are being cultivated and what are the types of on-farm irrigation methods?		This allows to weight the consumptive use of different crops with the efficiency of irrigation technologies being used. Combined with soil qualities, this also helps to target agricultural conservation strategies.
What is the consumptive use of crop types as compared with allocated water rights?		Farm profits in the Oasis can be compared with different crop scenarios, in which efficiency is promoted, liberating water for other uses.
What are the total and by farm yields of current agricultural production?		Related with the above, this gives a baseline for comparison with other crop schemes within the Oasis. Crop diversification and phasing between farm communities could increase the revenue base.
What are the patterns of dry-farms?	Change	Water rights that are not being used due to abandonment or land use changes, can be detrimental for neighboring farms, affecting their productivity. It also highlight critical areas for action.
What are the temporal patterns of agricultural activities: tilling, seeding, germination, irrigation, harvest?		Cultural practices play a big role when it comes to introduce variation in crops schemes. Calibrating new approaches with traditional farming is critical for success in agricultural conservation strategies.

SOCIOCULTURAL / ECONOMIC ATTRIBUTES

Figure 4. Preliminary Analysis: Oasis

maintaining a business-as-usual situation, in terms of how the stakeholders relate with the Oasis. This means that certain trade-offs in the way each stakeholder operates in the Oasis need to be negotiated. A final assumption is that decision makers at local, regional, and national levels are able to recognize this problem, and endorse a long-term planning perspective that secures a sustainable transition of Calama's Oasis in light of long-term regional climatic variations, and fluctuation in commodities.

3.2 Phase 2 - Preliminary Analysis

The analysis phase is the first spatial approximation to the problem without a particular direction in terms of assessment. The purpose is to reveal critical socio-ecological attributes of the Oasis and surrounding landscapes that will facilitate the diagnosis, and to identify the scales at which the planning phases are performed. It is, however, precise in the characterization of the landscape in order to get the right data for the diagnosis. The analysis phase seeks to understand the key ecological and hydrological processes, its patterns or the spatial imprints on the landscape, the temporal dynamics of such processes, and the scale at which these processes are important to the goals and the problem. Following the ecological analysis, the same process is repeated for socioeconomic and cultural attributes, with a particular set of questions. The sociocultural and economic attributes will define the spaces of opportunities and constraints, as well as the agency that stakeholders can harness to implement the practices and strategies proposed by the planning process.

Two scales are critical in Calama: the Loa River basin, and the Oasis as an agricultural system, including the functional connections with the city. The latter is influenced by the landscape dynamics at the basin level. Within the Oasis, other dynamics involving agricultural and urban uses take over to explain functional interlocks, and at the same time, they interact with the ecological and hydrological attributes of the Oasis and the Loa River. Figures 3 and 4 present the core questions and issues to be considered in this phase, and their translation to Calama's context.

3.3 Phase 3 - Landscape Diagnosis

The diagnosis phase is conceived as a screening process to reveal the potential of different landscape management strategies to be implemented. These strategies are in tune with the goals and problem defined in the first phase. This phase relies heavily on analytical tools in geographic information science and remote sensing. Objectives or spatial qualities that are deemed important for the incorporation of landscape and agricultural conservation strategies can be located by performing a spatial analysis of the ecological and socioeconomic attributes that facilitate them. Following the analysis, the defined areas can be ranked in terms of their potential to incorporate the strategies. This screening process serves as a prioritization system that weighs the degrees of landscape functionality with the socioeconomic factors that foster or hinder implementation.

OASIS AGRICULTURAL SYSTEM

GENERAL OBJECTIVES

To identify the patterns of processes of soil erosion, dry-up land, landscape fragmentation, and areas of high hydrological importance (function) for landscape and agricultural conservation.

To identify the on-farm and cross-boundary farm spaces for the introduction of conservation practices.

To identify the water consumptive use in each parcel or group of parcels to gauge how much water is used in the Oasis as compared with allocated water rights.

PRIORITIZATION QUESTIONS

What is the priority for landscape conservation strategies for the riparian and flood plain in the Oasis?

What is the priority for agricultural conservation strategies in the agricultural landscape?

SPATIAL PATTERNS FOR PRIORITIZATION

1. Metrics for riparian buffer fragmentation
2. Its proximity with farms and the stream channel
3. Spaces of non-productive patches,
4. Remaining biodiversity patches
5. Cross-boundary conditions
6. The network of dry-farms

1. Clusters of farm-productivity based on soil properties
2. Irrigation-capabilities
3. Current consumptive use.

1. Parcel-ownership structure
2. Economic expectations in the agricultural community
3. The water-governance structure
4. Potential linkages with current conservation efforts

Prioritization is based on the identification of critical landscape patterns and processes as the manifest through patterns of biophysical and sociocultural / economic attributes in the spatial context

SCREENING FUNCTION-CONFL

(+)

Socioeconomic Conflict

(−)   Landscape

1. Areas of high value conservation under dry-farm single community.

2. Areas of high value conservation under multiple uses other than agriculture

Diagram based on W. Huls Futures as an Integrativ Restoration of Large Rive Guidelines to Land Manager York: Springer-Verlag, 2001

Figure 5. Landscape Diagnosis

GENERAL QUESTIONS	CALAMA'S CONTEXT
What are the areas of possible non-point source pollution for sediment and nutrients source?	Parcels that are housing services for the mining industry such as storage, parking. Oils, and heavy metals can affect otherwise healthy agricultural soil in the Oasis.
What are critical cross-boundary pathways for sediment, nutrient and pollution delivery considering soil erodibility/drainage, slope and runoff pattern?	This doesn't apply much to Calama since overland runoff is rare. Nevertheless road access for parcels serving mining industry could be vectors of pollutants if connected with channels or river.
Are sediment or nutrient delivery the most threatening process for water quality?	Agriculture in Oasis is not industrial; nutrient loadings might not represent a threat for water quality. Leakage/discharges from tailings dams in the upper reaches of the river are bigger threat for water quality.
Are these processes augmented by irrigation methods and storm events regimes?	If flooding is the preferred irrigation method by farmers then point source pollution can spread across parcels and eventually reach the river or other farms in the Oasis.
Are the areas of sediment/nutrient transport buffered or functionally connected by the irrigation system with streams, wetlands, or riparian/floodplain areas?	Road access for parcels serving mining industry could be vectors of pollutants if connected with irrigation infrastructure or the riparian landscape.
Are the filtering buffer zones (land-water interface fringe), such as riparian forests/grasslands and wetlands, and aquifer recharge zones fragmented?	This is a measure of fragmentation. Riparian corridors are vital to buffer pollutants and as biodiversity corridors. Farm parcels seem to be close to the riparian corridor, affecting its continuity.
Are these zones diffuse or focalized?	If focalized it might be easier to stich the riparian corridor. As farming in the Oasis is pervasive, a diffuse condition seem to be the predominant.
What are the clusters of high farm productivity, as overlaid with suitable soil properties, such as soil suitability for less-consumptive crops, and soil-irrigation capability?	The mentioned ecological attributes can identify areas better suited for farming activities, which can be targeted with policies oriented to reinforce their agricultural function.
What are the clusters of efficient irrigation farms, as overlaid with soil-irrigation capability?	The use of high-end irrigation technologies is most likely not case in the Oasis. Soil properties can help to allocate subsidies for efficient irrigation and save water for other uses compatible with the Oasis.
What are the cluster of high-consumptive use, as expressed in crop typologies?	High water-consumptive crops can be compared with efficient crops in terms of revenues allowing the farmer to weigh the opportunity cost of having spare water for other uses compatible with the Oasis.
What are on-farm and cross-farm patches of biodiversity or non-cultivated land in which water conservation agricultural practices could be introduced?	This in-between spaces are high priority areas to introduce conservation strategies that enhance the landscape matrix. Small biodiversity patches can restore flood plain and riparian functions.
How does the latter connects with farm's cross-boundary conditions of dry-farms, and productive farms?	This further unveils the spaces of opportunities for landscape or agricultural conservation strategies. Dry-farms can be targeted for revelation through incentives, consolidating a landscape matrix.

ECOLOGICAL ATTRIBUTES

Are the diagnosed problems located in patterns of multiple individual ownerships (diffuse) or a few single ownerships (focal)?	Multiple ownerships need cross-boundary incentives to implement conservation strategies. A group of collectively administered land by indigenous communities can be easily targeted with conservation practices.
Are there governance capabilities to address the scale of the problem—such as ditch companies, land trusts or indigenous community groups?	Stewardship groups with governance capabilities can facilitate consensus building in the planning process when presented with alternative scenarios.
Are there current management efforts towards conservation embedded in the governance of landscape?	This needs to be corroborated on the ground, consulting with communities in the Oasis as well as advocacy and conservation groups in Calama or at regional/national levels, such as National System of Protected Areas.
What is the likelihood of farmers to implement practices that work through a collaborative paradigm rather than property and water rights paradigms?	Again, this needs to be gauged on the ground. Collective stewardship might be an installed capacity as indigenous communities in the Oasis maintain traditional irrigation and management traditions.

SOCIOCULTURAL / ECONOMIC ATTRIBUTES

3.4 Phase 4 - Scenario Modeling

As a proxy to Phase 4, the research presents an array of best practices in agricultural and landscape conservation that could be considered for the Oasis. A more calibrated set of strategies can be agreed upon by engaging directly with stakeholders and their specific set of goals. These management practices stem from varied fields – such as agronomy, soil science, hydrology, forestry, and landscape ecology. Thanks to development of spatial principles in Landscape Ecology, these practices can be operationalized on the ground by planning and design disciplines.

3.4.1 General Principles of Landscape Ecology

As mentioned earlier, one of the prime contributions of Landscape Ecology has been to add a spatial dimension to ecological processes, providing the necessary language to effectively ground ecological principles in planning.[14] In 1986, Forman and Gordon[15] proposed the patch-corridor-matrix model, which essentially spatialized the pattern-process relationship into recognizable landscape features that could be operationalized through planning and design. The model is instrumental in characterizing the structural (patterns) and functional (processes) qualities of the landscape, and "provides a handle for analysis and comparison, plus the potential for detecting general patterns and principles."[16] The authors note that the concepts were consciously chosen to facilitate communication with other disciplines. Later in 1996, and in an effort to translate landscape ecological principles into planning and design, Richard T.T. Forman et al.[17] developed a set of spatial recommendations that would account for key ecological processes, in order to maintain and enhance them. The simple spatial models proposed by Forman have permeated into design disciplines, especially Landscape Architecture, thus contributing to the emergence of ecological principles in the design and planning of the built environment. As a spatial syntax, the patch-corridor-matrix model has persisted as a rule-of-thumb to analyze, manage, and intervene in varied landscapes. From simple visual assessments to highly precise spatial metrics precipitated by the development of geographic information systems and remote sensing, the model has triggered the development of specific methodologies that are of common use among landscape ecologists, environmental planners-managers, landscape planners, and related disciplines.

Jianguo Wu[18] argues that Landscape Ecology is a pluralistic discipline. Natural pro-

---

14. Ahern, Botequilha, "Applying Ecological", 65-93.
15. Richard T.T. Forman and Michael Gordon, *Landscape Ecology* (New York: Wiley, 1986).
16. Richard T.T. Forman, "Some General Principles of Landscape and Regional Ecology," *Landscape Ecology* 10 (1995): 135.
17. Wenche Dramstad, James D. Olson, and Richard Forman, *Landscape Ecology Principles in Landscape Architecture and Land-Use Planning* (Washington DC: Island Press, 1996).
18. Jianguo Wu, "Landscape Ecology, Cross-Disciplinary, and Sustainability Science," *Landscape Ecology* 21 (2006): 1-4.

cesses position landscapes in a shifting dynamic state, making them permeable to cultural and ecological fluctuations. Landscape Ecology has embraced human agents as drivers of landscape change and sustainability. This recognition is important when considering the different vectors through which humans act over and interact with the land. The complexity of this relationship requires the involvement of several disciplines in an integrated fashion. This principle is evident in the development of Landscape Planning Frameworks.

Principles of Landscape Ecology come in the form of generalizations that, through research and testing, consist of particular patterns considered essentials for basic landscape/ecological functions.[19] The use of R.T.T. Forman's principles in planning and design has been pervasive. Using the spatial model of patch-corridor-matrix, Forman recommends particular patterns to enhance the ecological functions of the landscape: "Top-priority patterns for protection, with no known substitute for their ecological benefits, are a few large natural vegetation patches, wide vegetated corridors protecting water courses, connectivity for movement of key species among large patches, and small patches and corridors providing heterogeneous bits of nature throughout developed areas."[20]

Dale et al.[21] provide a comprehensive set of guidelines that account for ecological functions in land use planning. These are: (1) examine the impacts of local decisions in a regional context; (2) plan for long-term change and unexpected events; (3) preserve rare landscape elements, critical habitats, and associated species; (4) avoid land uses that deplete natural resources over a broad area; (5) retain large contiguous or connected areas that contain critical habitats; (6) minimize the introduction and spread of non-native species; (7) avoid or compensate for effects of development on ecological processes; and (8) implement land-use and land-management practices that are compatible with the natural potential with the area. Looking at Dale's guidelines, it is easy to see the similarities with Forman's recommendations, and also with important analytical and operational concepts like scale and change.

In summary, Landscape Ecology has provided a spatial methodology for analysis and action. It allows for the assessing of how the landscape is functioning, and for proposing a desired landscape structure performing specific functions. Even though the emphasis is on ecological process, Landscape Ecology has embraced a systemic understanding of landscapes that accounts for the functional relationship between

---

19. Richard T.T. Forman, *Land Mosaics;* Richard T.T. Forman, "General Principles", 133-142; Richard T.T. Forman, "General Principles", 133-142.
20. Forman, "General Principles", 140.
21. Virginia H. Dale et al. "Ecological Guidelines for Land Use Management," in *Applying Ecological Guidelines to Land Management,* eds. Virginia H. Dale, Richard A. Haeuber (New York: Springer-Verlag, 2001), 3-33.

human/urban processes, such as urban growth or agriculture, and ecological processes. As a natural evolution, Landscape Planning incorporates both ecological and socioeconomic/cultural attributes (see Figures 3, 4, and 5).

3.4.2 Landscape Management and Policy Strategies for Calama's Oasis

The City of Calama and the communities directly and indirectly involved with the Oasis could benefit from conservation strategies at the landscape and farm level. Landscape management with policy components could be used effectively towards water savings and water quality preservation through protection of vegetative mass, reforestation, riparian conservation, and agricultural best practices.[22] On-farm conservation practices – agro-conservation – such as intercropping, agroforestry, rotational fallowing, and irrigation efficiencies, could further save water, improve its quality, spark biodiversity by strengthening landscape connectivity and structural diversity, diversify agricultural production, and add up to a resilient multi-functional landscape. The strategies could be coupled with open space investment, improving the quality of life and environmental standards, thus extending social benefits to the urban population. Such outcomes are possible through the recombination of the strategies, which are designed to maintain and enhance specific ecological attributes and functions. At the landscape scale, a continuous landscape matrix from the river to the limits of the floodplain provides a template that enhances soil conditions contributing to overall soil health for farming activities. In case of a drought or extended fallowing periods, enough biomass will be available to maintain the topsoil through its root system. It also provides a system to filter pollutants within farms, protecting the water table. Water flows across farms can be managed through consistent buffering that protects the riparian edge of the Loa River. At the farm scale, agro-conservation practices can maintain key ecological attributes like soil moisture, structure, organic matter, and nutrients, thus avoiding soil erosion, increasing irrigation efficiency, and providing a suitable growing substrate.

Considering the allocated water rights for agriculture, a reduction of water consumption within croplands creates a positive differential in water availability that could be redistributed to promote a diversification of uses that are compatible with the Oasis landscape. Water-sharing schemes could be used for revegetation and the consolidation of landscape matrix that reclaims the flood plain and riparian ecosystems of the Oasis. Current dry farm-plots could be monetized by using water differentials. Moreover, the landscape matrix could be facilitated by providing cross-boundary incentives to farmers for recovering the connectivity of fragmented patches.[23] With the right incentives for water-sharing, agricultural fallowing could become a viable

---

22. Robert McDonald and Daniel Shemie, *Urban Water Blueprint: Mapping Conservation Solutions to the Global Water Challenge* (Washington DC: The Nature Conservancy, 2014)
23. Dale, "Ecological Guidelines," 3-33.

economic strategy for the farming communities in Calama. From a management perspective, fallowing with the introduction of local cover species could help to recuperate soil conditions and save water to initiate farming activities in dried-up parcels or allocate it for other non-agricultural uses, such as municipal demand, recreational activities, and industrial uses. Strategic phasing of fallowing coupled with landscape and on-farm conservation strategies could further maintain and increase the overall productivity of the agricultural system at Calama's Oasis.

Figure 6 displays the spatial implications and benefits of four management strategies that conserve water and improve land-water quality at the landscape and farm scale. Intercropping could reduce water consumption and improve soil conditions by combining water-intensive cash crops with water-efficient cover crops. The effect of trees species – by implementing agroforestry patterns – on water/soil could help to evaluate the viability of high-value but low-water harvests. Productive fallowing could liberate the land for soil recovery, improving the quality of the land for the next growing cycle, and increasing the long-term revenues from fallowing. It could also allow water allocation in higher demand periods to go towards other uses. Buffering could protect contributing streams, riparian corridors, riparian wetlands, natural embankments, farms, and aquifer recharge areas through a network of flood plains and riparian species. Herbaceous buffers can reduce non-point pollution, especially considering the establishment of potentially harmful activities that support the mining industry on the Oasis.

The strategies presented here are intrinsically spatial, therefore their potential impacts on landscape patterns and processes differ depending on the scale of application. Both the Oasis scale, and the Loa River basin scale could be addressed through this tool kit. Figure 7 reflects the different ecosystem services that can be harnessed in a progression of scales. Scalability becomes critical, and an evaluation of scenarios and strategies must consider the gradients of socioeconomic conflict that might affect implementation (see Figure 5).

4. Summarizing: Core Attributes of a Landscape Planning Approach and its Relevance for Calama

A Landscape Planning Approach operationalizes key principles stemming from Landscape Ecology in order to address the complexity of the Oasis landscape in Calama as a coupled socio-ecological system. Liu and Taylor[24] compiled a set of four core attributes related to Landscape Planning. These are a good reflection of ecological

---

24. Jianguo Liu and William W. Taylor, "Coupling Landscape Ecology with Natural Resource Management: Paradigm shifts and New Approaches," in *Integrating Landscape Ecology into Natural Resource Management*, eds. Jianguo Liu and William W. Taylor (Cambridge: Cambridge U. Press, 2002), 3-19.

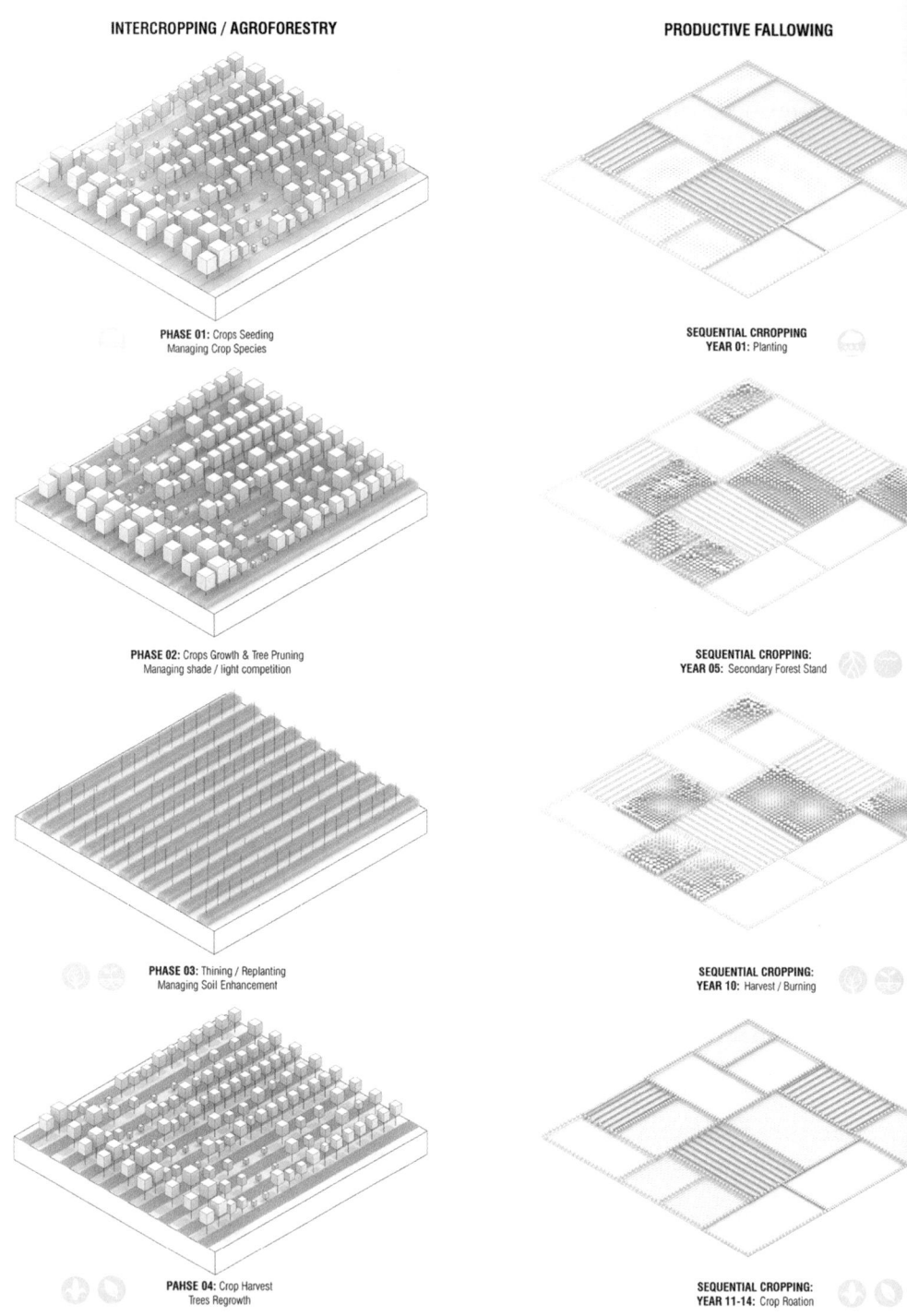

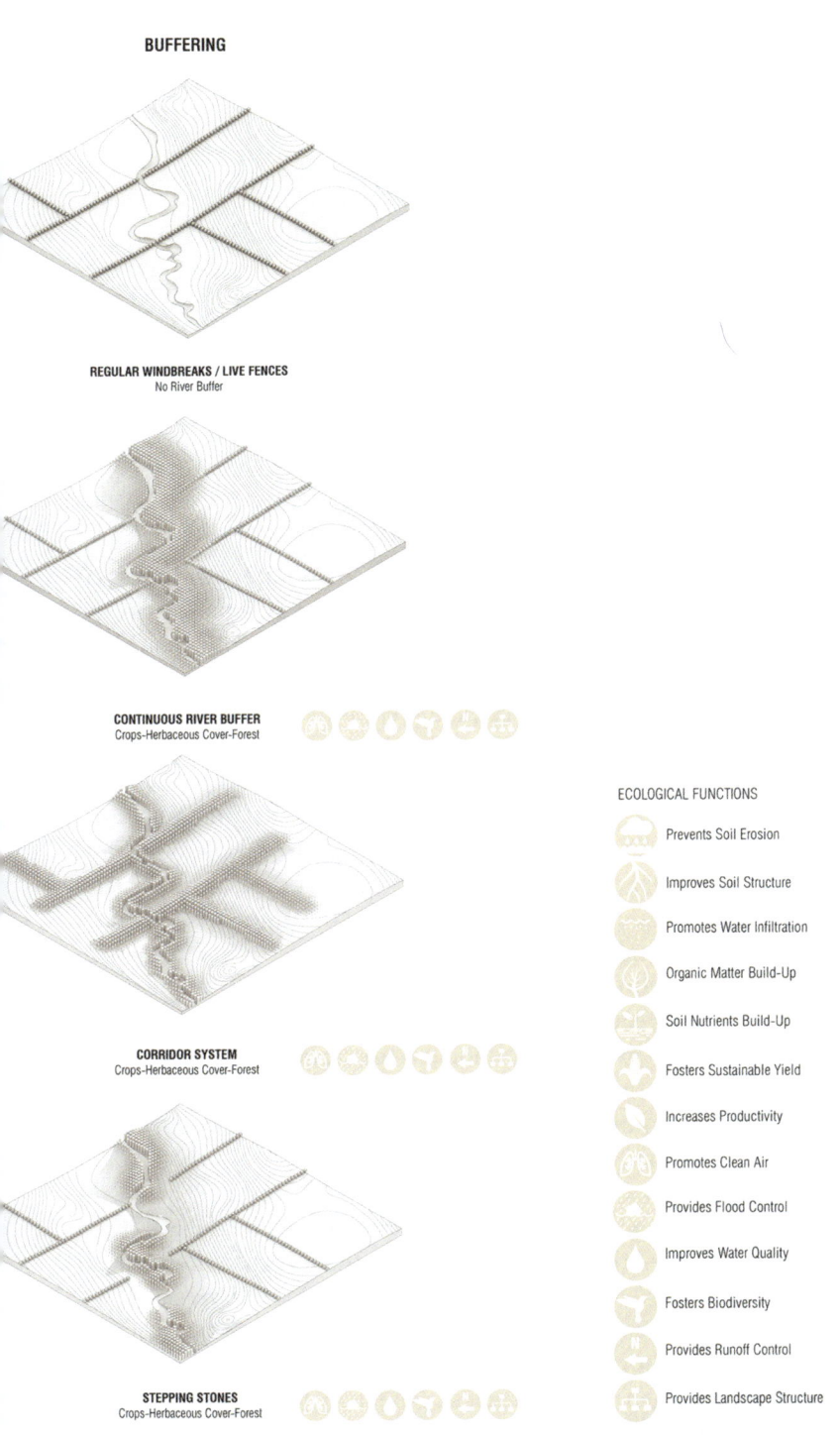

Figure 6. Land Management Strategies

A Landscape Approach for Calama's Oasis | 181

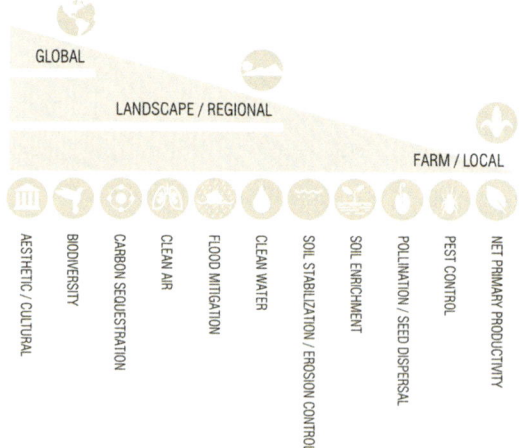

Figure 7. Scales of Influence

principles translated into operative planning principles. A summary of the attributes, as developed by Liu and Taylor, is presented below. The key for a Landscape Planning approach lies in the scale and change (time) variables. Usually, planning/management activities are framed by arbitrary spatial limits that do not account for the extent of socio-ecological processes. For example, the urban and rural divide in Calama leaves part of the Oasis outside planning policy. A Landscape Planning approach is (1) multi-scalar in nature and accounts for the mismatches between institutional/governance scales, and the scales of socio-ecological patterns and processes. Landscape patterns exist in nested hierarchies that influence each other through horizontal exchanges of matter, energy and organisms – as well as people, information and financial, social, and cultural resources. Traditional planning/management is conducted within the limits of land ownership, which does not account for the relationship between adjacent and nonadjacent patterns. Conservation strategies need to cut across individual and collective land ownerships in Calama. The Oasis conservation can benefit if the strategies are embedded in the farming and indigenous communities, which can act as active agents for a sustainable transition. A landscape approach is therefore (2) cross-boundary, such that it considers the reciprocal functional impacts or effects of one pattern over others.

As landscapes are interconnected in terms of function over different scales, single-goal approaches usually come with negative effects. For example, focusing only on riparian restoration to buffer pollution for water quality without regulating harmful land uses in the Oasis can create a false sense of security. Pollutants can seep down on the floodplain area – fostered perhaps by flooding irrigation regimes – and make their way to the Loa River through the water table. Focusing on uncultivated spaces between farm plots, abandoned or dry farms, and existing hedge groves, with a consideration of slope aspect and the infiltration capability of the soil, can provide a template for water quality management, and foster biodiversity and landscape regeneration within human activities in the Oasis. Thus, a landscape approach is (3) integrative, aligning several stakeholder's goals and functional scales in a systematic manner, negotiating the trade-offs between them, and taking advantage of the synergies of cross-boundary conditions.

Socio-ecological processes have temporal patterns of variability that are larger than decision-making and political timetables. They vary depending on natural and anthropogenic disturbances that usually have longer timeframes at different scales.[25] Traditional planning/management tends to capture dynamic processes in time, and do not account for uncertainty or cumulative effects resulting in undesirable outcomes (e.g. fire, flash floods, drought, soil erosion, etc.). Instead, a landscape approach is (4) adaptive, such that it continuously incorporates new knowledge in management practices to reduce uncertainty and increase the resiliency of the system over potential disturbances. Variations in seasonal floods and droughts in the Loa River Basin need to be incorporated in a flexible management of the Oasis that increases its resiliency. Either climate or water withdrawals for mining will fluctuate according to regional rain patterns and economic cycles; therefore, the Oasis needs to engage in an adaptive management. Moreover, Landscape Planning deals with incomplete information.[26] A complete and mechanistic understanding of cause and effect between patterns and function is unlikely to be achieved, and the landscape will eventually change due its dynamic properties. With pressing sustainability issues affecting land, water, agricultural, and cultural resources in the Oasis, Landscape Planning calls for action regardless of the lack of complete information or data confidence issues. Strategies and spatial scenarios can be quantitatively measured and serve as testable hypotheses to feed new information back into the planning process, and contribute to theory-building in a constant loop, expanding in conjunction the fields of Landscape Ecology, Landscape Planning, and Design. [27]

The authors of this paper press for an additional attribute: Landscape Planning is (5) spatially explicit. This attribute is suggested but not listed in Liu et al.[28] It is also outlined by other authors such as Ahern,[29] Steinitz,[30] Botequilha and Ahern,[31] and Nassauer.[32] It was added because it highlights the indispensable role of planning and

---

25. Dale, "Ecological Guidelines," 3-33.
26. Richard J. Hobbs and Robert Lambeck, "An Integrated Approach to Landscape Science and Management," in *Integrating Landscape Ecology into Natural Resource Management*, 412-430.
27. Liu, Taylor, "Coupling Landscape," 3-19; Nassauer, "Design in Science," 633-644.
28. Liu, Taylor, "Coupling Landscape," 3-19
29. Ahern, "Spatial Concepts," 175-201; Ahern, "Integration," 311-319; Ahern, "Theories, Methods," 199-131.
30. Steinitz, "A Framework," 136-143.
31. Ahern, Botequilha, "Applying Ecological", 65-93.
32. Nassauer, "Design in Science," 633-644.

design activities. First, it acknowledges that Landscape Ecology is spatial in nature, as it is devoted to the study of pattern, process, and change, in which the configuration and composition of patterns play a major role in unveiling functional interlocks. The latter facilitates the incorporation of ecological principles into spatial disciplines. Second, it acknowledges the instrumental role of planning, management, and design in translating ecological principles into practice. Third, a spatial methodology engages stakeholders towards specific goals, facilitating consensus-building towards the framing of sound policy. Considering the delayed nature of land/urban policy timetables in the face of a persistent shrinking of Calama's Oasis, Landscape Planning can move forward strategically and test patterns in order to operationalize ecological principles, policy mechanisms, landscape management strategies, and design strategies.

5. Challenges for Landscape Planning within Chilean Governance

The first challenge is the information gap in terms of data availability for ecosystems at different scales. The institutional information that exists is of poor quality, without systematization, and difficult to access. Since information is scarce, awareness, stewardship, and knowledge of ecological issues will not permeate into society, and in the case of Calama, into the communities and stakeholders associated with the Oasis. The first phase of Landscape Planning is concerned with gathering information and assessing the data to prioritize action. Such a task faces major challenges in the Chilean context. Nevertheless, pattern and process dynamics are also expressed at the landscape scale, thus the landscape approach could benefit from the methodological tools provided by Landscape Ecology. Open-source multispectral and elevation data sets from satellite sensing are readily available for anybody who wants to access it. Methods in GIS and remote sensing can unveil critical landscape interactions. Some information from government agencies is available at the landscape scale in Chile, and can be used as a starting point. The open-source methods would help then to offset data gaps in the institutional arrangement. A second challenge emerges when examining planning instruments. In Chile, urban development is regulated by zoning instruments at a communal and metropolitan level. Within these instruments, the notions of ecological processes, landscape patterns, and watersheds are not considered in planning and developmental activities; although they do include some elements like green areas, specific conservation areas, areas of agricultural value, and risk-prone areas. This situation creates scalar discrepancies when trying to conceive a comprehensive Planning Framework. For example, the basic problem of mismatches between administrative boundaries and ecological boundaries has not been incorporated into these instruments. Assessing and planning for landscapes, such as Calama's Oasis, could be challenging because it implies the overlapping of different administrations with ecological functions that do not follow such administrative divisions – a simple but important fact. Moreover, the tight urban-rural distinction made by these instruments encapsulates resources management and conservation in administrative and spatial silos, without any recognition of the functional and cross-boundary interlocks between urban development, landscapes, ecological processes, and management. The land outside the urban limit is regulated by different government agencies, such as agriculture, mining, water, and usually they act at the state level, disregarding specificity and local actors.

A final barrier is the deeply rooted idea of private property. Generally, subsidies and incentives in Chile are allocated to the demand, which has a clear spatial delimitation in the form of existing or potential property/land owners. Some advances have been made in housing planning, in which demand can be arranged in bundles to allocate subsidies and to secure private investment in affordable housing. Nevertheless, intermediate mechanisms that incentivize collaboration and organization among stakeholders are needed more than ever to engage in cross-boundary strategies that address the spatial extent of ecological processes. Chile has some examples of collective land ownership and collective administration of water resources. If applied to the Oasis, these governance structures could be harnessed to overcome the physical and cultural barriers posed by private property.

River Loa in Calama, Serena Dambrosio, 2015

The idea of landscape is the best instrument we have in order to understand an environment that is global but nevertheless cultural and specific. Landscape, like the Internet, allows us to look at the world as an environment, as a whole, in which the perspective and contribution of its inhabitants, individuals and collectivities, become essential for its transformation.
Franco Farinelli, 2015

Calama is a medium-sized city, with approximately 150,000 inhabitants according to the last census,[1] at the center of one of the world's most important copper, and not only copper, extraction sites. Chuquicamata and Rodomiro Tomic, the two biggest mines located within a 20km radius from the center of Calama, together provide about 30% of Chile's copper production, which equals almost 10% of the world's consumption.[2] Several other mines are located around Calama, all of which take advantage of the city's infrastructure – highways, airport, streets, accommodation, facilities, services, etc. – and contribute to its demographic and economic growth, its urban development, and its arising conflicts.

Located in the Atacama Desert, one of the driest deserts in the world, Calama is also the site of what was once the largest oasis in the world. In the pre-Hispanic era, the Inca Trail passed through the oasis of Calama, and the varied origins of some of the found objects prove the presence of nomadic groups that used the area as a stopover during their trips. For centuries, the oasis was used for agriculture and sustained the city and its surroundings until the development of the mining industry offered a valid counterpart. Mining has in fact been present in the region since pre-Columbian times. Activities significantly increased in the nineteenth century and were modernized and heavily industrialized starting from 1910, when the Chile Exploration Company of the Guggenheim Group started digging the Chuquicamata mine. In 1915, the town and extraction industry were set in Chuquicamata, and although most of the workers were living in the mining camp next to the pit, the development of the industry also drove the urbanization of the settlement of Calama: not only in terms of housing but especially in terms of infrastructure, land use, and resource consumption. Between 1997 and 2003, Chuquicamata was dismantled citing environmental reasons and encroachment from the mine's expansion. Its residents, about 25,000 people including the workers and their families, were relocated to Calama or started commuting from other cities. In 2002, Calama and Chuquicamata had a population of 138,402 inhabitants, which rose to 147,886 in 2012.[3]

---

1. According to the 2012 Census, Calama's population was 147,886 inhabitants.
2. See the "Calama as a Camp" chapter in this book.
3. Census data. In 1952, a population of 43,819 inhabitants was registered in the area, almost half of which lived in the mining town of Chuquicamata.

However, as previously mentioned, Chuquicamata is not the only productive site of Calama. Two more mines have been opened by Codelco in the area, and eleven other mines can be considered satellites of the city.[4] Thirty-nine flights a day arrive at and depart from its airport, the Loa Airport, generating a daily flow of around 11,000 people, almost 10% of the population. To which should be added the commuters from nearby regions, and the workers living in mining camps for shifts of 4, 7, or 10 days; workers that nevertheless use Calama as a hub for infrastructure, facilities, and services. Due to new operations linked to the exploration of new sites and the construction of underground mining in Chuquicamata, another 20,000 workers are expected to move to Calama before 2020.[5] And this is just one aspect of Calama's complexity.

Multiple Populations

The "populations" of Calama, to use Guido Martinotti's definition,[6] represent different interests and have specific impacts. In 1993, Guido Martinotti notably claimed that traditional models of human ecology – ones that described the social morphology of the city as derived from the conflict between different groups and that fighting for urban space created the social mosaic of the city – could not apply to those cities whose interests and are strictly intertwined with other spaces and locations, i.e. the metropolis (Milan in his study).[7] Only in the "traditional" city is it indeed possible to link the social form of the city to the social groups that inhabit it. The development of the contemporary metropolis (he was writing in 1993) should rather be defined as the progressive differentiation of *four* main *populations* that orbit around the town.[8] Thus, the first population represents the citizens and the space they occupy. A second population emerged in the first metropolises of the industrial age: the workers, or commuters, traveling to the city during the day and leaving for the suburbs or

---

4. Codelco (Corporación Nacional del Cobre de Chile or, in English, the National Copper Corporation of Chile) is a Chilean state-owned copper mining company. It was formed in 1976 from foreign-owned copper companies that were nationalized in 1971. It is currently the largest copper-producing company in the world and produced 1.66 million tons of copper in 2007, 11% of the world's total. It owns the world's largest known copper reserves and resources. Chuquicamata, for many years world's largest annual producer (recently overtaken by the Escondida mine, also in the Antofagasta region), Rodomiro Tomic, and Ministro Alejandro Hales are the three mines located in the Calama area. However, as highlighted by Ricardo Trufello and Luis Valenzuela's essay in this book, 14 mines can be considered related to and dependent on Calama's services.
5. The underground mine will start up in 2018 and when it reaches full capacity of 120,000 tons per day in 2030, the balance of the tonnage will come from the Alejandro Hales underground mine. It is estimated that extractable underground reserves below the present pit total 1.150 million tons of ore grading 0.76% copper and 0.052% molybdenum. Source: https://en.wikipedia.org/wiki/Codelco#cite_note-yaci-15.
6. Guido Martinotti, *Metropoli. La nuova morfologia sociale della città* (Bologna: Il Mulino, 1993).
7. Ibid.
8. The etymology of the world "metropolis" comes from the Greek: μήτηρ, *métēr* meaning «mother» and πόλις, *pólis* meaning «city» or «town."

nearby villages at night. Right after this, a third population arose, constituted by the people who use the city for their private and recreational use: the "city users," or metropolitan consumers. "City users" are different from the workers, of course, as they use the urban space only on specific occasions. They are present in most of contemporary big cities, and their presence is even more relevant in tourist centers.[9] Finally, a fourth population started to emerge at the end of the twentieth century, that of the "metropolitan businessmen," those individuals who use specific cities for their business affairs – something similar to the merchants of the Middle Ages. The latter is a very special synthesis of city users and commuters; it is a class of workers that has a large disposal of (corporate) money, usually flies to the city for specific reasons, and expects high-standard facilities and services, all of which considerably impacts the space of the city. Martinotti uses the term "population," rather than class or group, because it defines an aggregation of individuals that does not necessarily imply a collectivity or any rational connection between those individuals.[10]

So, as seen before and paraphrasing Martinotti's categories, in Calama too we can find a collection of populations, which are mostly indifferent to each other and whose interests are often in conflict. In the first place there are the citizens, the approximately 150,000 inhabitants of the town who live in Calama. They pay taxes, have the right to vote, and expect quality services and facilities.[11] The indigenous community is also struggling to get their voice heard; the indigenous are actually those whose ancestors have been living in the area for hundreds of years and whose relation to the landscape and resources of the area is very different from the contemporary notion of extraction. For centuries the oasis was cultivated, and it sustained the communities living in the Loa River valley, until mining offered an equally valid counterpart. It is important to consider the indigenous as a separate population because in Calama, as in many mining cities, being a citizen is often also a temporary condition – one that can range from a few months or years to a work life. A third population is constituted by the commuters, those employed by the mining companies or subcontracting service companies, who drive or fly to the city every day or every week or working shift. This population therefore includes all those people who live in Calama for a specific reason and for a temporary time that could also be years. Finally, there is a fourth population that is worth considering, which corresponds to Martinotti's metropolitan businessmen, and is represented by the executives of mining and subcontracting operations companies. This population flies sporadically to the city from the Chilean capital Santiago, but also from Canada, the United States, Europe, and

---

9. Martinotti refers to Venice, whose population in the center of around 80,000 inhabitants may double when adding the workers, but it had 7 million visitors in 1987, and over 27 million in 2014!
10. Guido Martinotti, *Metropoli*, 139.
11. Several protests and manifestations have taken place in recent years, asking for a better return of mining investment in the territory and city of Calama. See the articles by Luis Valenzuela and Felipe Vera and Rahul Mehrotra in this book.

Asia, for its business activities and expects high-standard facilities and services. In fact, this population is usually physically absent, but nevertheless makes most of the decisions in the territory: it manages the wealth and decides which projects are worthy of investment. It is easy to imagine the impact that the mining industry and all of its subcontracted operations – transport, energy, housing, food, waste, etc. – have on the landscape of Calama.

Calama may not be very big, but it certainly is a significant economic (and in part political and cultural) center in the northern regions of Chile, and an important hub for national and international connections, commerce, and communications. If it may be extreme to define Calama, or any other extraction town, as a metropolis, the concept is definitively useful for unveiling the complexity of the relation that characterizes their territories. And it is especially true when these "thematic" metropolises emerge as superimposed on areas that were already occupied and that rapidly urbanized because of the process of extraction and industrialization.[12]

One of the first issues that has emerged from the "Calama 2050. Territories of Extraction" research project, conducted by Luis Valenzuela, Felipe Vera, and myself, a collaboration between the Harvard Graduate School of Design and the Universidad Adolfo Ibañéz,[13] is the fact that any attempt made so far to solve the urban crisis of Calama has been unsuccessful because the "crisis" extends, and impacts, far beyond the boundaries of the municipality. If one wants to intervene in Calama, and this is true for any extraction site that involves more than one center or pit, one needs to consider the whole cluster. As Luis Valenzuela puts it in his article, "The site-specific determination of a mine hole is slowly replaced by the notion of a mining district."[14] And in this particular case, the mining district involves over fourteen mines.

A second point that has emerged from the research project is the fact that extraction territories cannot exclude temporality, or ephemerality, to use Felipe and Mehrotra's words, as part of the process of urbanization.[15] The very fact that mining settlements

---

12. For influential urbanists such as Patrick Geddes and Lewis Mumford, metropolitanism suggested an exploitative operationalization of the earth that was leading to a socially and ecologically unsustainable specialization of regions, reducing them to mere utilitarian links in a world system of exchange; see N. Katsikis, D. Ibanez, "Grounding Metabolism. Editorial," in *New Geographies* 6 (Cambridge: Harvard University Press, 2014). In the case of extraction, this naturally happens, since the whole development of regions is driven by a very specific sector, which in this case has its center in Calama.
13. The research project was granted a research grant by the Harvard University David Rockerfeller Center for Latin American Studies in 2014 ("Ephemeral Urbanism" Collaborative Research, Rahul Mehrotra, Felipe Vera, Luis Valenzuela) and a sponsorship by Codelco in 2015-2016 (Luis Valenzuela, Felipe Vera, Jeannette Sordi).
14. See Luis Valenzuela's article in this book.
15. See Rahul Mehrotra and Felipe Vera's essay in this book.

are organized as "camps" – with all which that implies – prevents them from evolving into a "city" and creating an enduring relation with the territory.

A third point is that a multiplicity of different scales and times coexist and overlap in territories of extraction. If we associate with each of the aforementioned populations one specific footprint, we can indeed begin to understand the scale of this urban/industrial realities.

In the case of Calama, the field of action of mining stakeholders (let's refer to it as group A) is absolutely global – spanning from North America where some of the mining companies are located, to Europe where design solutions also come from, to Asia where these solutions are often fabricated and the copper is sold. Workers and commuters (group B) are mainly Latin American: this includes Chilean citizens coming from the region and from all over Chile, but also many Peruvians, Colombians, Bolivians, etc. who travel back and forth from and to Calama for a day, a week, a few months, years, or a lifetime of work. Citizens (group C) coincide with the municipal boundaries of Calama and a bit beyond, which is also where stable workers – employed by mining companies, subcontractors or other activities – and their families live. Members of the indigenous population (group D) are also citizens, of course, but they live (in fact used to live) in a very specific area of Calama, in front of the river, where their ancestors have been living for centuries cultivating the oasis. One example of the conflicts that are created is the fact that the water of the oasis, on which indigenous communities have special rights, is reduced and polluted by the interests of A and the activity of B. At the same time, the new housing developments for C, previous inhabitants of Chuquicamata and now residents of Calama, have been built on top of the oasis land. Each population is also characterized by different time frames. In general, Calama's urban development is strictly linked to time, as the future of the industry is strictly related to the prime resource: copper.[16]

The availability of copper, the need for copper, the price of copper…the future of the city depends on these numbers, as well as on technological advancement and corporate decisions that could soon reduce the needed number of workers. It is not a secret that by 2050 most of the mining operations will go underground, drastically reducing the need for human workers.[17]

---

16. Many other minerals are in fact extracted together with copper, most importantly molybdenum, but also silver, gold, zinc, iron, etc.
17. It is now in the public domain that mining operations will transform towards underground extraction, as this article on the Codelco's website and even Wikipedia's Codelco page report: https://www.codelco.com/prontus_codelco/site/artic/20110706/pags/20110706103025.html and Wikipedia https://en.wikipedia.org/wiki/Codelco#cite_note-yaci-15:

This is influenced by geological and geographical conditions, in addition to the social and economic ones.[18] At the same time, and this is already on the table, the increasing social and economic costs related to urbanization, and the need to set up temporary housing for the construction operations, are pushing companies to opt for building more mining camps instead. Considering the different interests and actors that shape the urban space, it is very useful to reflect on how this will change the idea of common and public space, their scale and use, and for how long. In the case of the four populations of Calama, time is indeed very important to understand the dynamic of the city, in the short term as well as the long term. As mentioned before, stakeholders' interests are usually related to the availability of the resource, but workers' permanence on the territory may vary depending on the project they are working for and their contract, as most of mining workers work in shifts. In the same way, many families have become residents of Calama because of work opportunities, but never lost the relation with their previous hometown. As for the indigenous communities, and the oasis with which they identify, it should be a primary objective to ensure their permanence and flourishing in the region.

So, how to envision a development plan that includes multiple aspirations? In which the different actors can play a role in the near or distant future?

The interaction between the different populations, their scales and times, is creating a very complex landscape, which can itself become the medium through which to understand this territory. Landscape, in geographical terms, represents indeed "an entity comprising all the genetic, dynamic, and functional relations through which the components of every element of the terrestrial surface get connected among each other."[19] Landscape's complexity, therefore, is not only linked to the richness of its genetic patrimony and to its variability over time, but also to the functional relation being in force among its components. And landscape is also what the inhabitants identify with. Thus, landscape, as a concept and a resource, is where we, as designers, can find the vision to absorb, mitigate, and project the future of this territory from multiple and time-related perspectives. Landscape, as a medium, would allow us to consider a collection of disparate populations, characterized by different scales, interests, aspirations, and timelines and project its transformation into a community. In other words, landscape offers a way to overlap these different layers and understand – and over time promote – cohesion among the distinct actors of Calama. It can

---

18. One of the main reasons for starting the underground operations is, of course, the larger availability of copper that, in mines like Chuquicamata, is almost exhausted in the pit. However, secondary reasons include the need to reduce the environmental impact caused by dust generated in open-air operations, as well as the opportunity to reduce the number of workers doing high-risk tasks, as the majority of the operations would be conducted by drones.
19. Franco Farinelli, "L'arguzia del paesaggio," *Casabella* 575-76 (1991): 10-12.

set the rules, the narrative, the objectives, and the framework, within which each population can play its own game. The game is a metaphor, which we have literally explored.

The Calama Game

Games are very good devices through which to understand and imagine urban design dynamics. If we look at the work of architects such as Winy Maas and MVRDV, and the essays of scholars such as Ann Pendelton-Jullian, it is evident how a game can become a tool to experiment with different actors that represent different interests, set values and objectives, establish the space of action, construct narratives, set rules, and play them.[20] As Pendelton-Jullian has explored through her several studios, and as we have tested in the case of Calama with the 2014-2015 Landscape and Urbanism Studio at the Design Lab of Universidad Adolfo Ibañéz,[21] game design allows us to understand and design semi-complex relational structures. Games lead to the ability of successfully negotiating an entire range of parameters: programmatic needs, physical site constraints and opportunities, the cultural context in which the physical sites participate…approaching design as an emergent proposition within this dynamic field of behavior, as opposed to a static, formally imposed and planned response.[22]

If we imagine designing a board game (or a video game) about the city and the mining camp of Calama, we could easily start by defining a series of players or characters: the aforementioned mining companies, mining workers, citizens, and native communities, but also tourists, inhabitants of nearby towns, etc. The narrative could be built around the fights of Calama and its populations, their histories and challenges. For instance, constructing a story around the transition from what centuries ago was a settlement in the middle of the biggest oasis in the Atacama Desert to the first mine dug at the end of the eighteenth century. Or it could be remaking the relocation of the inhabitants of Chuquicamata to Calama in the 2000s. It could deal with the fight for water rights, the regeneration of the oasis, the development of new mining sites… and all that this implies. The board, i.e. the space of action, or the space of "design" in this case, could represent any of the spaces of the A, B, C, or D populations. And therefore include the globe, the Andean region, the Antofagasta region, the municipality, the oasis, the Loa River valley, or a couple of them. The scope of the way the game is played, i.e. its strategic logic and basically how you win or lose, could simply follow the principle of not affecting others. As MVRDV put it in their proposal for

---

20. Most notably MVRDV, *Spacefighter. The Evolutionary City* (Barcelona, Actar: 2007), Ann Pendelton-Jullian, Four (+1) Studios, 2010.
21. Jeannette Sordi and Felipe Vera, "Calama 2050. Landscape and Urbanism Studio," UAI 2015. The studio included the participation and advice of Winy Maas (MVRDV), Ann Pendelton Julian (Skype reviews), Josè Miguel Ansoleaga (Codelco), and Rodolfo Reygada (Calama PLUS).
22. Ann Pendelton-Jullian, Four (+1) Studios, 2010.

Freeland, the game could be based "on a set of parameters and simple rules that join individual desires with collective needs" and it could be based on "common sense: you can do whatever you want except harm others."[23] Thus, how to design the rules for a game/city taking into account that mining enterprises (A) may win if they find new valuable resources in the area and lose once the copper is exhausted or its price is too low to make it convenient to extract? Workers (B) may gain satisfaction and points if they get better facilities, services, infrastructure, at the cost and for the satisfaction of A? Citizens (C) are hurt by the mine activity but can hardly live without it. Their lifespan could potentially be infinite, but it is hard to imagine without A and B...

How to design rules that take into account individual desires with collective needs? Short-term necessities and long-term visions? How to give everybody the right to play and to play a role? How to save the game? How to dismantle it? How can the game dynamics suggest urban transformations that are equal and sustainable? The concept of sustainability for instance, and especially of sustainable transformation, is a controversial matter as we all know, as it implies that there can be transformations that have no negative impacts, for anybody or anything. As the document of the Union for Conservation of Nature (IUCN) highlights, not all entities have the same capacity of negotiation and adjustment.[24] In balancing sustainability, the environment is indeed always losing in favor of economic and social assets, both of which can be regulated by artificial mechanisms, which the environment cannot. Therefore development can be sustainable only if it is in the position of assuring the instruments with which to face the consequences of an unavoidable loss of natural assets.[25]

Chiara Rizzi, building on this assumption, suggests that landscape strategies and ecological objectives can be the key point for ensuring the sustainability of transformations, and highlights how tactics based on "potential" landscapes – what she calls "the 4th landscape" – are not designed to meet individual expectations, but to respond to a series of issues that the environmental crisis is raising.[26] According to Rizzi, this can only be prevented by the definition of an ecological 'budget' that a series of tactics, capable of responding to ecological needs and necessities that are not necessarily anthropocentric, can balance. Rizzi identifies these tactics in ecological restoration, mitigation, and compensation.[27]
However, thinking of *landscape* restoration, mitigation, and compensation offers an even more powerful lens and strategy with which to operate on urbanized territo-

---

23. See http://www.mvrdv.nl/projects/freelandalso, and "MVRDV, Freeland, Almere" in J. Sordi, *Beyond Urbanism* (Trento: Listlab 2014), pp. 176-179.
24. Union for Conservation of Nature, "The Future of Sustainability: Rethinking Environment and Development in the Twenty-First Century," 2006.
25. Ibid.
26. Chiara Rizzi, *The Fourth Landscape* (Trento: Listlab, 2015).
27. Ibid.

ries. Landscape is indeed not only a phenomenon of an ecological nature, but it also bears an organic and informative quality. Landscape, to use Almo Farina's words, is cognitive.[28] From a strictly ecological point of view, landscape can be intended as a "matrix" where both physical (earth, water, air...) and biological (populations, meta-populations, communities, meta-communities...) elements merge; if on the other hand, we refer to the organic aspect of the landscape, this represents the result of the interaction of the various organisms with the environment (or the matrix) to which they belong; but eventually, the landscape is also an informative phenomenon, as it is determined by the rules (functional or behavioral) of its composing organisms. Environment and rules are therefore two essential features of the landscape, but the latter does not exist if not through the perception of it.[29]

Landscape Rules
It is a few decades now that landscape has been defined as a medium for urbanism, especially when working in the case of complex natural environments, deindustrialized areas, and horizontal urbanism.[30] The notions of permanence, solidity, and continuity of the city have in fact been dismantled by the explosion of an irregular and unstable urbanization, both global and local. These conditions, and the development of information technologies, real-time data, GIS mapping, computation tools, as well as all the multiple and dynamic conditions of postmodernity, led to an increasing interest in the work of landscape designers and the notion and practice of landscape. In a few years, landscape went from being a background to the scenario to becoming an active element within the city[31] – a medium for urban, economic, and social order.[32]

As James Corner put it, "Suddenly, landscape became planetary, embracing and expressing the inter-relational tenets of ecology. The effects of local events on regional, continental and global ecologies was made emphatically clear, as the fluidity of water, air, and even movements of the earth's crust were revealed for all to see."[33]

---

28. Almo Farina, *Il paesaggio cognitivo. Una nuova entità ecologica* (Milano: Franco Angeli, 2008), p.16.
29. Ibid.
30. Charles Waldheim, "Landscape as Urbanism," in *The Landscape Urbanism Reader* (New York: Princeton Architectural Press, 2006).
31. Manuel Gausa, Interview with Jeannette Sordi in Jeannette Sordi, *Beyond Urbanism*, pp. 164-167.
32. Charles Waldheim refers to the disciplinary bases for urban design in the United States as established by José Luis Sert in 1956, at the occasion of a conference held at Harvard in 1956; Charles Waldheim, "The Other '56," in *Urban Design*, eds. Alex Krieger and William Saunders (Minneapolis: University of Minnesota Press, 2009), pp. 227–236.
33. James Corner, *Recovering Landscape* (New York: Princeton Architectural Press, 1999).

Landscape thus allows us to think on multiple and simultaneous scales with a holistic and time-related overview. As mentioned before, landscape is the result of the interactions of all the elements on the terrestrial surface: the structural elements composing the physical environment, their temporal dimensions, and their functional relations.[34] Intended as both the reality and its representation,[35] landscape offers an exceptional tool through which to understand the multiplicity of contemporary urbanization and its dynamics.

Going back to Calama – as an emblematic case of territories whose resources are highly impacted by temporary activities, and the Calama game as a model of the city's dynamics – landscape restoration, mitigation, and compensation can represent the rules for pursuing strategies and objectives with an overall benefit.[36] To mitigate, in ecological and planning terms, means to enact a series of actions and strategies that aim to avoid, reduce, and remedy the impact of alterations to the landscape.[37] To mitigate therefore refers to an action whose objective is to reduce the impact of another intervention, softening its effects and/or decreasing its magnitude. Actions of mitigation range from the design of "buffers," filters to mitigate the large-scale impact of industries, for example, absorbing dust, pollution, and noise, to "ecological corridors" that allow the movement and reproduction of small animals and vegetation, to ad hoc interventions tackling specific problems. In the case of Calama, one main issue has to do with mitigating the effects of dust and pollution on the inhabitants, for example, building a peripheral vegetation filter as suggested by Alejandro Aravena and Teresa Moller.[38] But in the case of Calama, to mitigate also means to reduce the impact of new urban development that is forecast for the next decade, a population that is then likely to significantly shrink in 2030 to 2050, when the underground automatic mining projects will be implemented and working. As Alexandros Tsamis and Mark Goulthorp suggested with the "Material Log(isti)c."

---

34. Franco Farinelli, "L'arguzia del paesaggio," 10-12.
35. The term "landscape" is being used in order to indicate both the thing itself and its representation; in the history of landscape, the representation of it precedes the original, i.e. the real one. (*Vorstellung* = concept, thought, representation).
36. Attempts are currently being made in Chile to preserve and compensate for the loss of biodiversity caused by extraction and industrial sites (CPB – Compensaciones por Pérdida de biodiversidad), so far only vaguely regulated by the Reglamento del Sistema de Evaluación Impacto Ambiental de Chile (RSEIA). Regarding the current Chilean legislation on environmental impact, and in particular the protection and compensation for loss of biodiversity, see Juan Ladrón de Guevara et al, *Guía para el desarrollo de compensaciones en biodiversidad en la Región de Tarapacá* (Tarapacá: Fundación Chile, 2015), p. 108.
37. See Chiara Rizzi, *4th Landscape*.
38. Calama Periurban Park, project by Elemental and Teresa Moller, design: 2013; construction 2014-; see: http://www.elementalchile.cl/en/projects/parque-peri-urbano-calama/.

In the Future Sustainable Mining Camp" workshop, the floating population could be allocated to camps that would be removed after an operation is done.[39] Working on the quality of these camps, their self-sufficiency, and the legacy they could leave on the territory – would avoid the current impact of a sudden increase in population and leave its legacy to the territory and its inhabitants.

Reclamation is instead an operation that happens after the end of activities that have been altering a particular landscape or ecology, with the objective of projecting it into the future. The issue of reclamation has proved very well the argument of the relation between landscape and urbanism. Notable examples of reclamation come from landscape interventions recovering after mining effects in the United States and especially from European de-industrialization processes. Among others, the case of the Emscher Park in the 1990s, where the reclamation of the contaminated landscape was developed in conjunction with a series of projects, architectural competitions, and private initiatives that had the final goal of not only restoring the landscape[40] but also of projecting the area into the future. In this sense, the overall goal has been pursued by framing a set of (game) rules that aimed at: 1) preserving the remaining leftover landscape; 2) linking up the isolated, separated areas in the agglomeration; 3) re-zoning separate areas as parkland; 4) coming to agreements both regionally and locally on individual projects with a long-term perspective; 5) maintaining and managing the new open spaces in a permanent regional park association.[41] The park was considered a model of urban architectural transformation. Ecological upgrading has been intended as the basis of a fresh economic impetus.

Compensation, in design and planning terms, means instead to generate *new* ecological, landscape, and social values that are equivalent to those that have been lost. It can be very specific, for example, to compensate particular ecological systems or ethnic groups, or generally aiming to set an overall framework. In Chile, recent research studies are aiming to provide a set of rules to encourage mining operations to also include actions of biodiversity compensation, at a regional level: for example, encouraging the investment in areas of high ecological value and biological diversity

---

39. Alexandros Tsamis, Mark Goulthourpe, UAI-MIT Misti research project, and "Material Logistics. The Future Sustainable Mining Camp" workshop, Calama-Santiago, June 2015.
40. Restoration is also considered to be part of reclamation actions, but it aims to bring a particular landscape or ecology back to its original status, initiating or accelerating ecosystem recovery with respect to the following characteristics: health status (functional processes), integrity (species composition and community structure), and sustainability (resistance to disturbance and resilience). See Almo Farina, *Principles and Methods in Landscape Ecology: Towards a Science of the Landscape* (Dordrecht, NL: Springer, 2006). Restoration is a very important process for the conservation of ecosystems and biodiversity, but it is not always successful, especially in environmentally sensitive areas, and it usually implies a large economic investment.
41. See Chiara Rizzi, *4th Landscape*.

as a compensation for mining operations carried out in areas of minor significance.[42] One very important precedent is the case of the Bayern Ökokonto system, established in German Bavaria in 2001.[43] Considering the fact that planning provides the necessary infrastructure to allocate new residents and activities, but not necessarily the benefits of it for the existing population, and actually in most cases environmental and cultural heritages are lost, stipulates that an ecological mitigation process must follow *any* territorial transformation. Rules and compensations strategies are established for the whole territory.[44]

Compensation always involves the exercise of the project, planning and strategic abilities, and an ongoing cross-referencing between the different scales. It requires determining a vision, or a set of values, that are at a higher level – for instance, preserving particular ecosystems or historical heritage – or that redistribute the benefits of the deployment of common resources. So, if one way is to work on the ephemerality of the construction – reducing the footprint of the activity – the other is to design the framework in which this "temporal activity" is happening: minimizing its impact and maximizing the benefit of what still remains a resource. In this sense, Alan Berger's definition of "Exterial Landscape" offers a very useful reference.[45] He coined the term to describe the altered environments caused by politico-economic decision-making processes that result in massive negative landscape spillover effects and externalities. As he claimed, "By chronicling the environmental and landscape system impact of first-order politico-economic decisions, and revealing and disclosing hidden externalized risks and costs created in their wake, better second-order decisions can be made that force more of the internalized costs to be borne by actors who neglect to calculate the landscape impacts of their actions. The design and planning field can take advantage of this gap by more fully understanding the outcomes of first-order decisions and preparing to intervene with more intelligent project responses. Only then, can better second-order decisions be made for more effective projects that take the burden off of society to pay for the destruction of public environmental resources."[46]

Environmental mitigation, restoration, and compensation are established practices in many countries, such as the United States, Australia, and Germany. In Chile, despite the many studies that have acknowledged the impact of mining on the environment, on biodiversity, and on communities, very few studies suggest ways to mitigate, restore, or compensate for these impacts, and the legislation remains very

---

42. Juan Ladrón de Guevara et al, *Guía para el desarrollo de compensaciones en biodiversidad en la Región de Tarapacá*.
43. See Bayern Oekokonto: http://www.lfu.bayern.de/natur/oekokonto/index.htm; and also Chiara Rizzi, *4th Landscape*.
44. Ibid. 45. Alan Berger, "Exterial Landscape," *Topos* 76 (Fall 2011).
46 Ibid.

vague. In general, there is no objective consensus on how to evaluate the impact on natural and cultural resources, nor are there unambiguous ways to evaluate and therefore regulate the benefits.

A solution will not be provided here. Yet, design should be able to change the rules, and reverse scenarios, re-creating these territories at the same time and after mining, for example, building on the quality of the landscape, the cultural and environmental patrimony, technology and innovation. Calama is for instance the gateway to the geological and archaeological wonders of Chile's high central desert. Chuquicamata, the village of San Pedro de Atacama, Valle de la Luna (Valley of the Moon), the Licancabur volcano, R. P. Gustavo Le Paige Archaeological Museum, Los Flamencos National Reserve, the Aguas Calientes Salt Flat, the Tuyajto lagoon, the El Tatio Geysers, the village of Chiu-Chiu...are all in a range of a few kilometers, not to mention the level of infrastructure and the highly qualified labor that the mining industry has been introducing to the region in the past decades.

Thinking of landscape – and its transformation, remediation, modification – as a lens, a paradigm, and a *program* of actions and interactions is a very powerful way to imagine new ways to plan and design for territories of extraction, and many other manifestations of contemporary urbanism. The interpretation of landscape as a relational system – a connecting infrastructure – is immediately associated with its condition of being a positive eco-structure and intra-structure with important implications for the new sustainable and environmental parameters of urban development: re-naturalization, green factors, air and visual quality and comfort, CO_2 equilibrium, etc. From being a formal and morphological entity, a decorative element within or alternative to the city, landscape has become the strategy through which to understand and organize territories on the geographical scale, managing programs and processes of transformation. It has become the place of relation of the city, in the concrete as well as symbolic way, on all scales: from the interstitial place between buildings to major ecosystems. As Manuel Gausa puts it, landscape is a medium for interaction, and interaction – among people, with the environment, between technologies and typologies, etc. – is the most important condition of our information era:[47] "Landscape is 'open' to change and transformation; it is malleable. It can offer multiple uses and is usually public; it is the place of relation of the city. However, notwithstanding the many contemporary reinterpretations landscape can assume, it will never lose its lyric and open-endedness, its holistic meaning, the horizon, the sky, the big lines and the large gazes, the lines of force, the environment solicitations: parameters of a new dynamic field conditions of our environments (*champ de forces*)."[48]

---

47. Manuel Gausa, interviewed by Jeannette Sordi in J.Sordi, *Beyond Urbanism*. See also Manuel Gausa. *Open* (Barcelona: Logica Abierta, Actar, 2010).

Today, we are thinking of the whole city, if not the world, as a landscape, a holistic entity to be rethought. Far beyond attempts to provide urban order and restore lost ecologies, landscape can provide a framework, and a series of rules, within which multiple actors and aspirations can play their game and envision more equal and enduring futures. As the geographer Franco Farinelli puts it, landscape is like the Internet: it is the only instrument that allows us to look at the world as a whole, or an environment, and at the same time make individual and collective contributions essential for the development of that environment.[49]

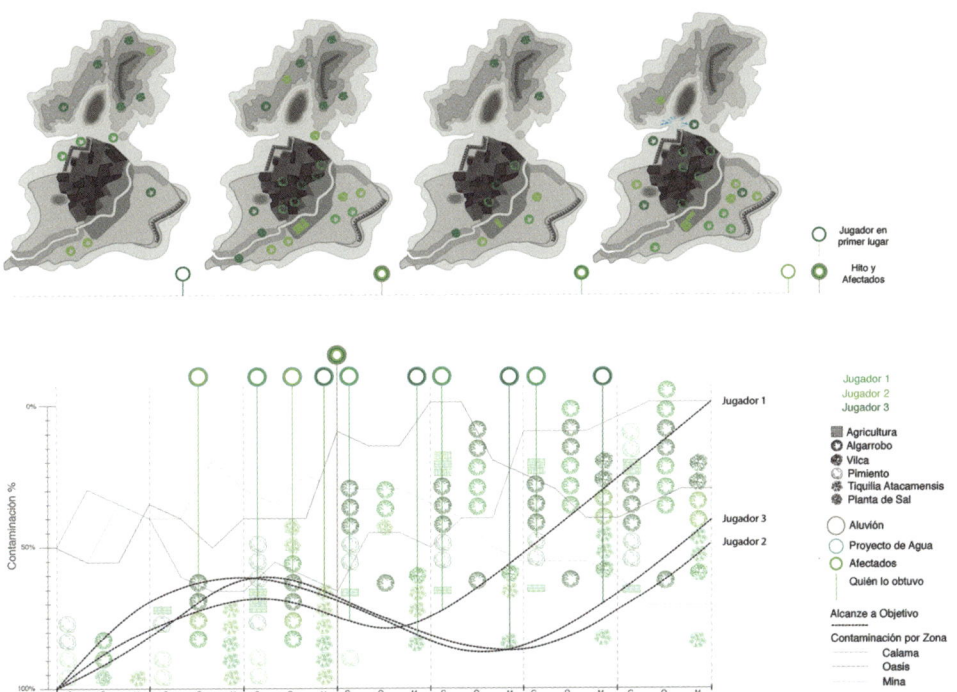

Landscape reclaimation game evolution, Daniela Prato, Sylvana Quest, Landscape and Urbanism Design Studio 2015, Jeannette Sordi, Felipe Vera, UAI

---

48. Manuel Gausa, interview with Jeannette Sordi in Jeannette Sordi, *Beyond Urbanism*.
49. Franco Farinelli, "Dal paesaggio al web. Discorso sul metodo," *Lettera Internazionale* 105 (2015): 25-28. 47. Manuel Gausa, interviewed by Jeannette Sordi in J.Sordi, *Beyond Urbanism*. See also Manuel Gausa. *Open* (Barcelona: Logica Abierta, Actar, 2010).

Landscape Rules | 201

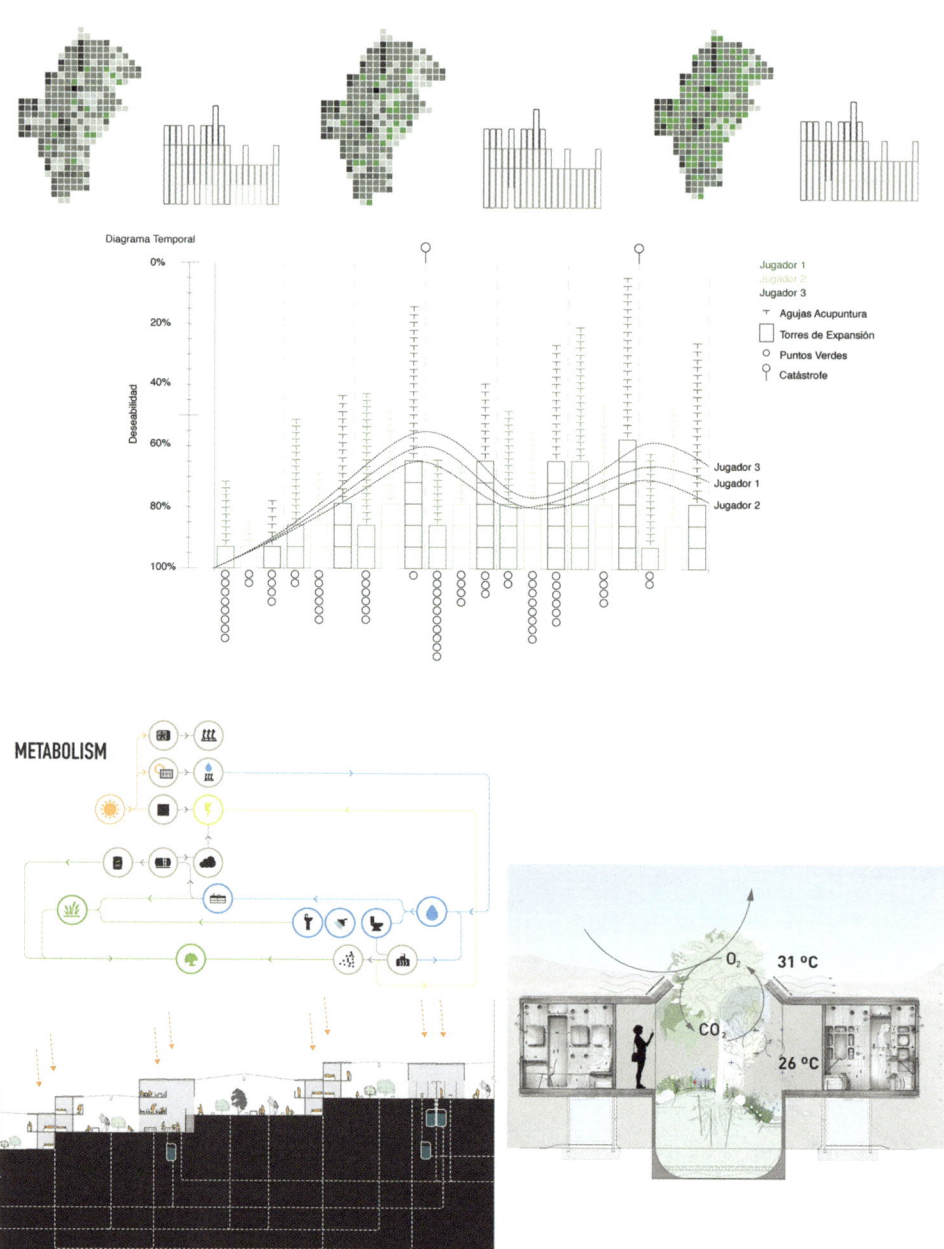

Above - Landscape reclaimation players impact, Daniela Prato, Sylvana Quest, Landscape and Urbanism Design Studio 2015, Jeannette Sordi, Felipe Vera, UAI

Bottom - Mining camp metabolism and afterlife, Material Logistic workshop, organized by Alexandros Tsamis and Mark Goulthourpe, UAI-MIT

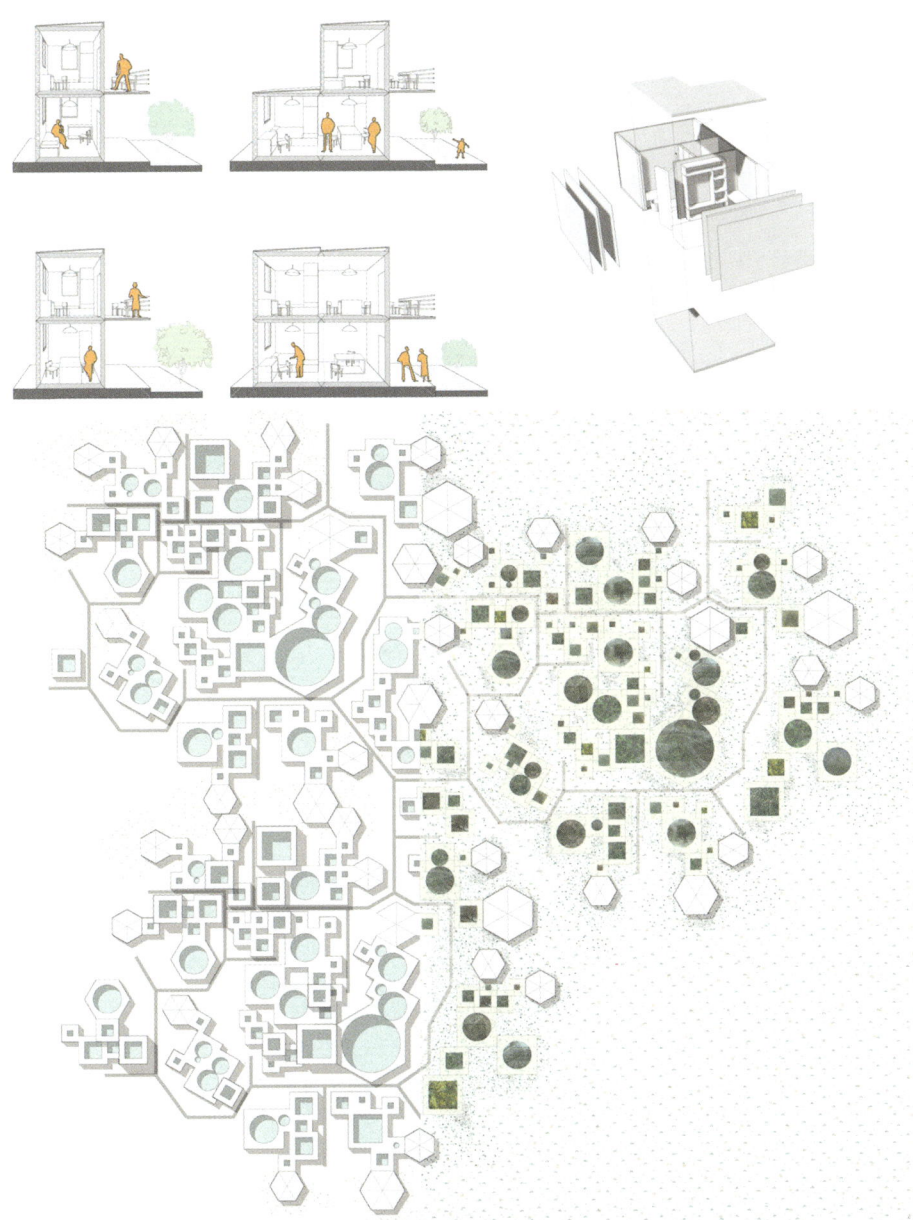

Mining camp assembly options, Material Logistic workshop, organized by Alexandros Tsamis and Mark Goulthourpe, UAI-MIT

Bottom- Organic Commixture as a vision for mitigation and future legacy by Monica Fontana, "Ephemeral Territorialism" Master Degree Thesis in Architecture, Politecnico di Milano, UAI, Advisors: Elisa C.Cattaneo, Jeannette Sordi

Scenarios of multi-scalar mitigation, recovery and reclamation for Calama and the mining landscape by Serena Dambrosio, "Chile as Geography in Movement" Master Degree Thesis in Architecture, Politecnico di Milano, UAI. Advisors: Elisa C.Cattaneo, Jeannette Sordi.

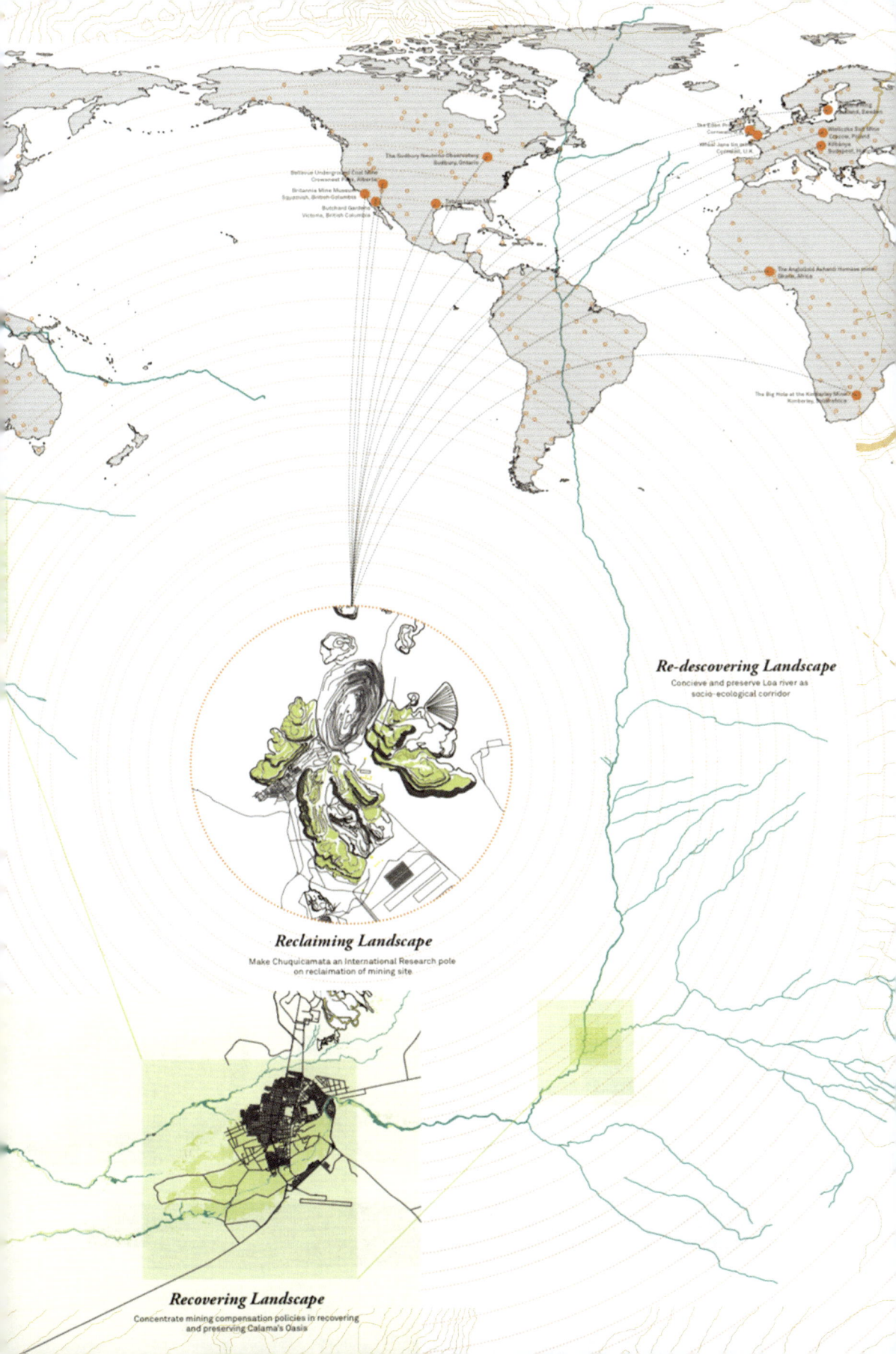

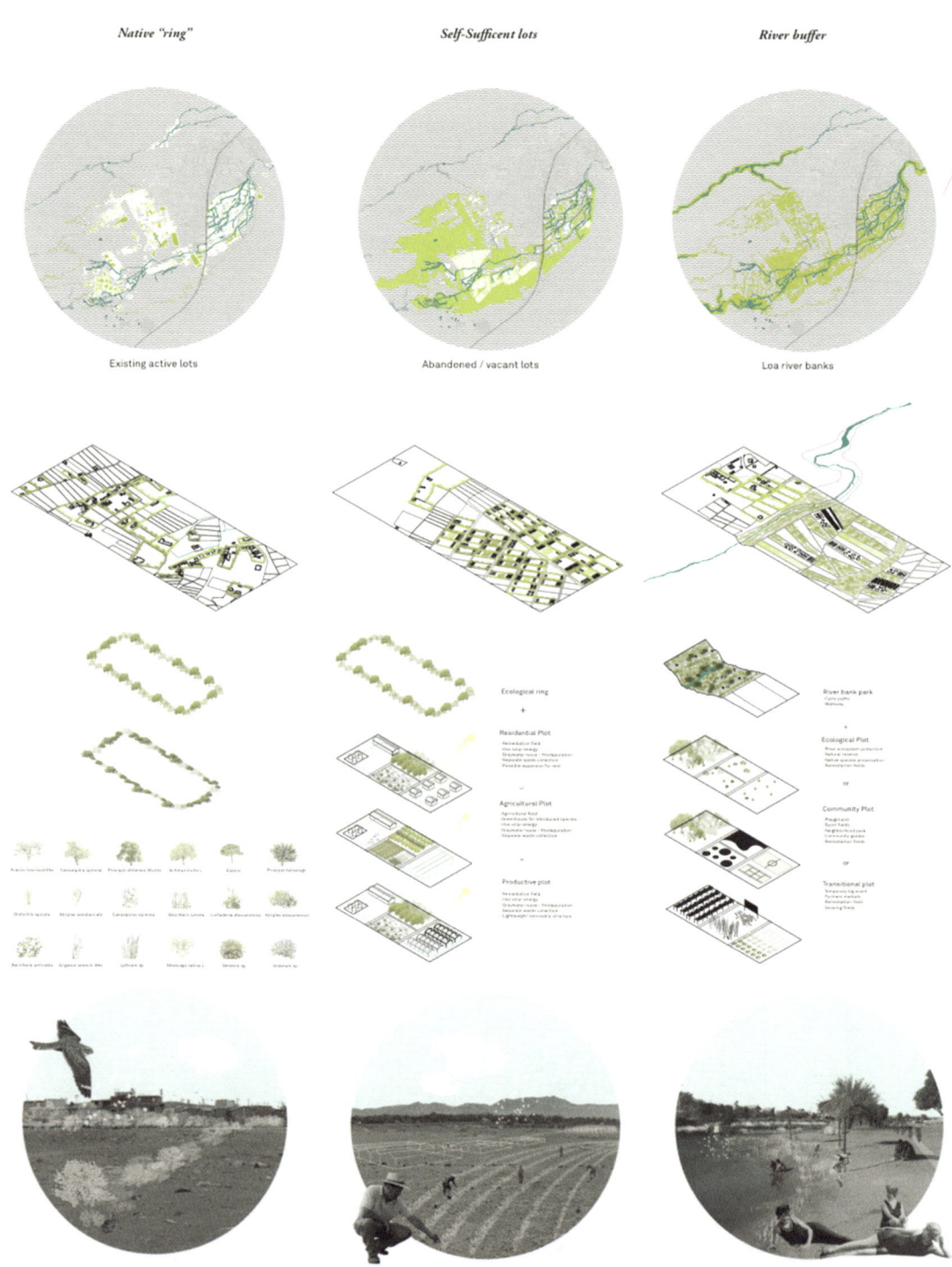

Scenarios of multi-scalar mitigation, recovery and reclamation for Calama and the mining landscape by Serena Dambrosio, "Chile as Geography in Movement" Master Degree Thesis in Architecture, Politecnico di Milano, UAI. Advisors: Elisa C. Cattaneo, Jeannette Sordi.

Landscape in motion

Calama occupied plots, Jeannette Sordi, 2015

Conflicting Spaces in New Territories of Extraction
Luis Valenzuela

Abstract
Many argue that since the mid-1980s and the beginning of the 1990s the extraction of mineral resources in Latin America took different and new forms compared to previous mining periods. This article takes a careful look at some of these new geographies of extraction, to consider whether they are a new perspective in the relationships between political, economic, and social factors with extraction issues and their transformations. Together with the increasing productivity of mining, the economic model became in each instance more complex and influenced by a broader territorial impact followed by the increasing social conflicts. Since the 1990s, the new dimensions of these extended territories of extraction are in part the result of historical struggles between mining and communities, but also because mining extraction has become more complex and intense by involving global mining companies, international mining outsourcing companies, and national service companies. The traditional mining model has evolved into a modern extractive business model. Under the mining boom, the articulation and tension of the uneven geography in the growth of natural resource extraction settings permanently submerge the real needs of daily life in local contexts, where social conflicts linked to the unequal territorial welfare arose, on one side due to spatial inaccessibility to public services and infrastructure, and on the other side, due to the concentration of poverty.

1. The Last Decades of New Transformations
Many argue that since the mid-1980s and the beginning of the 1990s the extraction of mineral resources in Latin America took different and new forms compared to previous mining periods.[1] As a result, in much of the Latin American Central Andean Region, extraction has become fundamental and dominant in its economic, political, and social dimensions.[2] Altogether with the increasing productivity of mining, its economic model became in each instance more complex and broadened its territorial impact, followed by an increasing intensity of social conflicts. Throughout the last 25 years, mining's social and economic contexts and fields have transformed, acquiring an incremental complexity related to extraction centers. The territories of extraction are grounds of changes between processes of globalization of mining companies, national and international mining outsourcing, services, local communities, indigenous rights, and social movements. Changes in a diverse range of dimensions around territories of extractions remain under-researched and under-theorized despite the worldwide scale of its industry:

---

1. A. Bebbington and J. Bury, eds., *Subterranean Struggles: New Dynamics of Mining, Oil, and Gas in Latin America* (Austin: University of Texas Press, 2014).
2. C. Ballard and G. Banks, "Resource Wars: The Anthropology of Mining," *Annual Review Anthropology 32* (2003): 287–313.

The exploitation of 'point' natural resources with large rents associated is likely, on the basis of the experience of the last few decades, and especially in countries with previously fragile political institutions, to generate both unexpectedly low rates of economic growth and a series of adverse effects on governance, including authoritarianism, militarization, regional secessionism, and socioeconomic inequality.[3]

Notwithstanding that the evidence demonstrates a lack of relationship between economic resources from extraction and a stalled local development, "The idea of a broad Resource Curse has become fixed in most people's minds. Extraction has been cast as a 'loser' sector by political economists."[4]

Since the 1990s, the new dimensions of these extended territories of extraction are in part the result of historical struggles between mining and communities, but also because mining extraction has become more complex and intense by involving global mining companies, international mining outsourcing companies, and national service companies. The traditional mining model has evolved into a modern extractive business model. While the overall trend of extraction panorama almost immensely increased doubling itself through two decades, the other significant transformation has been the conflict between communities, companies, and the state. Following the idea that these conflicts over extraction resources lead to a progressive change in institutional settings.[5]

2. New Spaces of Conflict in Territories of Extraction

Conflicts and extractive industries have long been linked; today such situations have become highly visible and explosive. Mining territories along the Andes region are no exception; it is a place of struggle against inequality, territorial control, and national distribution of wealth. One of the noticeable historical events is the copper mining labor strike in Mexico in mid-1906,[6] which gave birth to the social movement and revolution. The tensions that emerge are present in multiple dimensions and scales, from local communities' rights and the nation-state rights at the central level, between the legitimacy of indigenous communities and national territorial logics. The contrast of localized costs and national extraction revenues underlie tensions between local demands as victims of the extraction and the benefits for a greater collective interest,

---

3. J. Arellano-Yanguas, "Aggravating the Resource Curse: Decentralisation, Mining and Conflict in Peru," *Journal of Development Studies* 47 (4) (2011): 617–638.
4. G. A. Davis, "Extractive Economies, Growth, and the Poor ," in *Mining, Society, and a Sustainable World*, ed. J. Richards, (Berlin/Heidelberg: Springer, 2010), pp. 30-60.
5. A. Bebbington, J. Bury, *Subterranean Struggles*.
6. Michael J. Gonzales, "U.S. Copper Companies, the Mine Workers' Movement, and the Mexican Revolution, 1910-1920," *The Hispanic American Historical Review*, Vol. 76, No. 3 (Aug. 1996): pp. 503-534.

not only of the living population but also the development of future generations. These tensions among local and national, indigenous and global, costs and benefits, are contested in the occupied territories of extraction. Still, from a political point of view, a main issue of the theory of a recourse curse is that revenues provided by natural resources empower the central government system.

Despite the thesis of the Dutch disease on economies highly dependent on natural resources,[7] overall the evidence is not absolute in the relation between human development and intense extraction.[8] While some claim that countries specializing in mineral extraction growth are bad for the poor, others claim that it is particularly good for the poor.[9] The capacity of extractive economies to reduce poverty[10] has two effects on the poor: on the one hand it has an effect on the amount of income, as well as an effect on the distribution of income. Thus, this kind of economy is particularly bad for the poor unless strong local governments have a role when negative growth occurs. In periods with positive economic growth from extraction, the impact on the poor is no worse than non-extractive economies, yet for extractive economies with bad or negative growth, the impact on the poor is stronger than non-extractive economies. Since the national economy strongly depends on extraction, it "appears to be the failure of the extractive sectors to grow in a steady, persistent manner."[11] Indeed, some research suggests that the local government role is crucial in diminishing the negative impacts of bad growth. In the case of Chile, the recent strong economic growth has produced enormous gains for the state and multinational companies, and strong social conflict mainly due to the lack of strong local governments and because that growth spell is weak in extraction regions. Then the permanent damage to the poor in not receiving the benefits of growth is linked to the failure of having persistent and consistent development, and therefore conflict increases. Even more, the increase in the mining boom tends to decrease other economic sectors, as the extraction economy is able to replace income.[12] Indeed, it seems that policy has definitely turned to focus on a local scale, as many cases have emerged worldwide, in Latin America, and specifically in Chile related to mining: Creo Antofagasta and Calama PLUS are proof

---

7. J. Sachs and A. Warner, "Natural Resource Abundance and Economic Growth." NBER Working Paper 5398. Cambridge, MA, 1995.
8. G. Davis, "Learning to Love the Dutch Disease: Evidence from the Mineral Economies," *World Development* 23(10) (1995): 1765–1779.
9. G. Davis, "Learning to Love the Dutch Disease: Evidence from the Mineral Economies."
10. G. A. Davis, "Extractive Economies, Growth, and the Poor ," 30-60.
11. Ibid.
12. G. Bridge, "Contested Terrain: Mining and the Environment," *Annual Review of Environment and Resources* 29 (2004): 205-259, and G. Bridge, "Mapping the Bonanza: Geographies of Mining Investment in an Era of Neoliberal Reform," *The Professional Geographer* 56 (3) (2004): 406-421.
13. See Pablo Allard and Maria Ignacia Arrasate's chapter in this book.

of a new local policy perspective.[13] This new pattern has three leading elements:[14] a) a relatively compulsory distribution of mining revenues towards regional and local government, prioritizing localities with extraction points; b) a relatively formal process of participation for local communities to decide on the spending of revenues; c) a relatively broad motivation for stakeholders, key actors, civil society, and extraction companies to take part in locally based decision-making. Yet, there is a wide range of situations among countries, as well as among conflicts linked to specific economic productive sectors within the same country. Paradoxically, governments accept the policy components of a local perspective as an easy way to exhibit responsiveness towards their constituencies and also to the international community vigilant in the adherence to international treaties. In fact, the civil society activists and communities in mining extraction centers increased the pressure on companies to acknowledge and comprehend the impact of the operation in quality of life, although these leverage the benefits of people in territories of extraction.[15] Yet it is also a reaction to the international pressure of a new global policy climate, which is tending towards an increase of local control over natural resources. Much of the companies' emphasis on local mitigation is delivered as Corporate Social Responsibility (CSR), especially from the early 1990s when mining production stepped up and initiatives were focused on the local levels of citizens, governments, and NGOs.[16] There is a transversal recognition among mining companies that having a response capacity to local demands follows up a good business sense.[17]

Although CSR has been strongly advocated by local community rights defenders, as a method of devolution of natural resource extraction it does not yield a balance between communities and powerful companies. It is a compensation method that avoids tackling the power asymmetry, instead of seeking a balanced system of governance over the territory where different actors and stakeholders may pursue reciprocal beneficial processes and results.

> As long as inequalities persist communities will always be at a disadvantage in their relationships with MNCs [multinational companies] and they will be forced to rely on the goodwill of companies. At the same time, companies will have to devote time and money to defusing conflicts that have the potential to become increasingly violent as communities utilize disruptive weapons of the weak strategies. Thus, the solution to MNC and community conflict lies in increasing aware-

---

14. J. Arellano-Yanguas, "Aggravating the Resource Curse: Decentralisation, Mining and Conflict in Peru," 617–638.
15. C. Ballard and G. Banks, "Resource Wars: The Anthropology of Mining," 287–313.
16. Ibid.
17. L. Calvano, "Multinational Corporations and Local Communities: A Critical Analysis of Conflict," *Journal of Business Ethics* 82 (4) (2008): 793-805.

ness of community perspectives on the part of business leaders and bolstering the power of communities to challenge corporate actions.[18]

CSR practices, especially in extensive practices, tend to fail in the long run. Overall, local governments, communities, and people linked to territories affected by natural resources extraction operations do not counterbalance the revenues received by mining companies, service companies, and central governments. Even the activities of devolution themselves are a cause of conflict.

One of the possible reasons lies in the complexity of the territorial operation of extraction and the nature of conflicts. Accordingly, three kind of conflicts clearly emerged in the contemporary territories of extraction,[19] distinguishing main types with different sub-types.

First, there are conflicts with mining companies attempting to appropriate, or appropriating, resources of land, water, or other unpolluted local environment, in which communities resist or demand compensation for it. These conflicts may also involve issues of territorial control and local autonomy mixed with a diminished confidence in the central government. For these types of conflicts, generally the goal is to block the project, utilizing a referendum or community consultation strategies to decide on support for projects. Voting is also seen as form a communication or negotiation between local communities and the government. The case of Calama PLUS had a major public referendum, non-binding relative to the development of a project, but regarding public investment in a city highly impacted by mining extraction. This was the first community referendum in Chile related to mining extraction territories. Second, there are conflicts on mining driven to hold the greater possible share of benefits of the project development and operation. Methods may vary, such as employment offers to local residents – a recurring promise from companies –, distribution of revenues via royalties, or specific regional budgeting allocations by the central government. However, two new processes have taken place since the 1990s: on one side, mining in Latin America and in Chile require every time more highly skilled laborers, leaving behind the local population; on the other side, mining companies have shifted to subcontractors, and outsourced labor is shrinking its own permanent jobs. Today, the overall mining industry in Chile hires workers for one in four jobs and subcontracts the rest.[20] Third, there are conflicts related to the distribution of

---

18. Ibid.
19. S. Kirsch, "Afterword: extractive conflicts compared," in *Social Conflict, Economic Development and the Extractive Industry: Evidence from South America*, ed. A. Bebbington (London: Routledge, 2012), pp. 201-213, and J. Arellano-Yanguas, "Aggravating the Resource Curse: Decentralisation, Mining and Conflict in Peru," 617–638.

resources in localities in territories of extraction with the outcome that payments are strongly correlated with conflict levels; moreover, research suggests that this also increases local expectations, resulting in higher frustrations throughout negotiation processes. The distribution process demands greater management of expectations, since local residents and communities foresee a definite solution for long-term scarcities, yet when resources are allocated among many and over extended periods of time, the final sum seems quite smaller than expected:

> Thus management of expectations is not only a key ingredient of mining conflicts but also an important variable in the translation of social goals into policy reform.[21]

Mining conflicts claim territorial dominance in diverse levels or scales: by indigenous communities, by municipalities, or by the state. They operate both from a top-down logic, and also from a bottom-up one, and in this case a negotiation process has to be entered into, since the state hardly represents its constituency in many of these conflicts, since they receive important revenues that collide with local interests. This paradoxical situation ends in an increasing perception of an absence of the state in the territories of extraction, and consequently those local actors and communities must defend and negotiate themselves.

3. Geographies of Economies of Extraction

Mining production in Chile is highly concentrated in copper, and these resources are located in the three northern regions of the country: the Tarapacá, Antofagasta, and Atacama regions. Overall, these regions have concentrated 75% of the copper production as the main economic activity since the initial and last years of the 1990s.[22] Considering that on average Chile produces around a third of the world's copper, approximately 25% of that production comes from Chile's three northern regions.

Among the three regions, there are important differences in terms of the amount of production, and therefore the specific characteristics of local development also differ between each region. The region of Antofagasta has the most complex mining production and geological environment, generating on average 53% of the national production.[23] As a consequence, large flows of investment are concentrated in the region, and with it, multinational mining companies and their services, most possibly resulting in one of the most complex territories of copper mining, one that extracts around 12.5% of the world production – an exceptional territorial distinction.

---

20. P. Aroca and N. Rivera, "Escalas de producción en economías mineras: El caso de Chile en su dimensión regional," *EURE* 40 (121) (2014): 247-270.
21. S. Kirsch, "Afterword: extractive conflicts compared," pp. 201-213.
22. P. Aroca and N. Rivera, "Escalas de producción en economías mineras: El caso de Chile en su dimensión regional," *EURE* 40 (121) (2014): 247-270.

The region of Antofagasta not only concentrates a major part of worldwide copper production, it is almost entirely produced by large mining companies, with 97.3% of overall regional production. This is a significant difference of production size, since the implications of large mining companies have specific characteristics: they reach high efficiency levels of labor compared to the small and medium mining companies, and they are oriented toward an overseas market for trading. This highly efficient and international mining model has been installed in the region of Antofagasta, demanding a higher participation from the industrial sector in supplies and services, together with a demand for commerce, hotels, restaurants, transport, and communications sectors, all of them concentrated in the two main cities of the region: Antofagasta and Calama, and therefore with strong territorial consequences. The region of Antofagasta has received the highest concentration of investment in mining since the mid-1980s. Such capital has also involved the extraction of water, with consequences of decertification of wetlands, salt lakes, and rivers, located on the higher grounds of Calama's mining enclave.[24] Many of the territories affected by mining water withdrawals are also those that have been occupied for a long time by indigenous communities.

Calama is the exit door for approximately a fifth of world's cooper, yet experiences the lowest quality of life standards in Chile and probably the Andean Region. This city once had one of the larger urban oases of Chile and probably the world, but today the oasis is minimized and permanently menaced with disappearance. Such a paradox demands an improvement in the comprehension of both the city's and the mining cluster's problems in an integrated and holistic way. The most frequent approach to comprehending social tensions among mining communities has focused on the physical and tangible effects of mining on people and communities who are exposed to diverse hazards and diseases. Yet, again since the '90s, mining communities have shifted focus to social and environmental issues, "The preservation of cultural integrity and/or indigenous rights, and the ability to participate in decisions about mineral development from a position of prior informed consent."[25]

The new relationships of mining centers' development with communities is that people no longer blandly accept mining management or technical decisions in a neutral way. Mining, its community, and agencies are taking the debate of mining conflict around environment and revenues as part of a negotiation process. In the case of indigenous groups the conflict is taken to legitimate ownership and rights over the territory.

---

23. Ibid.
24. H. Romero, M. Méndez, and P. Smith, "Mining Development and Environmental Injustice in the Atacama Desert of Northern Chile," *Environmental Justice* 5 (2) (2012): 70-76.
25. G. Bridge, "Mapping the Bonanza: Geographies of Mining Investment in an Era of Neoliberal Reform."

4. Extended Territories of Urbanization

Until recently, mining – among other extractive activities such as agriculture and forestry – has been thought to occupy a small extent of land, and even its environmental effects are contained. Many have challenged this viewpoint of a localized extraction center by adopting an ecosystem perspective to address the environmental interaction of mining and pollution impacts far beyond the boundaries of its industrial processes.[26] More than the mine itself, mining modifies ecological processes over environmental areas such as air, water, and waste contamination, biogeochemical processes, and mining effects on regional habitat conversion and fragmentation.

These complex developments and interactions are much more than environmental. Mining extraction overall is a process of moving and shifting elements throughout the territory.[27] Inherent to all extraction activity is the necessity of moving elements, whether it be earth, trees, fruits, or fish. Yet to extract a resource is also the need to move other inputs such as fuel, machinery, fuel, chemicals, energy, and labor among many others. Throughout this movement of elements "mining (is) a form of landscape modification,"[28] that has two differentiating characteristics: a quantitative flow of materials and energy as form of different inputs and outputs to the mining operation, and a flow of labor at local, regional, and global scales dedicated to the extraction activities, outsourcing, and services. The physical alterations of the landscape and movement on the landscape are in themselves a registration of the extraction process, and it shows the intense mining territorial model's complexity, sometimes interpreted as the overburdening of extraction that has a spatial dimension.

The flow of materials, labor, waste, products, resources, and energy construct a new and dual territorial reality of extraction and urbanization. The magnitude of associated flow is so massive that its extension overspills the extraction point, and even its surroundings of milling and smelting, radically reframing the local geography. In the midst of these transformations, both natural and man-made elements have been deeply affected. Vegetation, waterways and bodies of water, dust growth, and large-scale topographic alterations are natural sceneries that change. The introduction of new structures, large-scale economic capital investment, logistics facilities, and networks of infrastructure are some of the explicit man-made consequences of extractive economy operation grounds:

---

26. Ibid.
27. Conceptual expression used by Professor Alexander Tsamis, DesignLAB Faculty at the Universidad Adolfo Ibañez.
28. G. Bridge, "Mapping the Bonanza: Geographies of Mining Investment in an Era of Neoliberal Reform."

The mining industry requires not only capital and labor, but food for its workers and physical inputs for its operations. Consequently, mining activities tend to integrate surrounding regions into a single economic sphere.[29]

The territorial setting of the overall mining operation arranges a series of infrastructure urbanization out of the settlement's borders. The site-specific determination of a mine hole is slowly replaced by the notion of a mining district. If before, mining had an extraction together with milling and smelting processes settings, today mining operation adds the combined relationship with industrial facilities, transportation and communication infrastructure, extraction operation services, camps, roads, railroads, and highways, which together build a novel territorial scale. In a way, it is a new organizing principle in the concept of urbanization: the operational formation of an economic activity in a broader spatial scale than known before.

The new territorial notion is not only a physical modification of the space, but also a new attachment in the symbolic relations of mining communities and their changing landscapes.[30] This identity is closely related to the isolation of mining settlements, like, for example, the highlands in the Andean Region. There are also new tensions that arise as the mining impact expands itself throughout the territory. Preservationists are closely looking at all transgressions specifically taken by large multinational mining companies relative to several issues such as natural preservation, environmental protection, and indigenous cultural inclusion, among others.The significance of territories of extraction has become especially intriguing due to the unexpected superimpositions of elements in a simultaneous time and space situation. The enclave of Calama, like many others in the Andean Region, is a new territorial notion of geography that challenges conventional perceptions of space, governance, and cohesion. These conflicting spaces in new territories of extraction have been summarized as a "new geography of extraction"[31] in the sense of its spatial form of social expression, in juxtaposition to the production processes that have expanded throughout the territory resulting in an increasing occurrence of conflicts.

> The range of landscape modifications introduced by mining includes pits, waste piles, built structures (headframes, stacks, aqueducts, tramways) and secondary (i.e., downstream) geomorphological features, such as debris fans, sand bars, and turbid rivers. Frequently described as "visual intrusions," the interpretation of these landscape features as "unsightly or even repellent" is far from universal.[32]

---

29. R. Godoy, "Mining: Anthropological Perspectives," *Annual Review of Anthropology* 14 (1985): 199-217.
30. G. Bridge, "Mapping the Bonanza: Geographies of Mining Investment in an Era of Neoliberal Reform."
31. A. Bebbington, J. Bury, *Subterranean Struggles*.
32. G. Bridge, "Contested Terrain: Mining and the Environment," p. 209.

The new geography of extraction is not only due to the conflicting spatial superposition of heritage rights of indigenous cultures with extraction concessions over the land. It is also because of the intense interaction of extraction in the territory as it mobilizes elements across its space in a particularly intense manner.[33] Extraction is fundamental to the continental, national, and territorial processes of transformation that produce tensions with natural resources, the environment, cities, and settlements. In territorial terms, the flow of input of materials and labor, and the outputs of products and waste, is a continuous movement across boundaries and frontiers. Together they build a complex system that operates over the territory. Extraction is a complex coordinated operation of a set of activities that operates over the territory, according to a strong rationale of a minimum effort to maximize the production of a commodity. Labor moves from continental origins to the extraction pits and different operations; fuel and acid are transported, and energy and water are supplied. From the extraction centers, waste and products are delivered to deposits or to final market destinations.

The overlapping extraction territories diagram explains the different and diverse flows' interaction in terms of scale and cycles in the operations of mining. It shows flying patterns, with labor being the most intensive, from other cities, countries, and regions towards the logistics city or extraction center as a floating population. The extraction labor force is divided among mining company workers, mining outsourcing company workers, and mining extraction workers. All of them generate flights in and out of the mine's closest airport facility. Outsourcing and services companies represent a large part of the mining economic model when based on multinational companies' operations. Therefore, they are also the most demanding in terms of labor, many of whom fly in and out according to the work shifts. The following diagram, part of the Floating Population map, shows 24 hours of flights, both arrivals and departures, into and out of Calama's airport, named Loa Airport.

Year	Passengers
2004	247,821
2005	273,275
2006	315,725
2007	99,061
2012	1,071,445
2013	1,441,566
2014	1,296,650

Source: Junta Nacional Aeronautica Civil and Dirección General de Aeronáutica Civil

---

33. Roderick G Eggert, *Mining and the Environment: International Perspectives on Public Policy*. John M. Olin Foundation, Resources For The Future, Inc. (1994) Washington, DC, USA.

With a floating population of such large numbers, other resources need to be transported and distributed to the different mines, settlements, and cities. Food, water, fuel, acids, and other resources follow the movement of materials over the territory towards the extraction point. Earth material is drawn out to process waste minerals, wastewater, and waste fluids, and other wastes are part of the cycles of operation. Finally, the mineral itself is transported and shipped to overseas markets. The overlapping extraction territories diagram shows an order of scales that ranges from local to global. Yet it also shows certain uncommon loops that would not occur in a more diversified economic basis. In the case of a complex mining enclave, services tend to be local or national, while outsourcing has trended towards highly qualified international companies. Mining companies themselves are multinational corporations, yet with property ownership and extraction concessions over very specific locations within the territory.

5. Extractive Urbanization's Critical Domains

There has been a recent change in the social struggle and policy focus toward an attention on the local, which in the case of Calama can be fixed on the day that the city's population flowed into the streets in a protest against the country led by the Mayor. This social awareness and local policy orientation pattern is based on three concepts that have emerged from a series of case studies[34]: i) one of the most common and pressing was the necessity to redistribute the resource revenues towards the local level where extraction centers are located and operate; ii) the effective participation of local residents and indigenous communities; iii) regional and local level decision-making by institutional actors and the active involvement of civil society. The change in policy, along with these three main concepts, has directly impacted the urbanization phenomenon of territories of extraction. The recent local focus, with active participation in decision-making, implies taking into consideration several relevant critical domains. These range from economic, cultural, social, and infrastructural perspectives. Extraction requires impressive infrastructure provisions and an increased mobility of services for the most extreme industrial processes of extraction, yet it does not uniquely impact the mine but disseminates an extensive and broadly connected network across which diverse matters are continuously moved, changed, or relocated, such as fuel, workers, mineral, acids, water, among others. The emergent paradox of a territory, defined by the tone of the most profitable global extraction businesses, is functionally linked to the locals' segregation and the indigenous communities' struggle for development with a precise spatial allocation and operation in the territory, one that extends beyond solely the urban setting and production areas defined by the direct and indirect economic impact of mining.

---

34. J. Arellano-Yanguas, "Aggravating the Resource Curse: Decentralisation, Mining and Conflict in Peru," 617–638.

Mining, during its early phases and currently more intensively, has been a labor-intensive operation. Consequently, one of the first and most important requirements of the mining industry has been the procurement of an ample and reliable supply of laborers. The evidence suggests that migration to the mines in diverse regions such as Africa, Latin America, and North America occurs on a more frequent basis and for longer periods of time. Until recently, the net transfer of wealth flowed from the rural to the mining sector. In recent years, however, that subsidy has been reversed, with mining wages soaring upward through multinational global capital, and increasingly international and specialized mining outsourcing companies, while services to the industry adjust themselves to provide for the local market. Despite all economic scaling development and growth, this is followed by a rapidly decomposing indigenous subsistence structure. Historically, the copper mining industry in Calama has been highly extractive and unidirectional with regard to labor, resources, and the natural environment. Resources leave the site, largely benefitting the producer and the purchaser. The prearrangement and establishment of an extended urbanization for the purposes of extraction have remained largely invisible despite the massive over-scaling of mining operations, except for growth pressure within urban areas. Yet, until a broader and more inclusive perspective of the real urbanization scale of extraction is initiated, problems in the inner city or in the outer landscape will not be properly solved. Consequently, the landscape environment's degraded condition is also followed by the intense effect of mining production within urban areas. Conventional planning undertaken solely for the administrative determination of urban land areas will leave its infrastructures and its public spaces unattended to the real pressures to which they are subject and will be seen as conventional urban development.Infrastructures and structures have progressively taken steps toward strong and also non-responsive territorial integration throughout the processes and services of extraction, and outside the scope of long-term planning. It has happened that communities, stakeholders, municipalities, and governments resist more effectively contributing with management, planning regulations, and proper monitoring and control mechanisms. The result is a fragmented territory divided into socially and culturally uneven geographies. Throughout the mining boom, the articulation and tension of uneven geographies in the growth of natural resource extraction settings permanently submerge the real needs of daily life in local contexts, where social conflicts arose linked to the unequal territorial welfare, on one side due to spatial inaccessibility to public services and infrastructure, and on the other side, due to the concentration of poverty. In the long run, it is necessary to deliver a theoretical framework to enable a conceptual and operational construction aiming to understand the relationship of mining enclaves with their surroundings, the effects on social and economic conditions, transportation, water, energy, fuel, food, and other needed inputs for mining production. In the short run, the recognition of tangible and physical conditions becomes the way to build a discourse.

Chuquicamata, Jeannette Sordi, 2015

Calama, view from the east, Jeannette Sordi, 2015

Calama, view from the east, Jeannette Sordi, 2015

CALAMA AS A CAMP
Agustina González Cid

The world today consumes around 50% more natural resources than only 30 years ago, at about 60 billion tons of raw materials a year.[1] The extraction of these materials transforms specific areas of the world into producing/extracting machines, creating urbanities that are unique to their kind. From the planetary scale at which minerals are commercialized to the scale of an anode, this section of the book analyzes Calama: a city located in the Northern Region of Chile, at the center of a global copper extraction enclave. Because of Calama's strategic location, above one of the world's largest copper deposits, mining companies have transformed the city into a camp, outsourcing in the city some of the activities that used to be taken care of by these companies in earlier versions of camps, forcing the city to deal with the externalities of the extractive activity that surrounds it. The photos, maps, and info-graphics created by the book team are meant to help grasp the intensity of the extractive activity in the territory around Calama.

Like most territories of extraction, the Calama enclave suffers from both external and internal pressures: on the one hand, the external pressure of keeping up with the hungry world's demand for natural resources and, on the other, the internal pressure of receiving, in exchange for materials, the incoming revenues so important to the country. This is the case of copper in Chile, whose revenues account for 11,99% of its GDP,[2] making the country's economy highly dependent on the global price of the commodity, and whose mining has transformed its Northern region into a territory of extraction, creating an artificial topography that materializes the copper apparatus at a national scale.

Although minerals are distributed all around the planet, due to geological processes that happened between 30 and 40 million years ago,[3] more than 42%[4] of the world's copper is located in the Andean region.

The world consumes around 22 million tons[5] of copper a year and around 34%[6]

---

1. Friends of the Earth, "OVERCONSUMPTION? Our Use of the World's Natural Resources," Friends of the Earth (2009), accessed December 2015, http://www.foe.co.uk/sites/default/files/downloads/overconsumption.pdf.
2. SONAMI, "Sociedad Nacional de Minería: Tradición Minera con Visión de Fututo," SONAMI, accessed December 23, 2015, http://www.sonami.cl/index.php?option=com_content&view=article&id=221&Itemid=109.
3. Codelco, Guided Tour Chuquicamata: "Gran Vecino, Buen Vecino," n.d., accessed August 2015, https://www.codelco.com/codelco-buen-vecino-tour-por-chuquicamata/prontus_codelco/2011-08-01/174444.html
4. Alejandro Carranza, "Mantenimiento del Módulo 'Precios del Cobre' del Modelo Macroeconométrico 'The Economist'" (Master's Thesis, Universidad Tecnológica Metropolitana, 2005).
5. Metales y Metalurgia, "Metales y Metalurgia," Metales y Metalurgia (April 21, 2014), accessed December 20, 2015, http://www.metalesymetalurgia.com/?p=363637.
6. Alejandro Carranza, "Mantenimiento del Módulo 'Precios del Cobre' del Modelo Macroeconométrico 'The Economist.'"

of it comes from Chile, transforming the country into the world largest copper producer, while the second largest producer is the U.S., with only 8.5%.[7] Apart from this, Chile owns 39%[8] of the world's copper reserves, with CODELCO (Chilean Copper Corporation) alone owning 9% of the total amount. Extracting this high percentage of the world's copper, excavating open pits (sometimes up to 1 kilometer deep) and underground mines (with tunnels that can reach depths of 7 km), demands a colossal physical effort: an invasive process that involves explosives, blasts, particles thrown into the air, huge amounts of water and rocks moved by trucks, all creating an artificial landscape that becomes the postcard of the place.

As an emblematic example of this physical transformation, after being intensely mined for 100 years, Chuquicamata still offers 932.5 metric tons of copper a day,[9] becoming the world's largest open pit copper mine with a hole that is 4.5 km long, 3.5 km wide and 1 km deep. Furthermore, although open-pit Chuquicamata is expected to stop being productive in the next decade, there is a project to transform the mine into a set of underground tunnels from where an estimate of 1.7 billion tons of copper will start being extracted by 2019, accounting for more than 60% of what was mined in the last 90 years,[10] extending the mine's life.

Although the impacts of mining are mostly associated with economic, social, and environmental issues, there are also territorial impacts affecting the urbanizations immersed in the middle of the territories of extraction. These mining effects materialize in Calama, located 20 km south of the Chuquicamata mine, in the Atacama Desert, one of the driest places on earth but also one of the richest. In this context, Calama is a city working as an "outsourced" camp, hosting people and infrastructure while performing the command function for the region. The long history of mining in Chile has shown different models: from the first camps in the hands of American companies to contemporary miner hotels, the different typologies have been selected to best serve an industry highly determined by national and international conditions. Mining companies changed from a paternalistic model that took care of every service related to extraction itself and to employees, to outsourcing these same services to other companies and even cities. The "camp" is now a territorial shapeless occupation covering whole enclaves. Calama works as a new form of camp, serving mining companies and subcontractors but being almost totally independent from them.

Previous camp models had a contained order, encapsulating the whole mining apparatus under one company's umbrella. However, after so many structural changes, this

7. Ibid.
8. Ibid.
9. "Codelco," codelco.com, accessed December 11, 2015, https://www.codelco.com/.
10. Ibid.

enclosed system was left behind, becoming impossible to return to. Apart from this, it is not only the business that was transformed; people's demands changed, too. In Chile, mine workers and their families now prefer to live in other more central cities like La Serena or Santiago and commute weekly by plane to the mines. On top of this, labor demand increased exponentially since the '80s, attracting workers from regions further away and even from other neighboring countries. The flow of different companies, workers, supplies, and revenues results in a mining apparatus that is now spread throughout the whole national territory with a strong epicenter, in this case, in the city of Calama.

Chuquicamata's Mining History

The history of intensive copper mining in the area started at the beginning of the twentieth century with the Chile Exploration Company, owned by the Guggenheim family. These first camps in the hands of American companies were based on models for utopian societies and company towns around the world. By the time the Chuquicamata camp opened in 1917, around three percent of the Chilean population (60,000 employees) were living on housing provided by the companies they were working for.[11] These camps and company towns provided for their employees, creating an intense sense of community and solving everything from housing to public spaces and education.

The Industrial Revolution together with the uncontrolled growth of cities had led some thinkers like Charles Fourier to reflect on different ways of living and working in less alienating environments, generating utopian models that would inspire real towns to come. Apart from this, there was a need from different industries to work in remote sites, either because of the location of natural resources or because of the availability of cheaper land far away from urbanized areas. Company towns appeared in the nineteenth century to solve the lack of labor in the proximities of the work sites. Company towns like Pullman (1880, Chicago, United States) and Hershey (1903, Pennsylvania, United States) commonly had modern public buildings and infrastructures, with every aspect of the employee's life covered by the company.[12] With these utopian models and company towns as precedents, Chuquicamata started working during its first period as an industrial enterprise, producing the first copper bar in 1915. Chuquicamata was by then the largest camp in Chile[13] and was designed to create a community neighboring the mine. It had two different camps three kilometers away: Hillsite (known as the "American Neighborhood") mostly occupied by people coming from the United States and the "Campamento Nuevo" for Chilean workers.[14] With time, public buildings appeared in the camp and by 1950, apart from a third Camp (O'Higgins), there were shops, a bar, a drugstore, a church, a coed school, social

---

11. Hardy Green, *The Company Town: The Industrial Edens and Satanic Mills That Shaped the American Economy* (New York: Basic Books, c2010).
12. Ibid.
13. Eugenio Garcés Feliú, Marcelo Cooper Apablaza, and Mauricio Baros Townsend, *Las Ciudades Del Cobre: Sewell, Chuquicamata, Potrerillos, El Salvador, San Lorenzo, Pabellón Del Inca, Los Pelambres*, 1. ed., Investigaciones (Santiago, Chile: Ediciones Universidad Católica de Chile, 2007).
14. Ibid.
15. Ibid.

clubs, a theater and an auditorium. Some of these buildings were exact replicas of other buildings in the United States and the sports were also based on U.S. preferences like basketball and baseball. By 1970, there were 24,000 people living in the camp,[15] out of which approximately 5,600 were workers and the rest were workers' families, police officers, public workers, teachers, and shopkeepers.

The second period started in 1971 when, during Salvador Allende's presidency (1970 – 1973), Chile's National Congress unanimously approved the nationalization of copper. Thanks to this, in 1976, the National Copper Corporation (CODELCO) was created as a state company in charge of extracting and commercializing the country's main mineral from every working mine. From that moment on, CODELCO has maintained its position as the world's largest copper producer.[16]

In the 1980s, Chuquicamata's third period arrived in hand with neoliberalism, changing the whole mining enclave. During Pinochet's presidency (1974-1990), mining was again opened to private companies. Moreover, following a strong global trend, many of the services that had been until that moment in the hands of Codelco were outsourced to subcontractors. This meant not only private companies working the mines, but also many subcontractors appearing to outsource other mining-related activities. This transformation in the work format is still present today and of all the people that directly or indirectly work for Codelco (66,979 people), only 29% (19,242 people) are part of the company's staff, while the remaining 71% (47,747 people) are employed by subcontractors.[17]

The fourth and current period is marked by the closure of the Chuquicamata camp. In the beginning of the 1990s, Chuquicamata started showing signs of its long life as a working mine, forcing the company to make some changes. On the one hand, the air in the camp was proven too polluted to breathe and, on the other, Codelco had run out of space in proximity to the mine for the allocation of waste. Because of this, in 1997, Codelco decided to close the Chuquicamata camp and moved its workers and their families to Calama. The company spent US$200 million to build houses and infrastructures for "New Calama."[18] Most families started moving in 2004, with the last families abandoning the camp in 2008. The new houses, for which Codelco had paid 75% of the total cost, were owned by the employees and located in the oasis. From that moment on, it was the city of Calama that had to deal with public spaces and transportation, health, and security demands for the recently enlarged popula-

16. "Codelco."
17. Codelco, "Codelco, Orgullo de Todos," Codelco, n.d., accessed December 11, 2015, https://www.codelco.com/codelco-orgullo-de-todos/prontus_codelco/2011-09-28/182001.html.
18. "Codelco."
19. People of Calama, Interviews to People of Calama for Class Territorial Inteligence, Spring 2015, Harvard Graduate School of Design, Paper Questionnaire, n.d.
20. Maria Josefina Valdes Cobo, "Parque de Recuperación y Tratamiento de las Aguas en el Oasis de Calama" (Master's Thesis, Pontificia Universidad Católica de Chile, 2007).
21. Ricardo Truffello and Luis Valenzuela, "De Geografías Superpuestas a Relaciones Territoriales Funcionales: El Caso del Cluster Minero de Calama, Chile" (Universidad Adolfo Ibáñez, December 2015).

tion. Still today, when asked, people from Calama consider the time of the closure of the Chuquicamata camp and the arrival of 4,000 families in the city as the moment when all services collapsed and the situation became chaotic.[19] The population went from 117,068 inhabitants in 1996 to 141,581 in 2006 and the surface area of the city grew from 1,359 ha to 1,923 ha, mostly over the Oasis.[20] Calama now deals with the externalities of being an "outsourced" camp for around 26 mines located in its proximity,[21] while the main decisions regarding what happens in the area are taken in other cities and the "payment" received for its "service" never seems to be enough. After the last families abandoned the camp, Chuquicamata became both a ghost town turned into a museum and a dumping place: the most iconic buildings and public spaces were kept intact for the general public to visit while mountains of inert material covered the regular houses (not without a previous struggle between former residents and the company).

Dealing with the Externalities
Hosting such an intense activity brings consequences for the territory. The physical footprint of the productive chain is clearly present around the enclave, and it extends its influence all over the country, from the pits around Calama to the headquarters in Santiago.
In Calama, there are two main minerals: copper oxide (found in more superficial areas in contact with water) and copper sulfides (found in deeper areas), each following a different industrial process. Although many mines have both types of minerals, some of the mines in the Calama enclave have only one type. The process of copper starts in the pit with the blast to make way towards the minerals. With these explosions, the air is filled with particles and, on windy days, dust is felt around downtown Calama. Weather does not help in preventing this; scarce rains and insufficient forestation help dust to freely find its way into the city.

Once removed from the pit, inert material is taken to big mountains of waste, becoming part of the artificial landscapes. As with every aspect of the camp, waste is part of its planned pragmatism: price and availability of land define where these mountains will grow.[22] In fact, after the closure of the Chuquicamata camp, the place was transformed into a dumping area, proving it was easier to move people and their associated needs than daily tons of waste. These mountains over the old camp are around 50 meters high, covering whole neighborhoods.

Rocks with high concentration of copper are taken to a series of automatic mills where the material is broken into smaller pieces. Then comes the flotation process, adding water and injecting air into the rock powder, making copper float to the surface. For this part, each drop of water is recycled and used up to 8.5 times.[23] The powder from the surface is later taken to drying ovens, reducing the humidity from 12% to

---

22. Garcés Feliú, Cooper Apablaza, and Baros Townsend, Las Ciudades Del Cobre.

23. Codelco, Tour Chuquicamata: "Gran Vecino, Buen Vecino."

0.2% and after which a concentrate of 33% copper and 1% molybdenum is obtained. Molybdenum is usually between four and five times more expensive than copper and, by selling it, Codelco covers the expense for producing all the copper extracted from the mine.[24]

The last steps in the process are meant to increase the copper purity. The copper is melted three times and later transformed into a 420-kg. 99.7 % copper anode. From here the anodes are taken by railway to the refinery were they are immersed inside a big pool with water, alternating one anode and one stainless steel sheet for the electrolysis process. After nine days of electricity inside the pool, all the molecules are transported from the anode to the stainless steel sheet, obtaining two copper cathodes of 99.99 % purity.[25] Chuquicamata has the capacity of producing 8,500 cathodes a day, requiring 140,000 daily tons of untreated material. These cathodes are grouped in sets of sixteen and later taken by railway from Chuquicamata to the Angamos port from where they are exported to the world.[26]

These copper exports account for nine million dollars a day, exclusively coming from Chuquicamata. Since Codelco is owned by the Chilean state, the revenues go directly to the national coffers from where they are redistributed. This long series of physical and chemical processes not only leaves mountains of waste behind but also tailings where the water that cannot be used anymore is deposited. These tailings are open-air tanks with impermeable bases, strictly controlled to minimize environmental damage in case of spills.

The main copper vein runs under Calama, and future projects for underground mining will start excavating underneath the city.[27] Calama will be then entirely surrounded by the extractive activity and the transformations it brings to the environment. However, the territory of the copper apparatus goes much further than the few kilometers around the mine and includes every step of the productive chain. Apart from depleting the earth of its valuable resource, the industry demands – from very diverse providers – influxes of people, food, machinery, explosives, and water: supplies that are brought to the site from long distances to keep the industry running. For every one of these needs, there are one or more companies taking care of a specific link of the chain. All these companies repeat a very similar structure; many of them include international headquarters, extended productive chains, national and international suppliers, short-term contracts in the area, subcontractors, and a floating population. The complexity is then multiplied and the territorial influence reaches global levels. The floating population also extends the territory of mining across the country. Mining is the activity that carries the largest floating population in Chile, with people specifically travelling on a regular basis from central areas to the North, where the activity is mostly developed. On a regular day, there are around 39 flights to and from Calama. This means that in one day an average of 11,895 people will go through the Calama Airport. This is especially

---

24. Ibid.   25. Ibid.   26. Ibid.   27. Ibid.

high compared to the 138,722 people that, according to the 2012 census, live in the city. Many of the workers stay there from Sunday to Thursday. On Thursday evening, the local airport is packed with the red pickups that are usually used in mining, and they stay there until Sunday evening when their owners come back to start another week. These are the 4-3 shifts that are most common with higher rank employees. However, most miners normally have a 10-10 shift, with ten days working and ten days off. These are especially designed for those miners whose families live so far away that the commute would not make sense with shorter shifts. These fly in - fly out miners mostly live on camps or in miner hotels. These "new" camps have little in common with older versions based on utopian communities; they are just simple pavilions directly connected to the airport by private transportation hosting workers but without their families. Many of these employees only use Calama as an airport, spending their time in the area exclusively on the camp. In most of these camps, employees have everything they need until their shifts are over. Amenities include gymnasiums, alcohol-free bars, and playrooms. However, not everyone working in the mining industry has the same luck; there are many differences in the conditions under which people work in the area depending the position they have and the company for which they work.

Another way to host floating populations are miner hotels. These hotels offer companies the hosting of their employees and taking care of their well-being. The "Hotel Minero by Park,"[28] as one of the many examples, is located in the middle of the Calama Oasis. According to its website, it offers guests a playroom, a native garden with resting areas, a TV room, a small store, and a gym. Renting hotel rooms is a way of outsourcing lodging and having the least infrastructure, but still keeping the employees comfortable. With new camps and hotels, companies separate themselves from any social responsibility with the city and the employees' families.

Apart from camps and hotels, people from Calama themselves "invisibly" host workers in rooms especially built for rent. These rooms are mostly built on a second floor, on top of an existing home, many times with a private bathroom and its own independent entrance from the outside. Signs of rooms for rent are easily found in different shops around downtown. Apart from renting rooms, since mining is an activity that runs 24/7, in Calama, it is possible to rent a "warm bed" to sleep by the hour, enabling up to three people to use the same bed in one day.

At an urban level, the floating population brings a lack of investment in local housing as well as a lack of cultural demand. Most people, even those who are given whole houses to live in while in Calama, consider another city home. Calama for them is just the place where they sleep between working hours. Furthermore, floating population does not count in the national census. Since

---

28. "Hotel Minero by Park," Hotel Minero by Park, accessed December 27, 2015, http://www.hotelminerobypark.cl/.

the Chilean national budget is assigned according to population and people who work in Calama are counted in the census in other cities, Calama is missing the budget for around 30% of its population that does not appear on the official numbers, preventing the city from receiving the subsidies it deserves.

Apart from the influx of people, there is an influx of food and supplies. As an example of this, the Philadelphia-based company Aramark has become the main food and service provider in the Calama enclave, serving 25,000 daily meals to almost every mine in the area. It has business around the world, specializing in remote sites and resource extraction. The company claims to focus on clients' needs and on how to enable them to perform their business without worrying. Aramark considers itself the "nanny" of camps, taking care of everything from food to making beds and entertaining employees.[29]

The Aramark productive chain occupies the whole Chilean territory; products are bought from different areas of the country and gathered in Santiago from where trucks leave full of supplies to every remote location they serve. Although fresh food is served in every camp, in response to the mining companies demands, Aramark tries to do as little as possible on site and prepare everything in advance, either in Santiago or Calama. The company has 18,000 workers in Chile, with approximately 1,800 of those living and working in Calama.[30] The company does not use camps in the area but rents houses in the city for their employees to live. Aramark is just one of the many companies that use Calama as a center from where to distribute services to the different mines.

The Urban Extension of the Camp

Calama is used as a camp, hosting activities and logistics related to mining while dealing with its own externalities. Since the beginning of intensive mining in the area, every decision connected to the city and its environment was taken with strong consideration of the industry.

However, there is more to Calama than just mining. In the next chapter, Calama as a City, another face of the same area will be shown. The chapter focuses on the oasis working as a counterweight for the extractive activity, extending its timeframe, and the efforts made to create city-ness in this remote environment.

---

29. Interview with Sandra Miranda conducted by the author, Aramark, October 27, 2015.

30 Ibid.

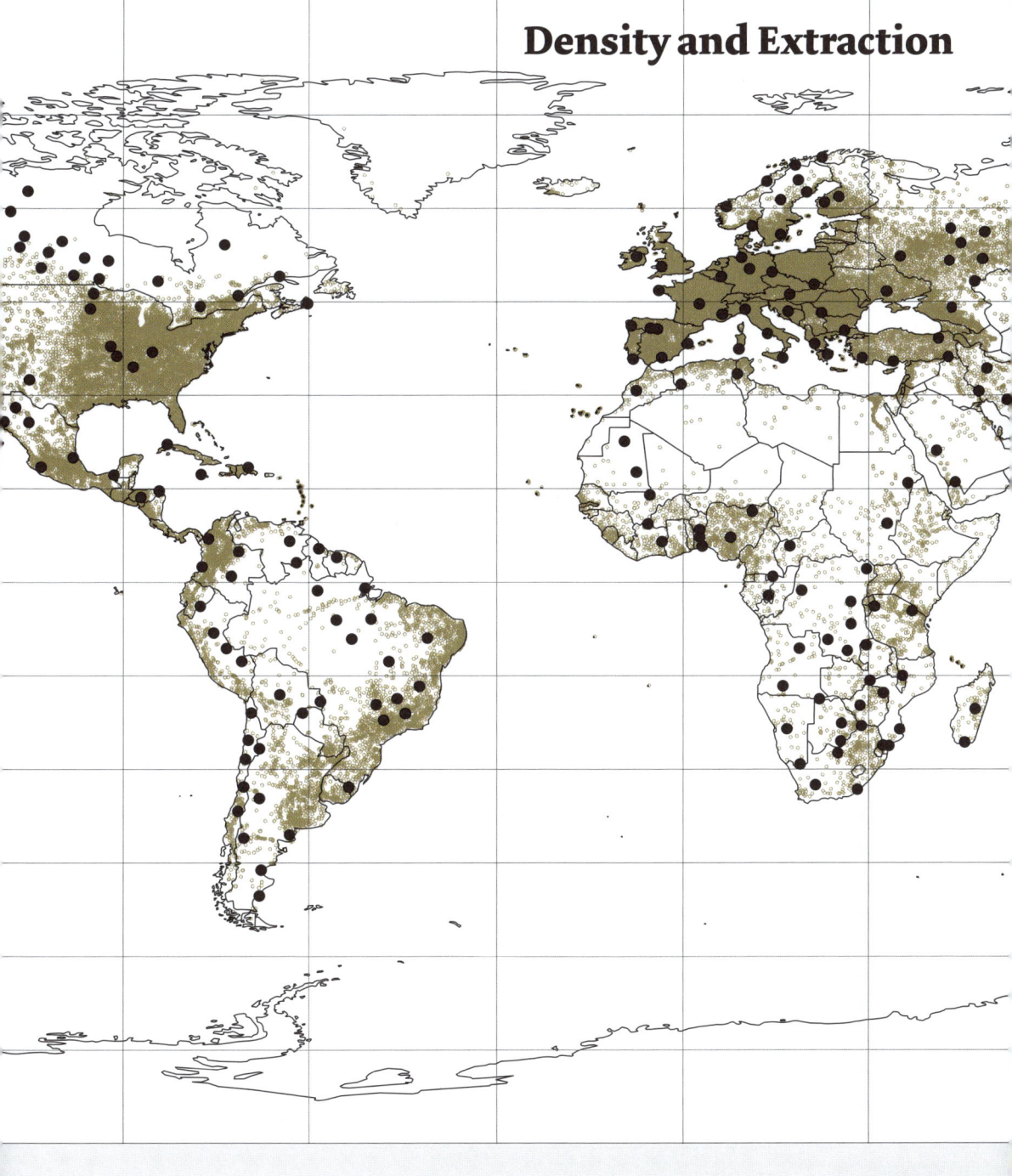

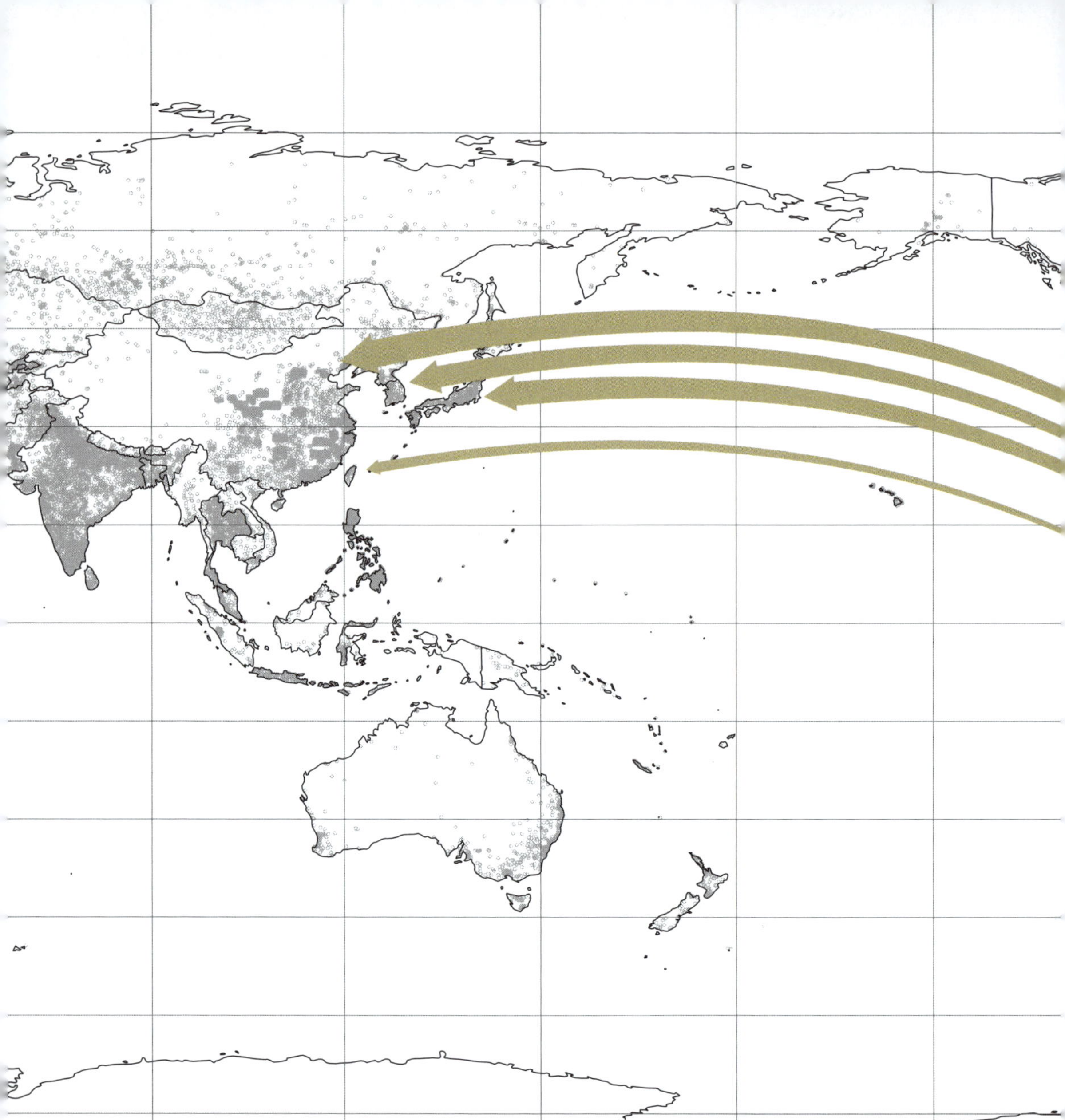

(Source Modulo "Precios del Cobre" del modelo macroeconometrico "The Economist," Thesis by Alejandro Cesar Landra Carranza)

World copper production

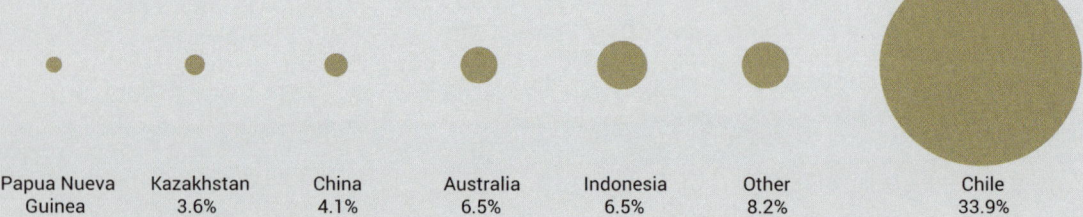

Papua Nueva Guinea	Kazakhstan	China	Australia	Indonesia	Other	Chile
1.6%	3.6%	4.1%	6.5%	6.5%	8.2%	33.9%

(Source: Modulo "Precios del Cobre" del modelo macroeconometrico "The Economist", Thesis by Alejandro Cesar Landra Carranza)

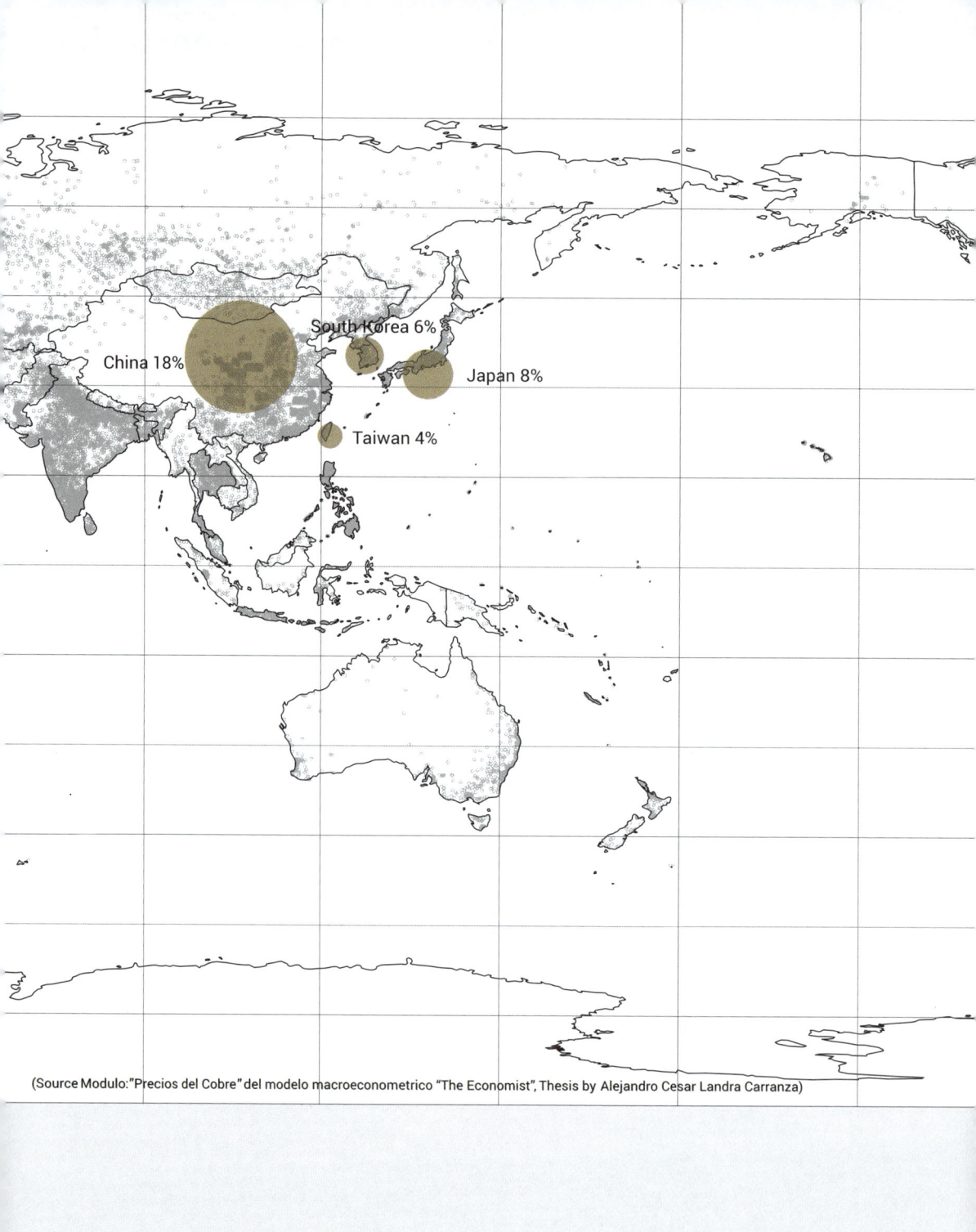

(Source Modulo:"Precios del Cobre" del modelo macroeconometrico "The Economist", Thesis by Alejandro Cesar Landra Carranza)

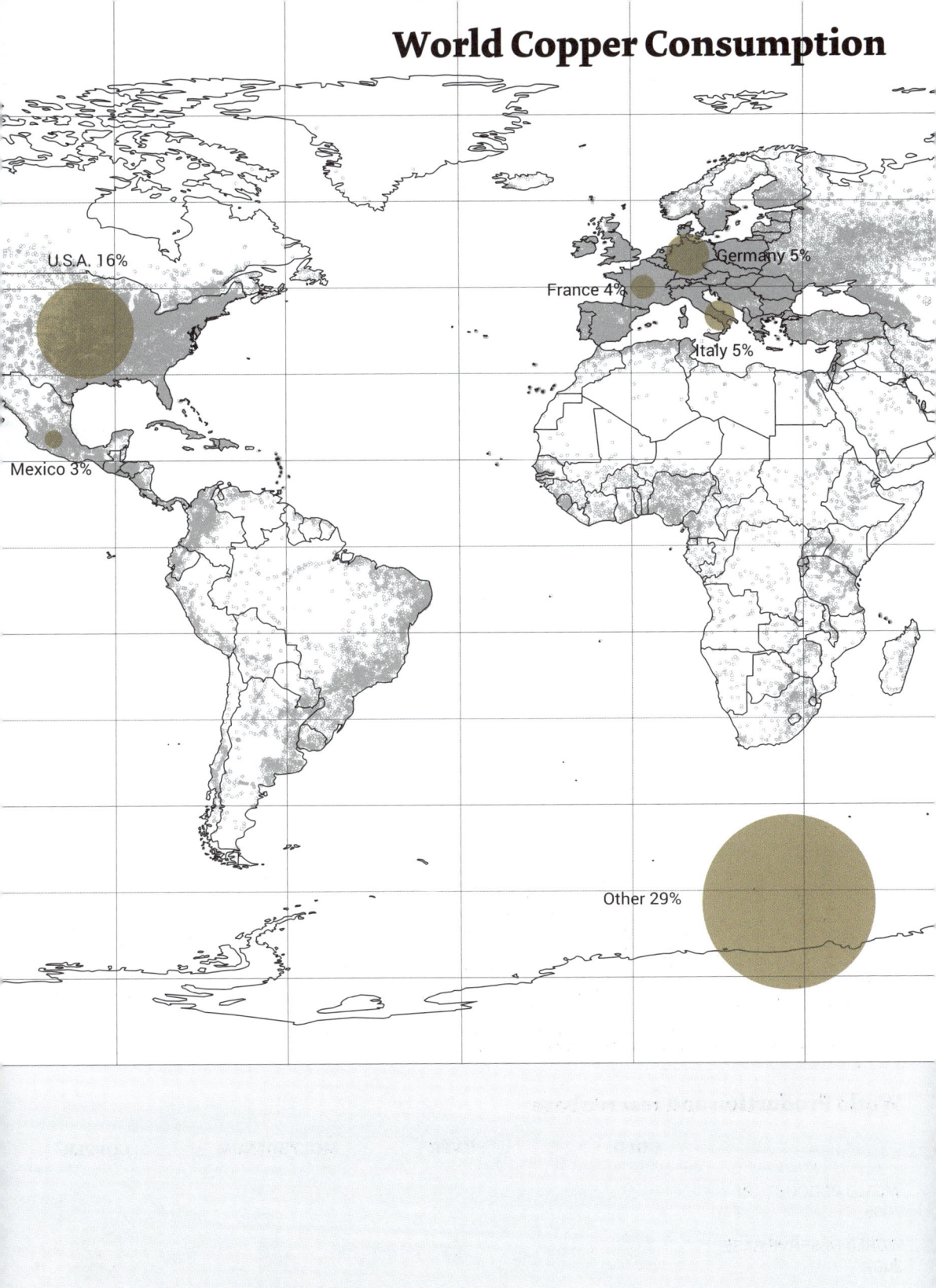

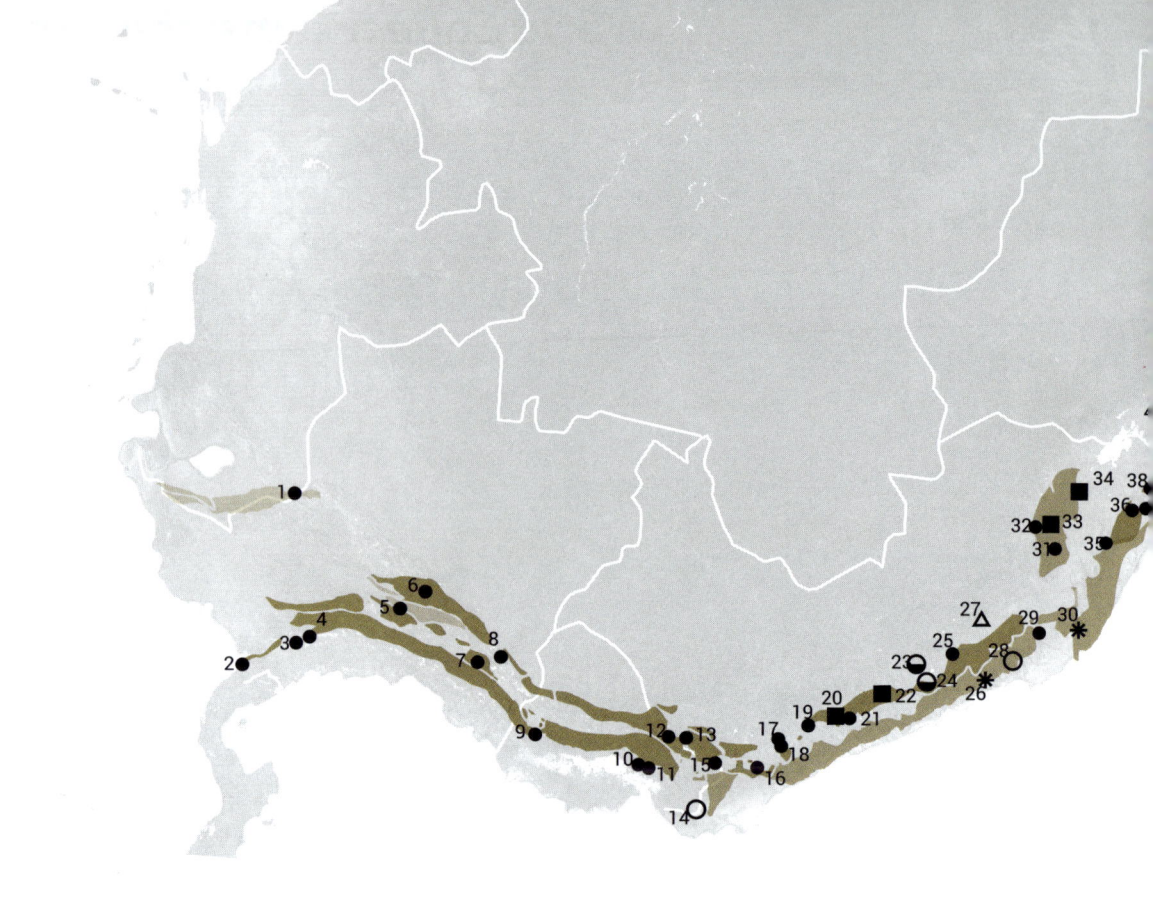

1. California
2. Acandi
3. Murindo
4. Pantanos-Pegadorcito
5. Infierno-Chili
6. Dolores
7. Piedrasent Ada
8. Mocoa
9. Junin
10. Chaucha
11. Gaby
12. San Carlos
13. Mirador
14. Tambogrande
15. Rio Blanco
16. La Granja
17. Minas Conga
18. Yanacocha
19. Michiquillay
20. Magistral
21. Pashpap
22. Antamina
23. Cerro de Pasco
24. Marcapunta
25. Toromocho
26. Raul-Condestable
27. Cobriza
28. Cerro Lindo
29. Puquio
30. Mina Justa
31. Los Chancas
32. Cotabambas
33. Las Bambas
34. Tintaya
35. Zafranal
36. Cerro Verde-Santa Rosa
37. Cachuyito
38. Cuajone
39. Toquepala
40. Corocoro

Map based on "Quantitative Mineral Resource Assessment of Copper, Molybdenum, Gold, and Silver in Undiscovered Porphyry Copper Deposits in the Andes Mountains of South America" USGS Open-File Report // Sillitoe and Perello 2005

World Production and reserve base

	GOLD	SILVER	MOLYBDENUM	COPPER
WORLD PRODUCTION 2006	≈3 TMT	≈20 TMT	≈0.2 TMT	≈20 TMT
WORLD RESERVE BASE 2007	≈90 TMT	≈560 TMT	≈19 TMT	≈940 TMT
UNDISCOVERED ANDES	≈12 TMT	≈250 TMT	≈20 TMT	≈750 TMT

(Source: Quantitative Mineral Resource Assessment of Copper, Molybdenum, Gold, and Silver in Undiscovered Porphyry Copper Deposits in the Andes Mountains of South America: USGS Open-File Report 2008

Andean Copper Deposit

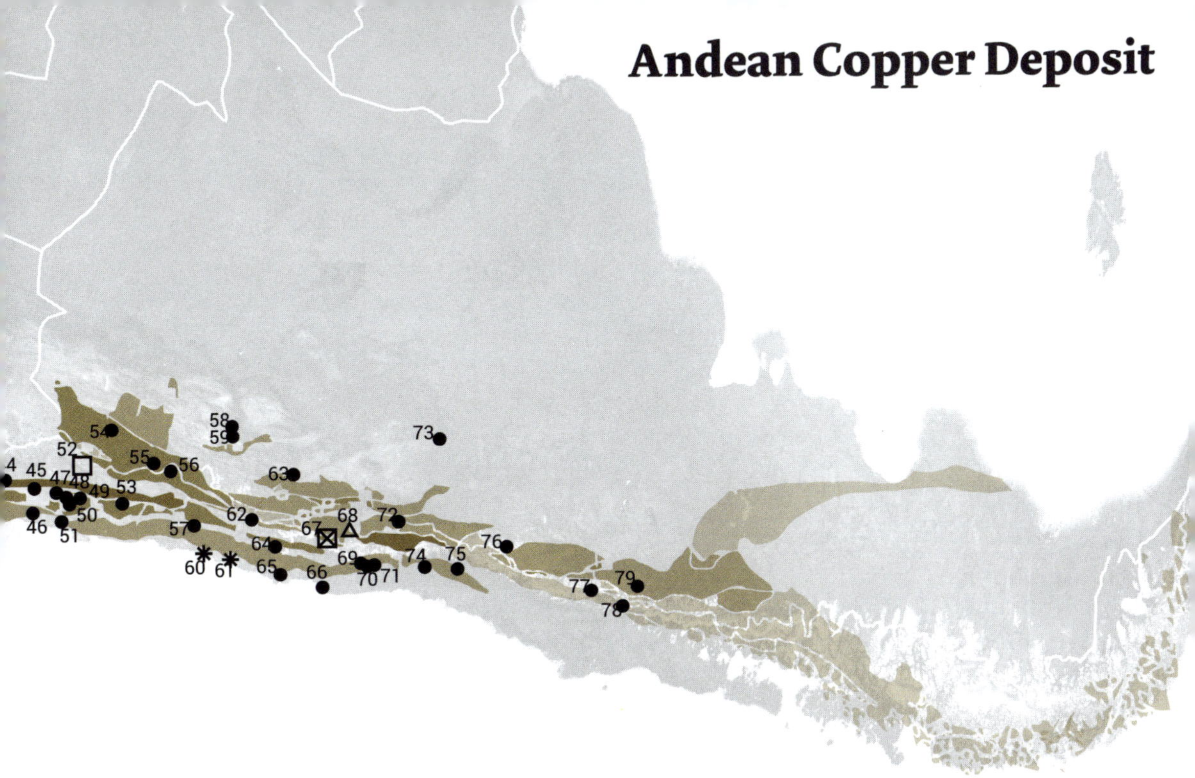

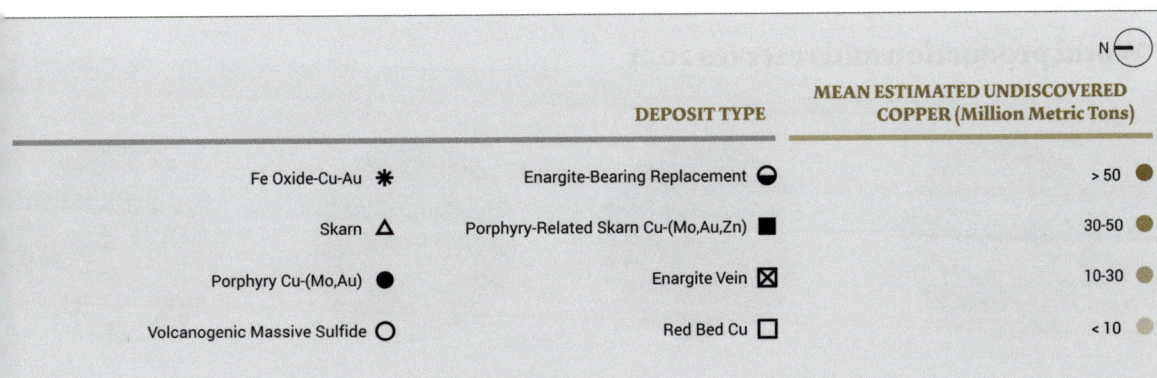

41. Laurani
42. La Mancha
43. Cerro Colorado
44. Collahuasi District
45. El Abra
46. Puntillas-Galenosa
47. Chiuquicamata
48. Toki
49. Esperanza
50. Spence
51. Buey Muerto-Antucoya
52. San Bartolo
53. Escondida
54. Pancho Arias
55. Taca Taca Bajo
56. Cerro Samenta
57. El Salvador
58. Bajo de la Alumbrera
59. Agua Rica
60. Mantoverde
61. Candelaria
62. Cerro Casale
63. Fatima
64. La Fortuna
65. Domeyko
66. Andacollo
67. El Indio
68. San Francisco de los Andes
69. Los Bagres Sur
70. El Altar
71. Los Pelambres-El Panchon
72. San Jorge
73. Diente Verde
74. Rio Blancos-Los Bronces
75. El Teniente
76. San Pedro
77. Campana Mahuida
78. Galletue
79. La Voluntad

N

DEPOSIT TYPE

- Fe Oxide-Cu-Au ✱
- Skarn △
- Porphyry Cu-(Mo,Au) ●
- Volcanogenic Massive Sulfide ○
- Enargite-Bearing Replacement ◒
- Porphyry-Related Skarn Cu-(Mo,Au,Zn) ■
- Enargite Vein ☒
- Red Bed Cu □

MEAN ESTIMATED UNDISCOVERED COPPER (Million Metric Tons)

- > 50
- 30-50
- 10-30
- < 10

Production and Price of Copper 2003 - 2015

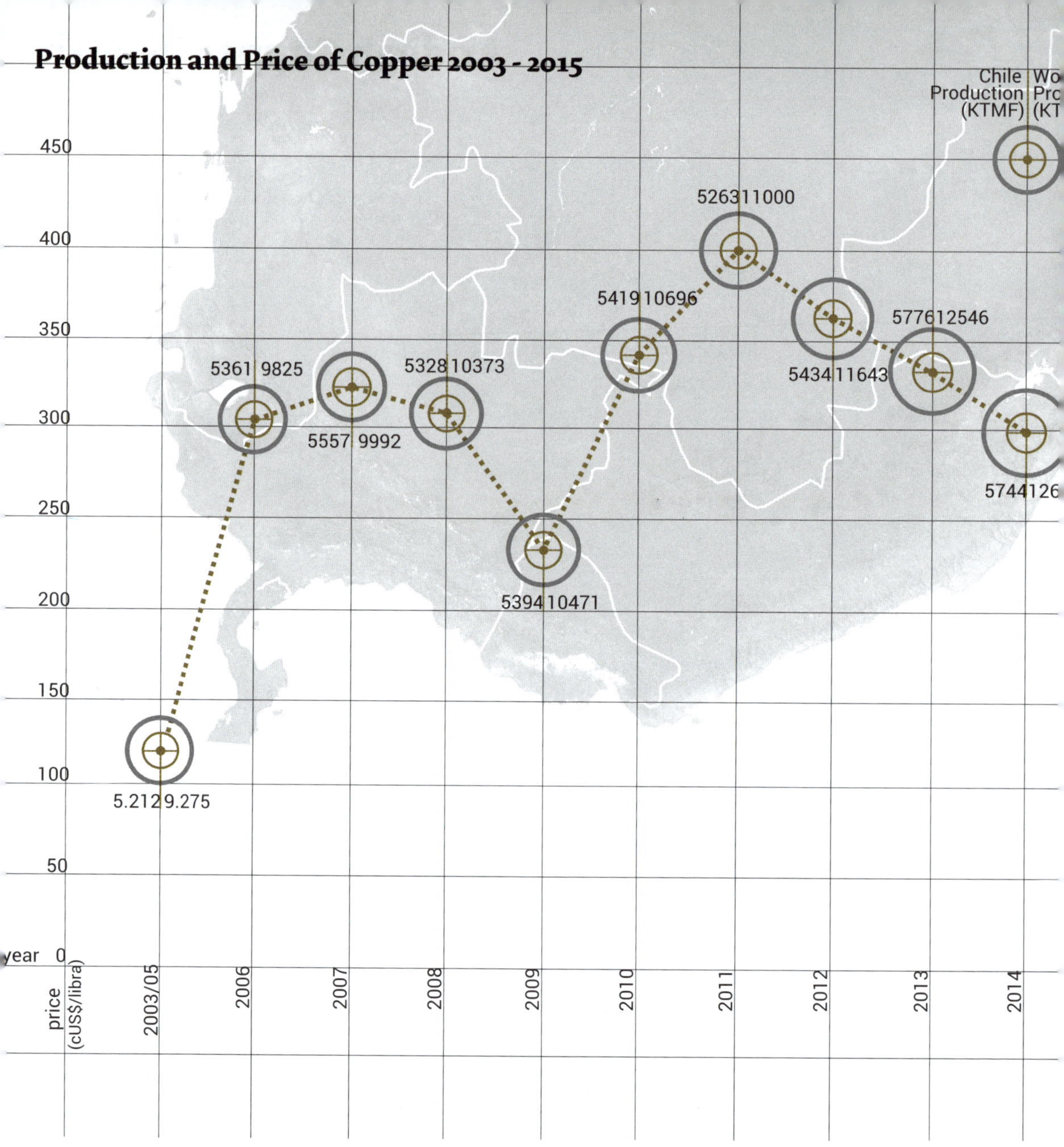

- 450
- 400 — 526311000
- 350 — 541910696 — 577612546
- 5361 9825 — 5328 10373 — 5434 11643
- 300 — 5557 9992
- 250 — 5744126
- 200 — 5394 10471
- 150
- 100 — 5.212 9.275
- 50

year / price (cUS$/libra): 2003/05, 2006, 2007, 2008, 2009, 2010, 2011, 2012, 2013, 2014

Chile Production (KTMF) | World Production (KT)

(source "Mineria en Cifras", Consejo Minero)

World production and reserves 2014

GOLD — WORLD Production Chile 2% | WORLD Reserve Chile 7%

SILVER — WORLD Production Chile 5% | WORLD Reserve Chile

(source "Mineria en cifras", Consejo Minero)

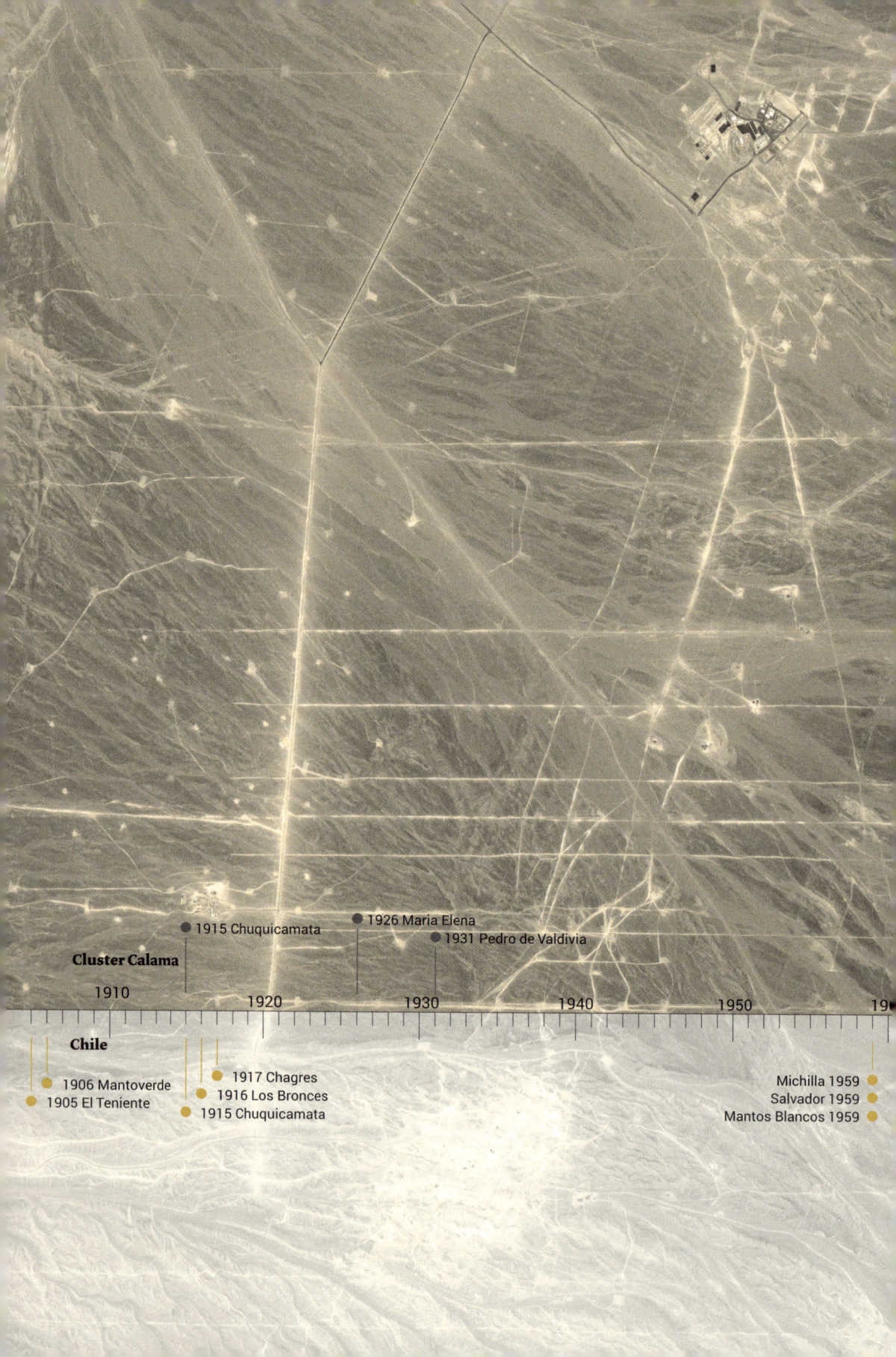

● 1926 Maria Elena
● 1915 Chuquicamata
                  ● 1931 Pedro de Valdivia

Cluster Calama

1910   1920   1930   1940   1950   19

Chile

        ● 1917 Chagres   Michilla 1959 ●
● 1906 Mantoverde   ● 1916 Los Bronces   Salvador 1959 ●
● 1905 El Teniente   ● 1915 Chuquicamata   Mantos Blancos 1959 ●

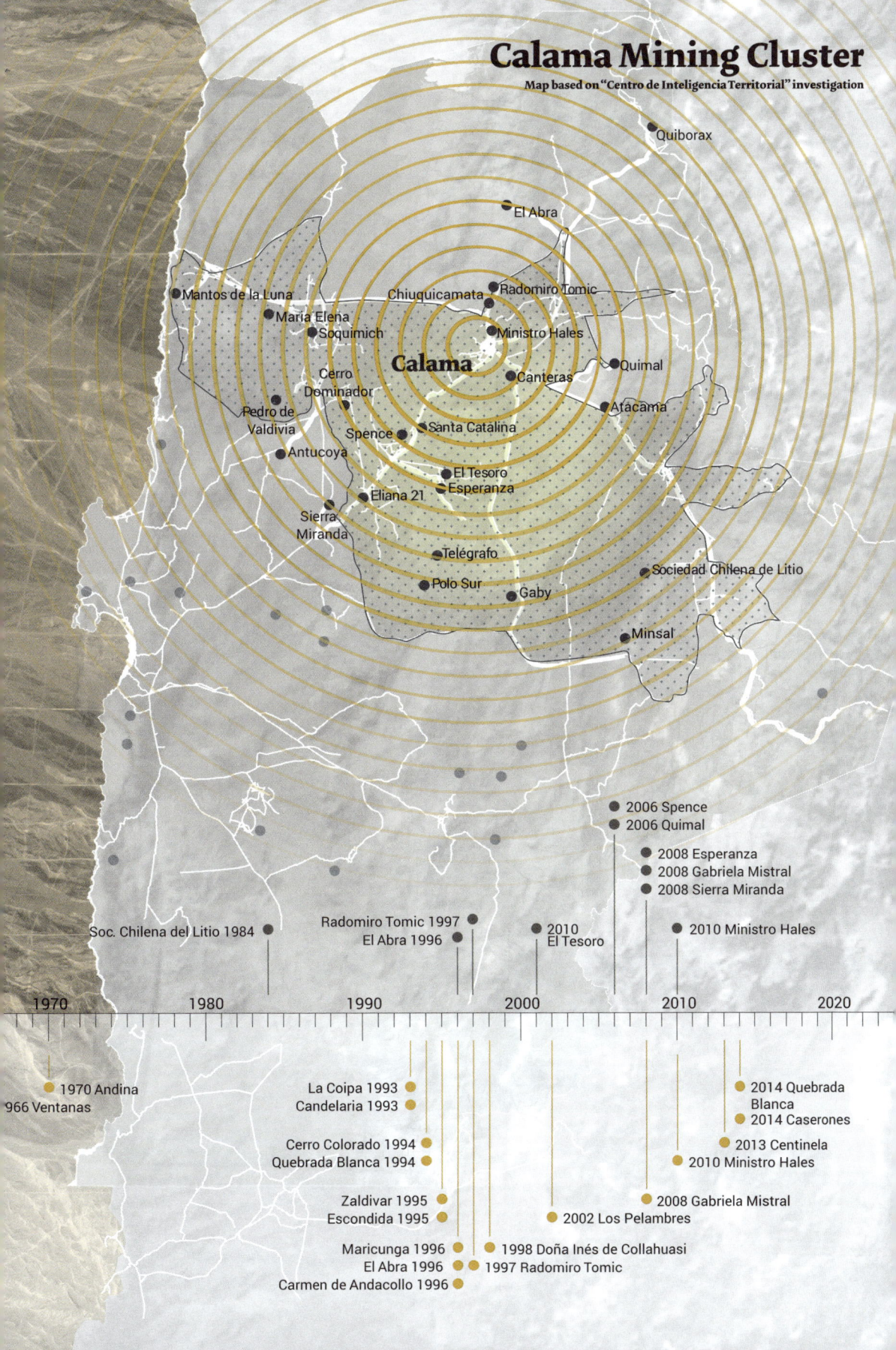

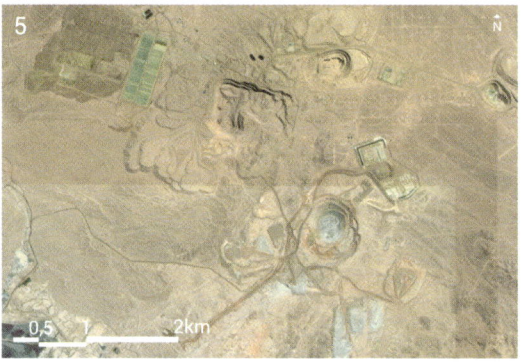
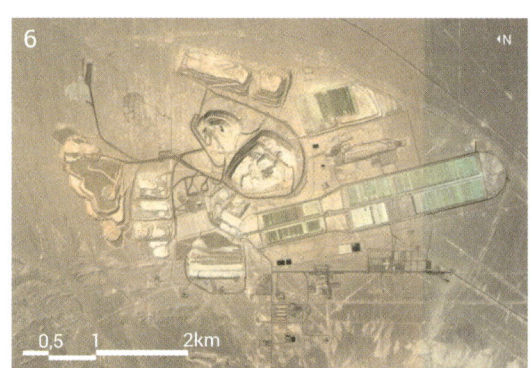
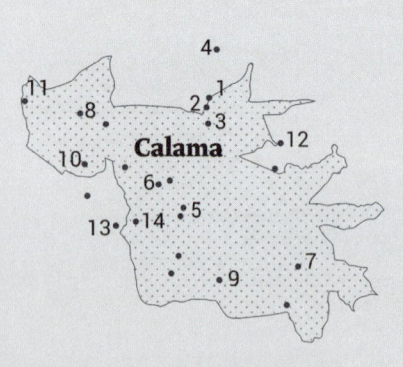

26 MINES in the Calama Cluster
21 COPPER Mines
3 NITRATE Processing Plants
1 QUARTZ Mine
1 LITHIUM Processing Plant

Major Mines from Calama Cluster

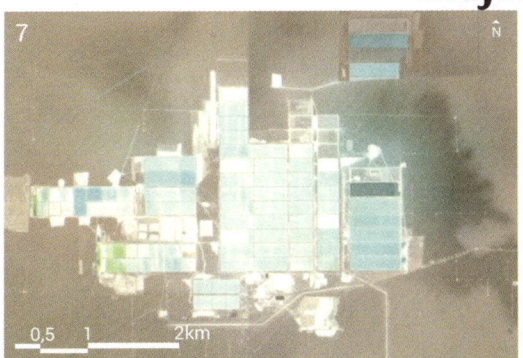

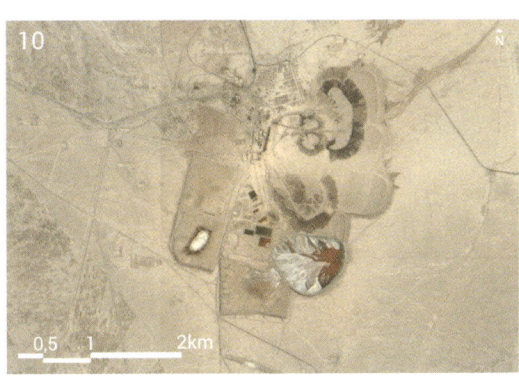

1. Radomiro Tomich - COPPER
2. Chuquicamata - COPPER
3. Ministro Hales - COPPER
4. El Abra - COPPER
5. El Tesoro - COPPER
6. Spence - COPPER
7. Sociedad Chilena del Litio - LITHIUM CARBONATE
8. Maria Elena - NITRATES
9. Gaby - COPPER
10. Pedro de Valdivia - NITRATES
11. Mantos de la Luna - COPPER
12. Quimal - COPPER SULPHATE
13. Sierra Miranda - COPPER
14. Eliana 21 - QUARTZ

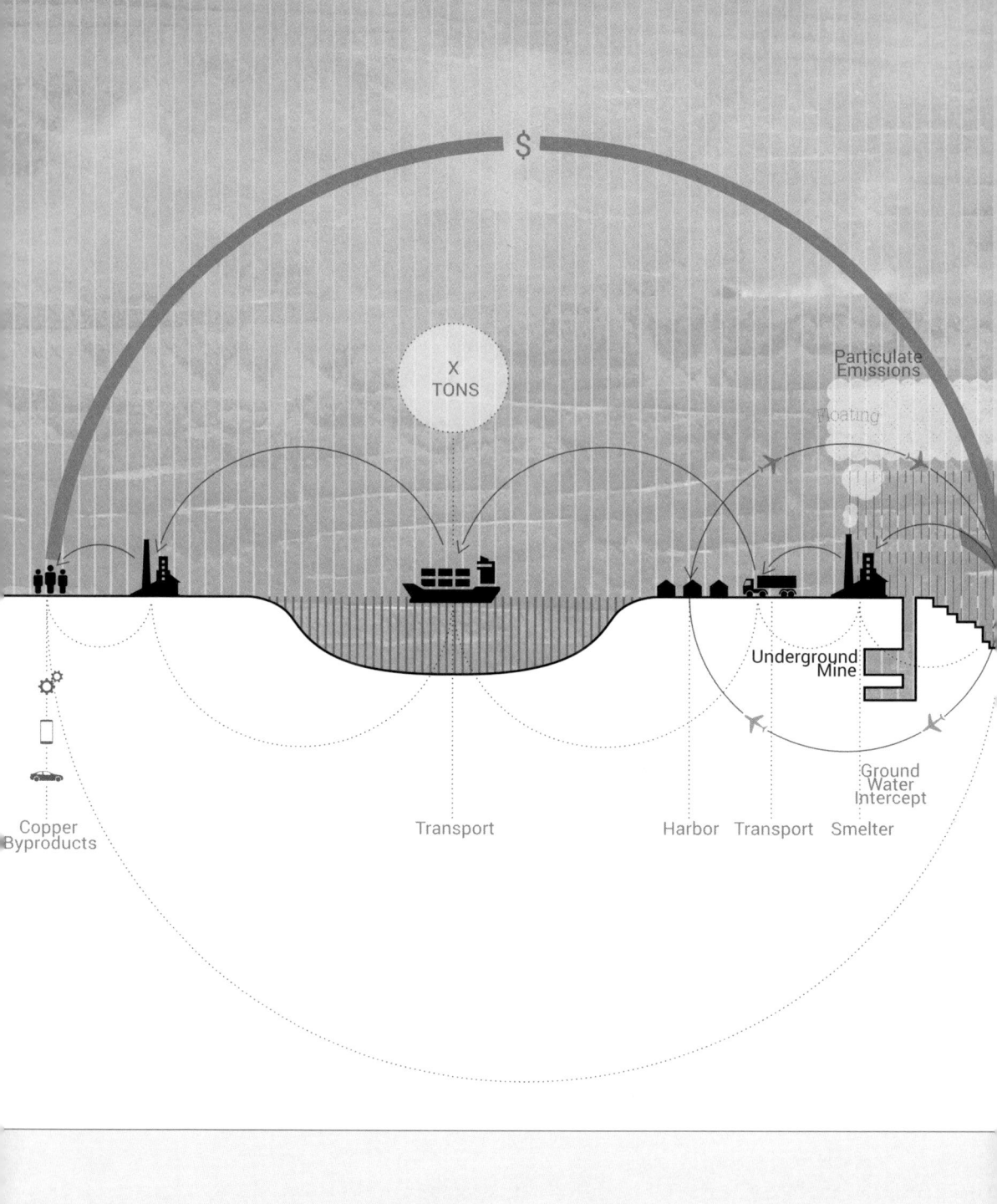

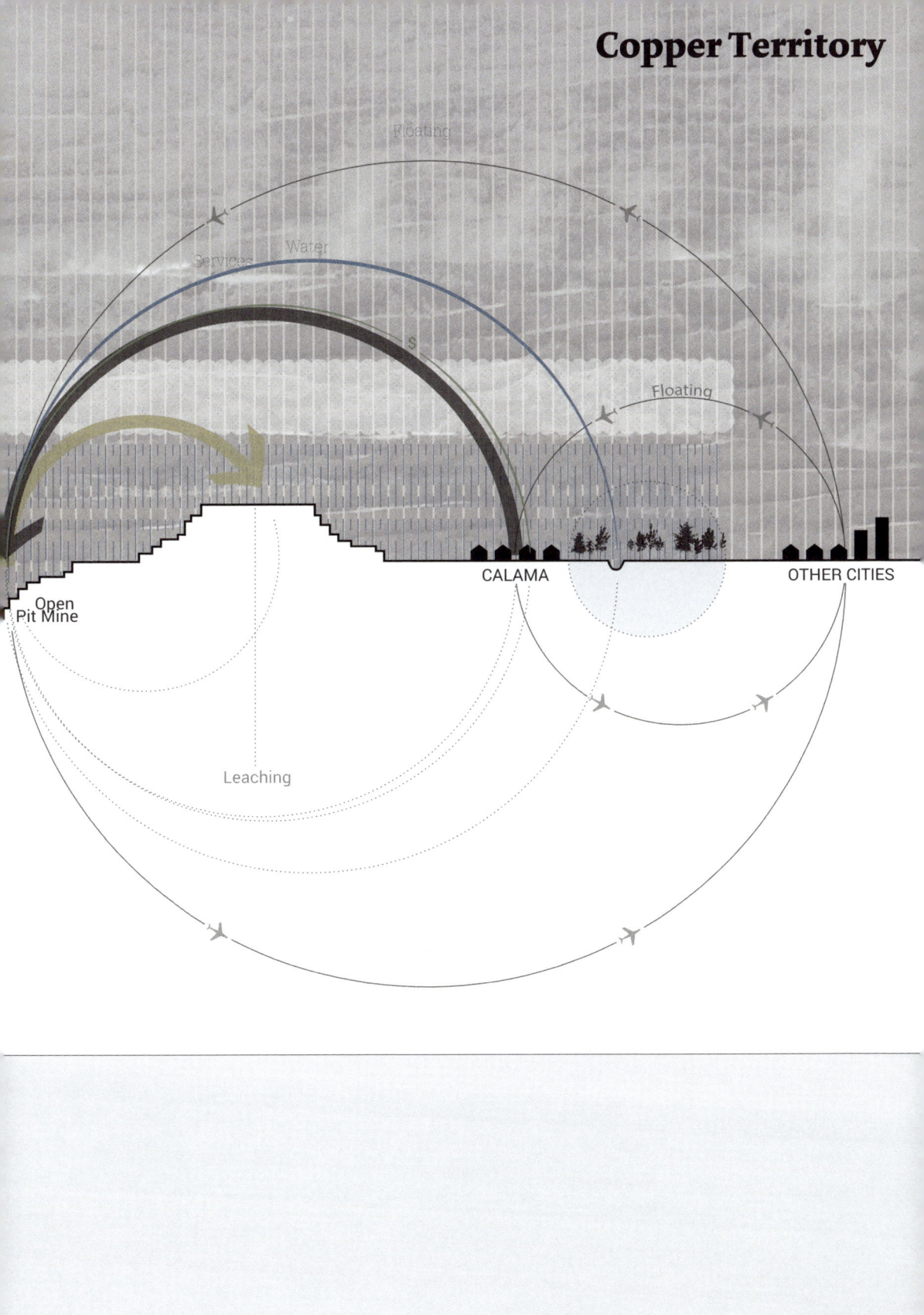

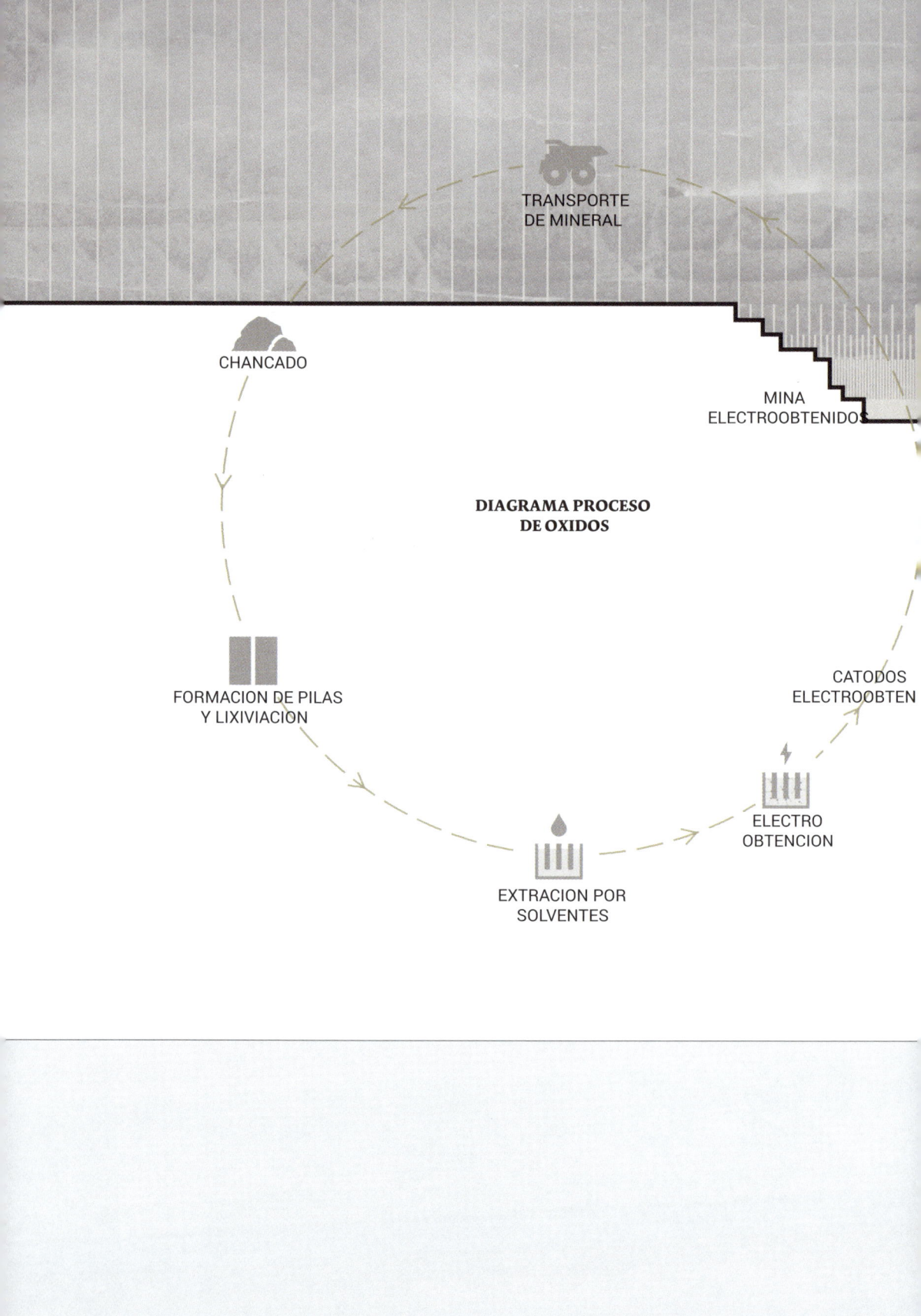

Copper Production

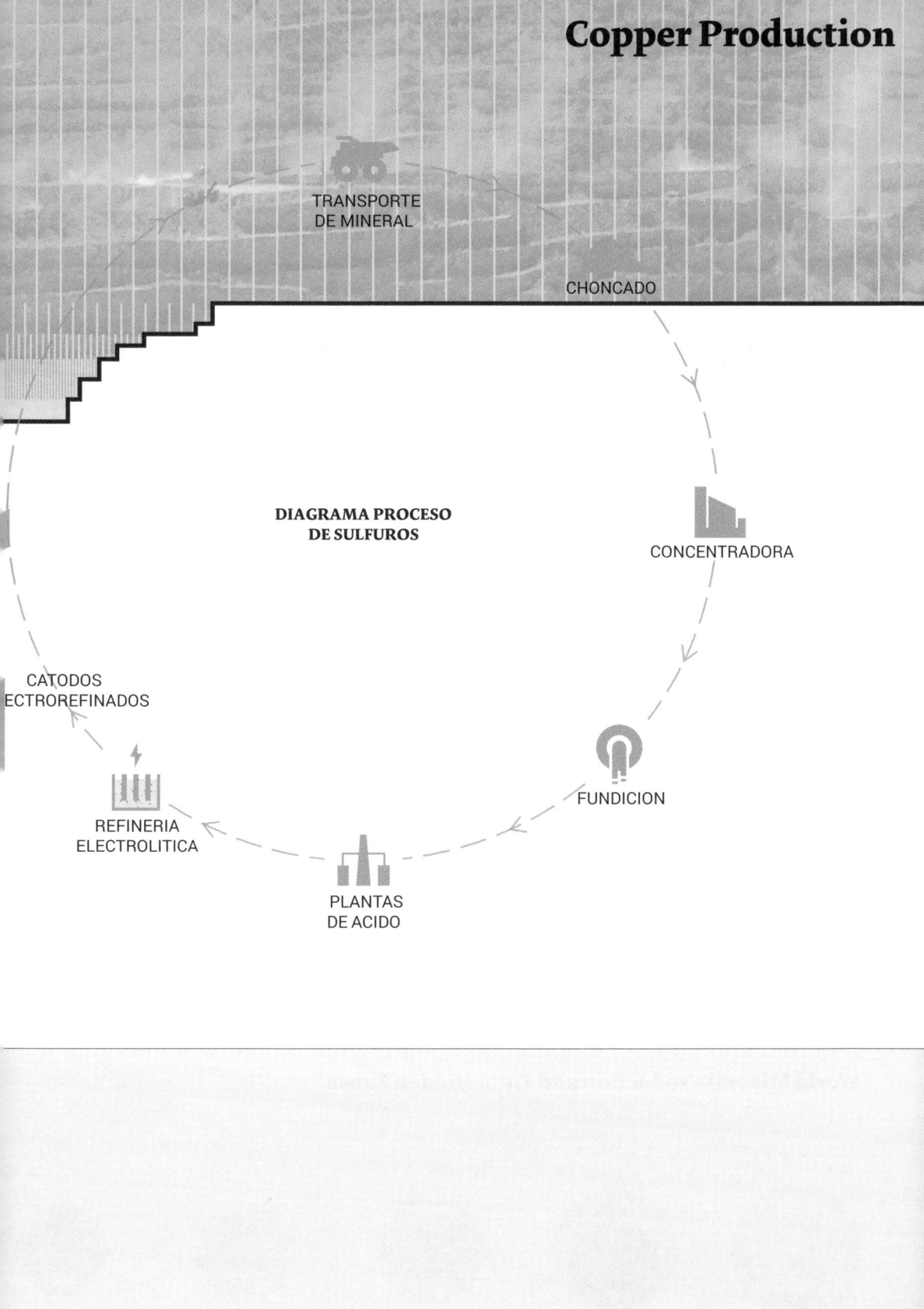

Environmental Impacts of Copper Production

(Source U.S. Congress, Office of Technology Assessment,
Copper, technology & competitiveness, Environmental Aspects of Copper Production_Office of technology Assessment)

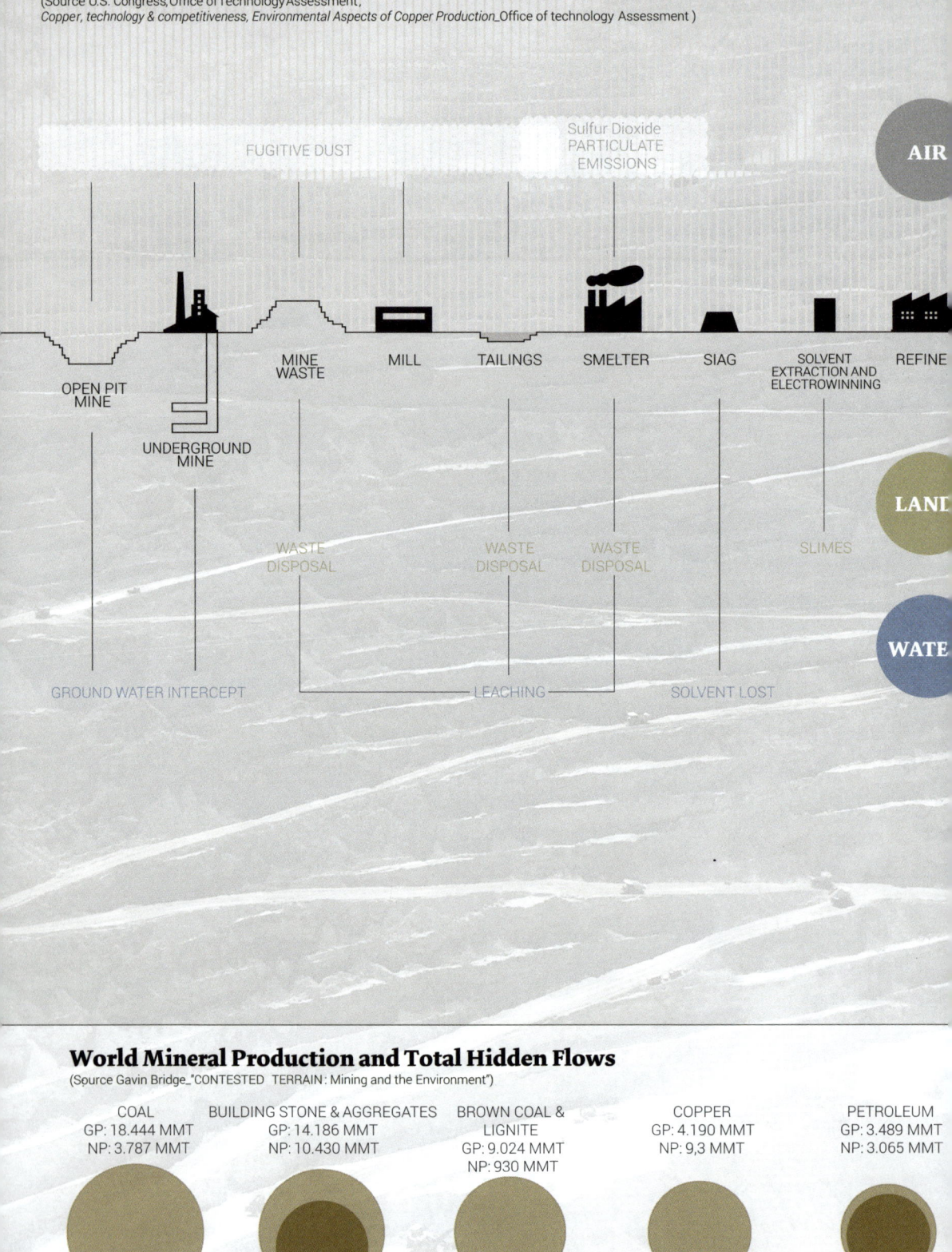

World Mineral Production and Total Hidden Flows
(Source Gavin Bridge_"CONTESTED TERRAIN: Mining and the Environment")

COAL	BUILDING STONE & AGGREGATES	BROWN COAL & LIGNITE	COPPER	PETROLEUM
GP: 18.444 MMT	GP: 14.186 MMT	GP: 9.024 MMT	GP: 4.190 MMT	GP: 3.489 MMT
NP: 3.787 MMT	NP: 10.430 MMT	NP: 930 MMT	NP: 9,3 MMT	NP: 3.065 MMT

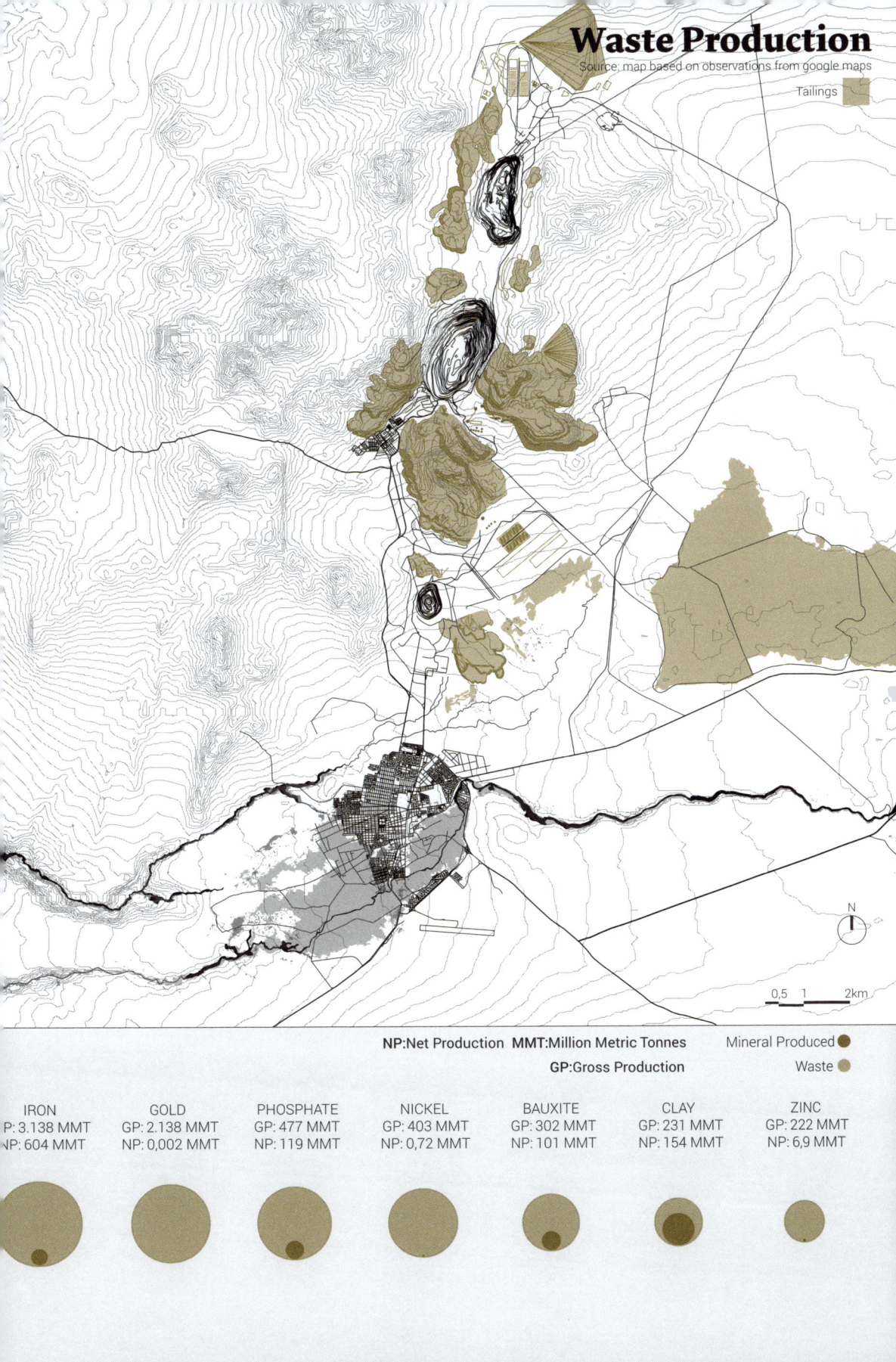

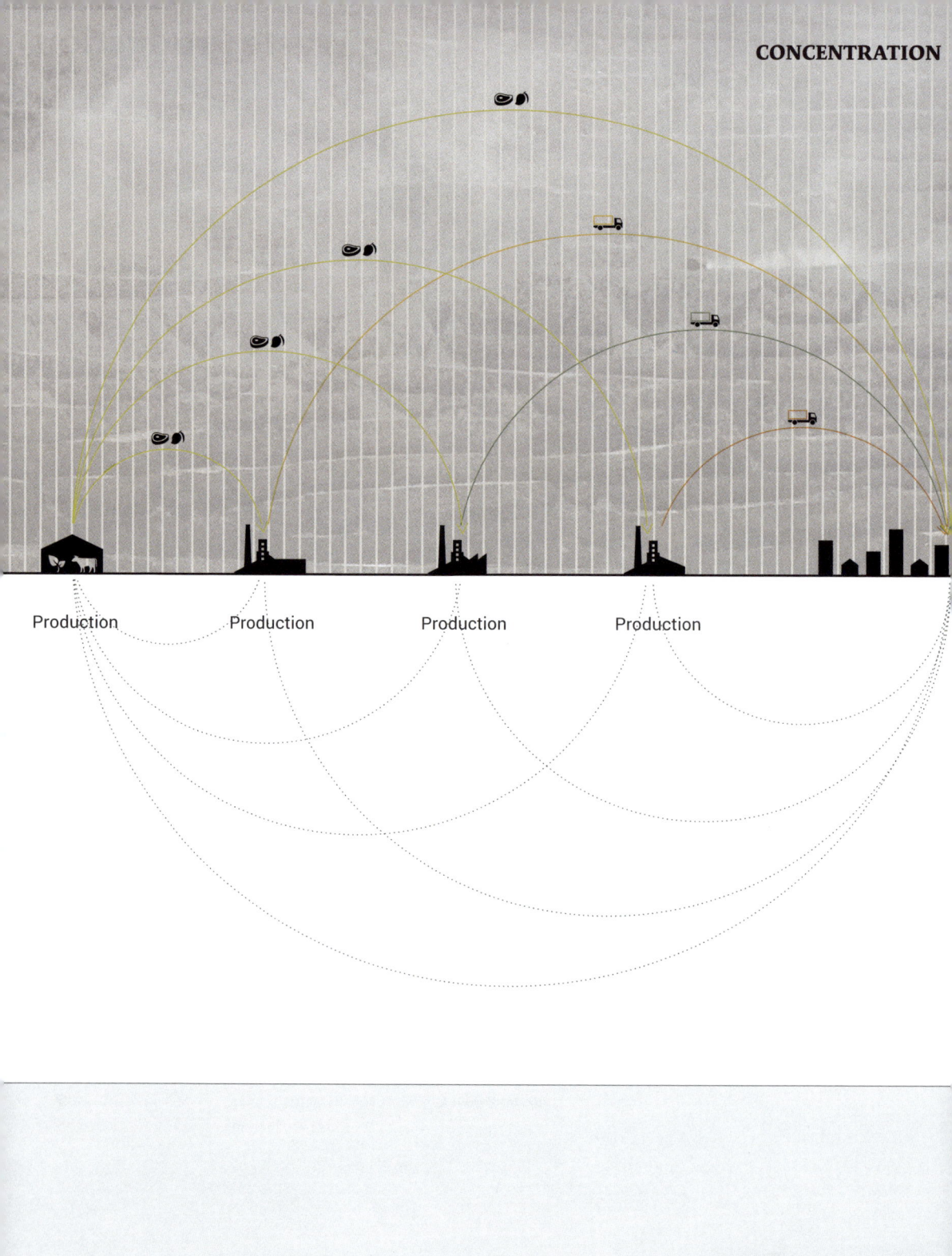

REDISTRIBUTION
Food and Supplies

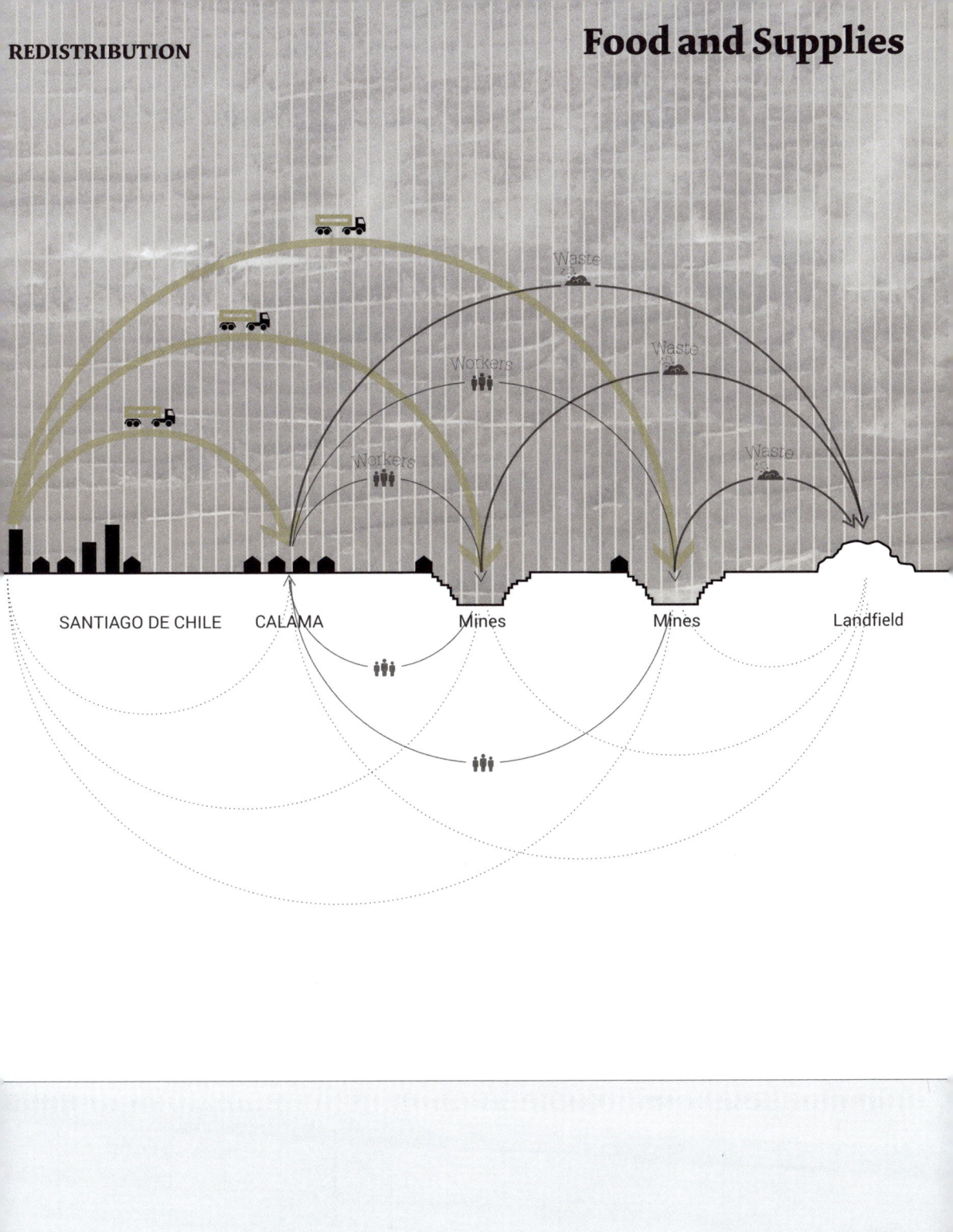

Daily Flights to and from Calama

Based on flights for Tuesday 1st of September, 2015

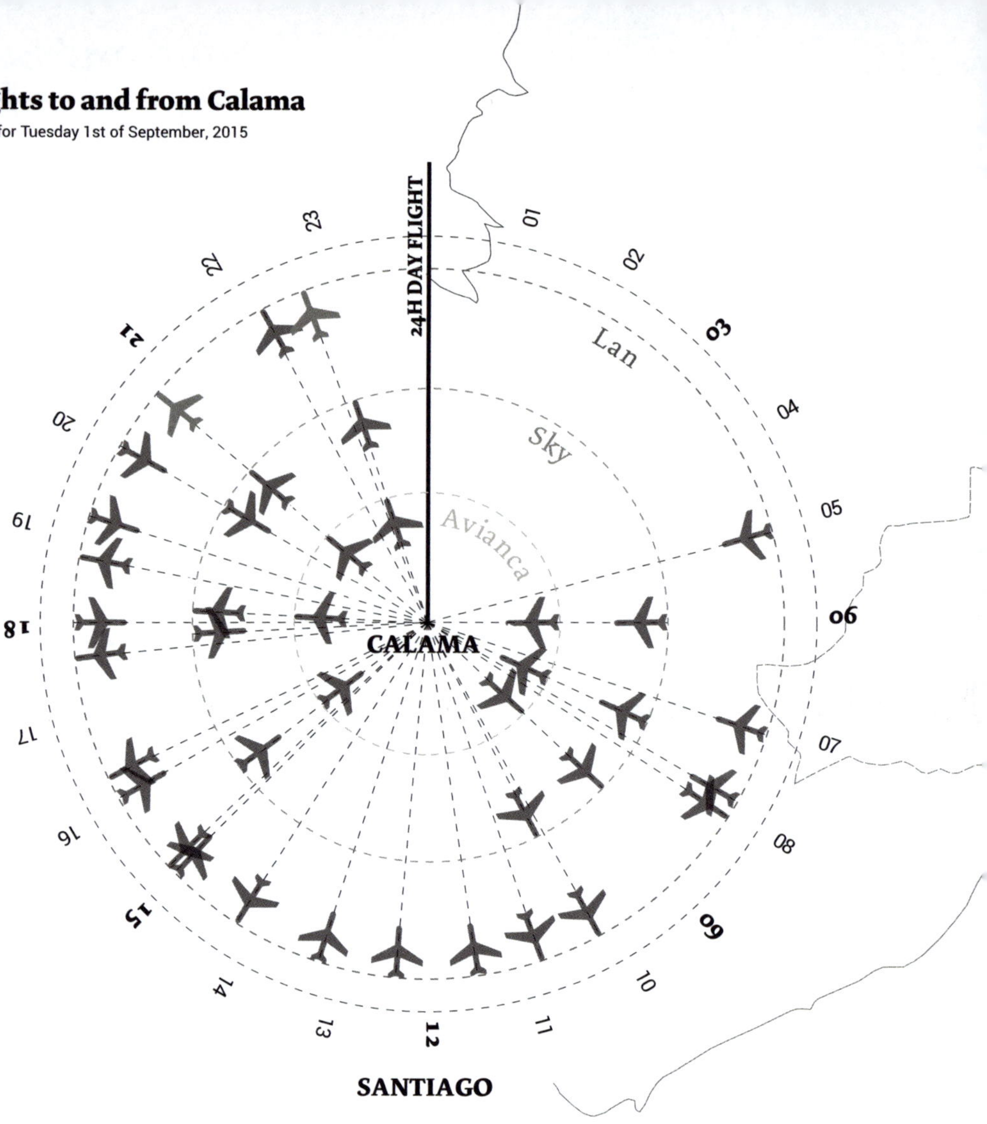

24H DAY FLIGHT
01
02
03
04
05
06
07
08
09
10
11
12
13
14
15
16
17
18
19
20
21
22
23
Lan
Sky
Avianca
CALAMA
SANTIAGO

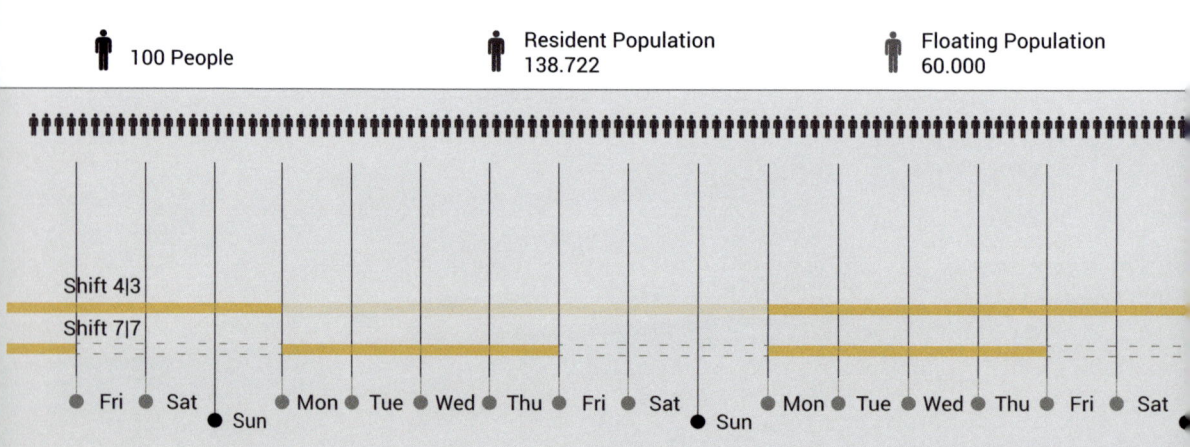

100 People
Resident Population
138.722
Floating Population
60.000
Shift 4|3
Shift 7|7
Fri
Sat
Sun
Mon
Tue
Wed
Thu
Fri
Sat
Sun
Mon
Tue
Wed
Thu
Fri
Sat

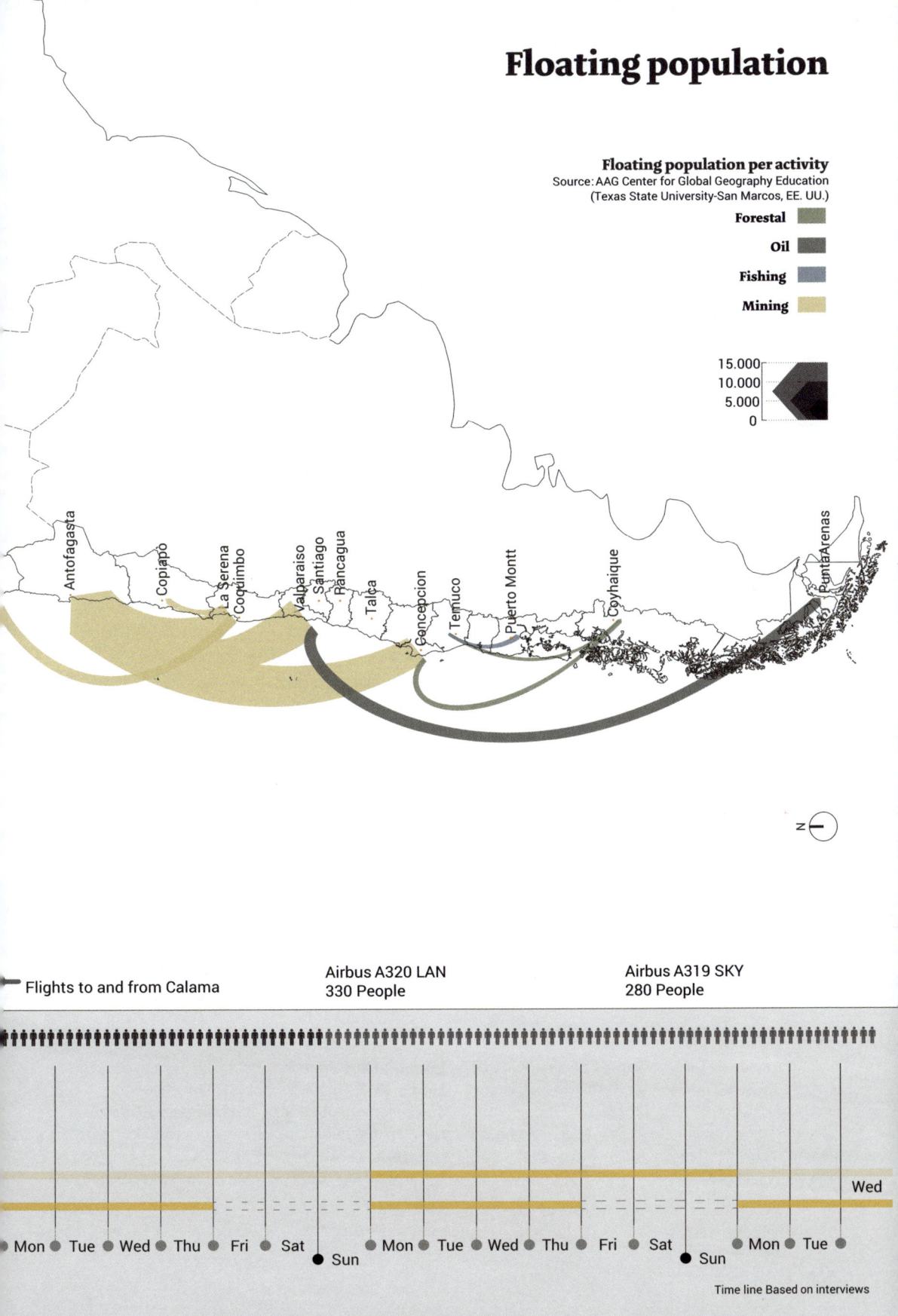

CALAMA AS A CITY
Agustina González Cid

It all started with an oasis: a green area in one of the driest deserts of the world where locals lived and travelers stopped to rest; and, although today people from Calama proudly recognize the city as an oasis and as the mining capital of Chile,[1] while mining continues to grow around and under the city, the oasis is facing disappearance. This natural "refuge" is, in a certain way, both the reason why settlements appeared in the area before mining and the hope for the city after the extractive activity ends. On the borders of the Loa River, the green area extends the temporality of Calama beyond the presence of minerals, requiring from every actor involved a higher level of commitment and a long-term sustainability plan for the city. This chapter focuses on the extended temporality of the city of Calama beyond the time frame of mining due to the presence of the oasis. While the extraction of non-renewable materials necessarily implies an expiration date for the mine and the entire infrastructure that supports it, a well-kept oasis can last forever, contributing to the sustainable future of the city. The historical graphic visualizations presented in this chapter show the different moments of the oasis and the city, from an estimated first stage, prior to the beginning of intensive mining, to its current situation. Maps set their emphasis on the oasis, its water, and its flora and fauna to understand the complexity the presence of this rich ecosystem adds to Calama's city and its territory of extraction. The oasis owes its relevance to its surrounding environment. Located 3,000 meters above sea level, with the highest UV radiation on Earth, Calama has a great daily temperature variance, with the average low of 2ºC and a an average high of 22.9°C. It gets only 35mm of rainfall per year, and people from the city acknowledge the lack of sufficient water as one of Calama's main problems.[2]

The oasis has an important concentration of biodiversity composed of birds, mammals, reptiles, and plants, creating a unique biological corridor. Apart from the natural habitat, 400 hectares of the oasis are used for agriculture, mostly producing corn and alfalfa. The oasis also serves as a humidifier for the city and it is responsible for making the place easier to live in. However, in spite of its importance, the area is being deserted and, if nothing changes soon, the oasis will disappear. The Atacama region, in the North of Chile, has been desert for almost 40 million years,[3] and the oasis has always been part of the lives of the people of Calama and the surrounding areas. The first archeological remains found in the area date from around 10,000 BC.[4] The oasis was funda-

---

1. Corporación de Desarrollo de la Provincia de El Loa, PROLOA, Costumbres y Tradiciones Agrícolas del Oasis de Calama, 1st ed...(Calama, Chile: Asociación de Agricultores Calama, 2014).
2. People of Calama, Interviews with people of Calama for the class Territorial Intelligence, Spring 2015, Harvard Graduate School of Design, written questionnaire, n.d.
3. Corporación de Desarrollo de la Provincia de El Loa, PROLOA, Costumbres y Tradiciones Agrícolas del Oasis de Calama, 1st ed...(Calama, Chile: Asociación

mental as resting area for those making the pilgrimage between inland and the coast. In fact, the Inca Trail, a path connecting the main cities during the Inca Empire, passed by the Calama oasis. The different origins of some of the found objects prove the presence of nomadic groups that used the area as a stopover during their trips.[5]

Since pre-Hispanic times, the oasis was used for agriculture,[6] an activity that still continues today, albeit on a smaller scale. The first settlements started appearing on the eastern coast of the Loa River (now called El Peuco, Chorrillos, and Topater[7]). After this period, a long process of occupation and consumption of the oasis began. In 1825, Bolivia declared its independence, including the province of Atacama within its boundaries. During this time, Calama was a key stop in the path between Cobija, located in the northern area of Bolivia, and Potosi, located in the south of the Bolivian territory. However, the place was still not intensely mined for copper.[8] After the Pacific War in 1883, the area became Chilean territory, marking the beginning of a new period based on copper extraction. The wild oasis was transformed into productive land to feed the increasing number of miners. At the same time, native trees were cut down for their caloric energy for melting, putting some species at risk of disappearance. From this very beginning, mining was eating the oasis, while competing against Calameñans for its valuable resources.

Balancing the Camp

Temporality is embedded in the very nature of resource extraction. Since it implies the depletion of materials and consumption of areas of the planet, territories are transformed into extractive machines for certain periods of time and then left behind, creating ghost towns abandoned in the middle of deserted areas. In this context, the Calama oasis acts as a counterweight for mining, maintaining Calama as a city and separating it from the exclusive idea of a camp. The oasis stretches the time frame of Calama beyond mines and camps, strengthening the city as such. In addition to this temporal autonomy of the city, in a large sense, because of the oasis, not everyone in Calama works for the mine.

The oasis complements Calama's arid surrounding landscape with an ecosystem that enriches the economic, social, and ecological life of the city, shaping its strong identity. Apart from native species, even before mining, there was agriculture in the area, and the descendants of those groups still work in the Calama oasis, adding variety to this "one company town." Although beneficial in other aspects of life, the mixture of different actors depending on one single territory creates fierce competition for the already shattered oasis and its resources. Neither the mining industry nor the city respects the oasis, continuously growing over and under it and reducing its size. The decline of

---

de Agricultores Calama, 2014).

4. Ibid.
5. Ibid.

6. Ibid.
7. Ibid.

8. Ibid.

the vulnerable green landscape threatens its native flora and fauna as well as the incomes and lives based on agriculture.

Apart from the growth of mining and buildings in its proximity, the oasis is also threatened by the increasing drought. Water is scarce in Calama, limiting development in the area. The oasis, which has enabled life in the area for thousands of years, is one of the several oases present along the Loa, a 440-kilometer-long river that ttraverses the Atacama Desert, providing the cities of Calama, Tocopilla, Mejillones, and Antofagasta with water. Water is used for human consumption, agriculture, and mining, which use 35% of its total flow.[9] Although the use of water for copper production has been reduced from 1.09 m3/ton in 1988 to 0.47 m3/ton today,[10] it is still problematic considering the desert conditions in the Calama territory. Even if the oasis is one ecosystem, it works as two different entities treated in different ways. Today, the territorial division results in half of the oasis being considered urban and the other half rural. Because of this, there is no organization or public office clearly in charge of policing the oasis as a whole, controlling both the natural and the built infrastructures. On top of this, very few people care about the natural oasis enough to work towards its survival. In the city of Calama it is hard to find records of the natural flora and fauna of the place.

As seen in the previous chapter "Calama as a Camp," when people from Chuquicamata were moved to Calama, most of the new construction took place in the oasis, an already vulnerable territory, not protecting the natural heritage and transforming it in part of the city. Now, the oasis is mostly occupied by condominiums and warehouses owned by outsourcing companies. Apart from this, there are also some illegal occupations in the oasis related to agriculture. The oasis as a pristine natural mirage does not exist anymore and was transformed into a suburban sector of the city of Calama. The oasis is now mainly composed of private land not accessible to the public. The historical sites have been left to decay, and only some people from the indigenous group care about them. Sadly, the oasis has become the backyard of mining instead of the heart of the city.

Creating City-ness

Although some mining companies think of themselves as totally independent from the city, they all use Calama's infrastructure, services, and oasis in some way or another, mostly as a logistical base, hosting workers and distributing services. These private companies consider their presence in the city of Calama and its surrounding oasis as temporary underestimating the impact they have on the territory. On top of this, these companies are not regarded as responsible for their impact and negative externalities, left alone as free-riders, doing business and benefiting without caring about its present and future. As a consequence of this, the city faces social conflict, high prices, income and rights inequality between different social

---

9. Maria Josefina Valdes Cobo, "Parque de Recuperación y Tratamiento de las Aguas en el Oasis de Calama" (Master's Thesis, Pontificia Universidad Católica de Chile, 2007).

10. Codelco, "Codelco, Orgullo de Todos" Codelco, n.d., accessed December 11, 2015, https://www.codelco.com/codelco-orgullo-de-todos/prontus_codelco/2011-09-28/182001.html.

groups, violence, water scarcity, and environmental pollution. In an attempt to reverse the accumulation of these mining side effects on Calama and its oasis and compensate Calameñans for the "historical debt,"[11] after a major strike, Calama PLUS (from the Spanish for Plan for Calama's Sustainable Urban Development) was created in 2011 as a public-private initiative involving many of the mining and outsourcing companies. Codelco, as the main stakeholder in the area, decided to call Elemental, an architectural and urban office led by Alejandro Aravena, to create a participatory urban plan to "dismantle the social time bomb."[12] After several failed attempts and ideas rejected by the general public, 25,000 people (around 50% of all voters in Calama) voted during the open election, and the first prioritized projects for Calama were selected. Calama PLUS still works today as a public-private consortium, with the mission of coordinating efforts to achieve the sustainable development of Calama. Calama PLUS is also in charge of following the advancement of projects brought to the table by the different private partners.[13] However, Calama PLUS faces now its lack of being a legal entity: a consortium with many actors involved, which can only count on the intentions and good will of its partners.

A Future Beyond Mining
Codelco, Calama PLUS's main partner, while operating in the area, is already working on plans for the after-mining, looking for alternative business opportunities for the area. One of the main elements in the future of Calama is its oasis, since it can provide a source of income and fresh food as well as improve the quality of life in its proximity. The mining industry is both responsible for the oasis' current situation and powerful enough to help with its protection and remediation. Altogether in 2013, Codelco invested US$211 million in environmental projects, surpassing the investments for the previous ten years.[14] Apart from this, US$20 million was invested in projects towards helping neighboring communities in the areas of extraction. In the Calama PLUS plan, there are projects for sustainable development to enhance the oasis and the agricultural activities that take place within it. Apart from this, they offer workshops and seminars about clean energy and other ways of improving the sustainability in the area and enhancing agricultural activities. Also, there is a project for waste management, recycling inorganic materials, and composting. Furthermore, Calama PLUS proposes an urban water recovery system to water plants and green areas both in the oasis and in the interior of the city. This program also encourages the reuse of grey water in private or public buildings in order to reduce water consumption.[15] All these projects have a more sustainable future in mind for Calama and its oasis.

---

11. "Elemental," Elemental, accessed December 16, 2015, http://www.elementalchile.cl/en/projects/calama-plus/.
12. Ibid.
13. "Calama Plus," Calama Plus: Plan de Desarrollo Urbano, Calama Oasis, Moderna y Sustentable, accessed December 16, 2015, http://www.calamaplus.cl/.
14. Codelco, "Codelco, Orgullo de Todos."
15. Ibid.

| 10,000 B.C. | | 1500 B.C. | 0 |

9000 B.C. — Settlement of nomadic populations in the territory

400 B.C. - 100 A.D. — Intensification of agriculture and livestock in the area

Pre-Columbian Period

Original Prehispanic Settlement

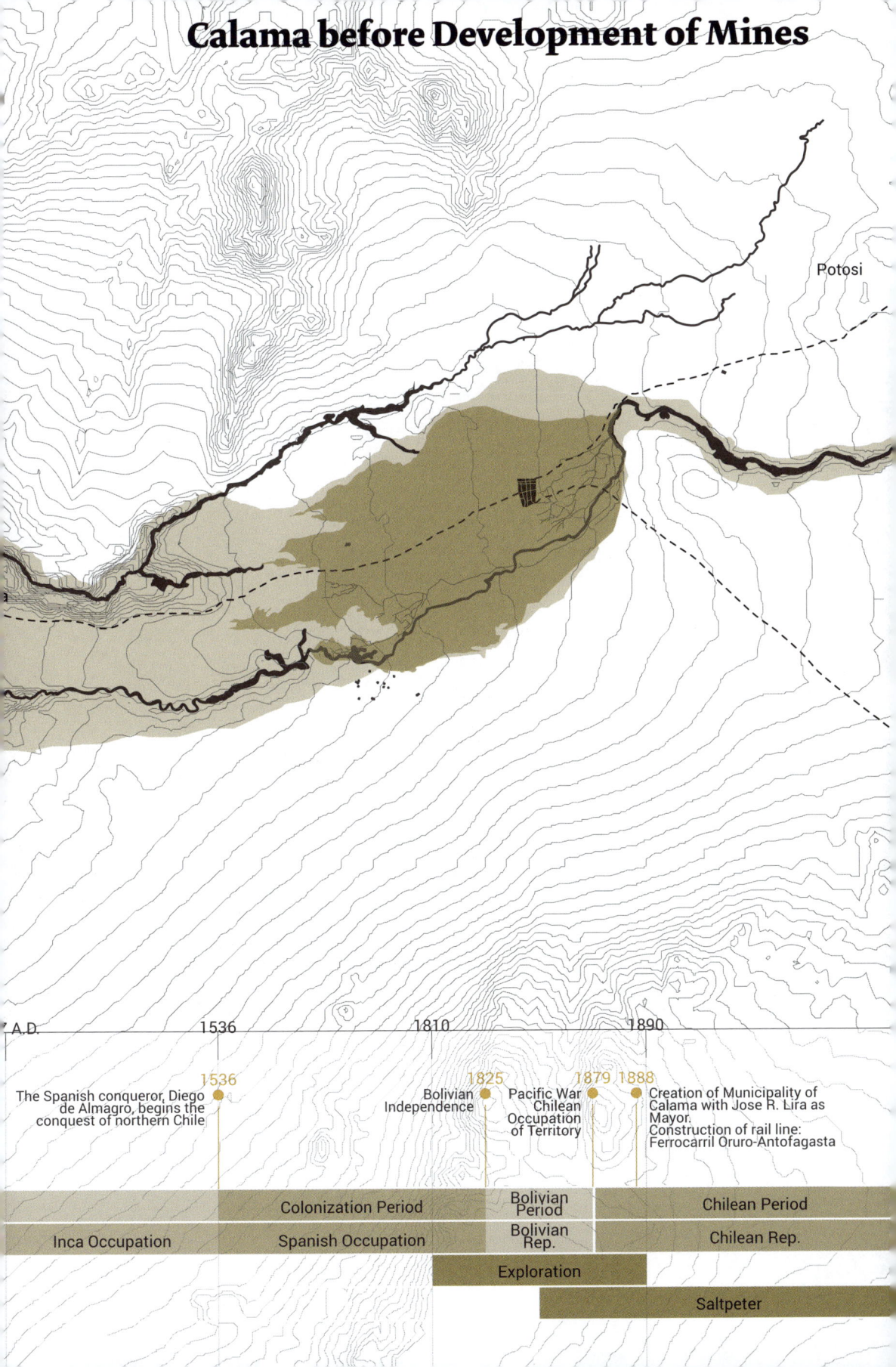

Calama: Before the Disappearance of Mines

Calama's Archaeological Sector

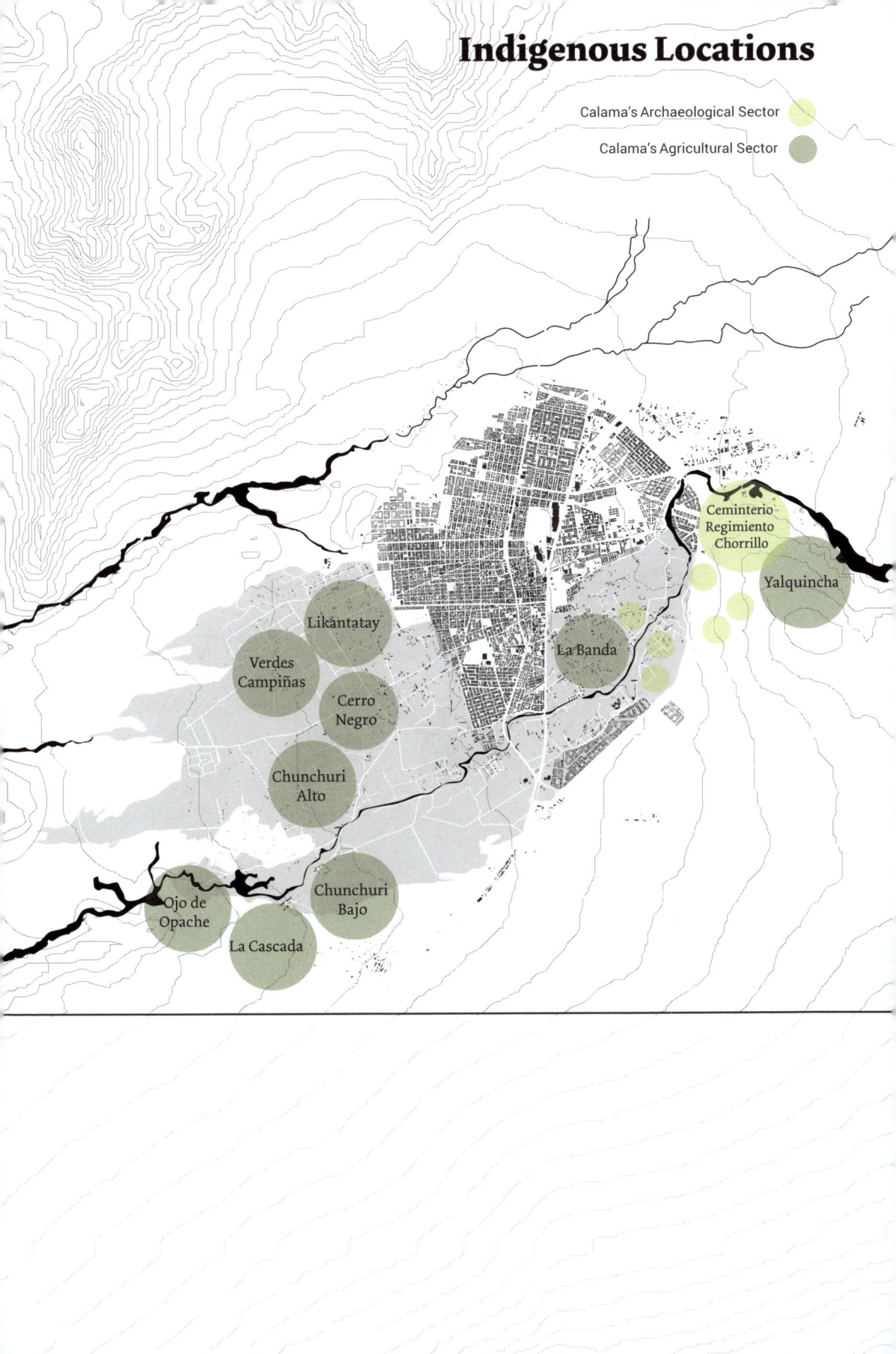

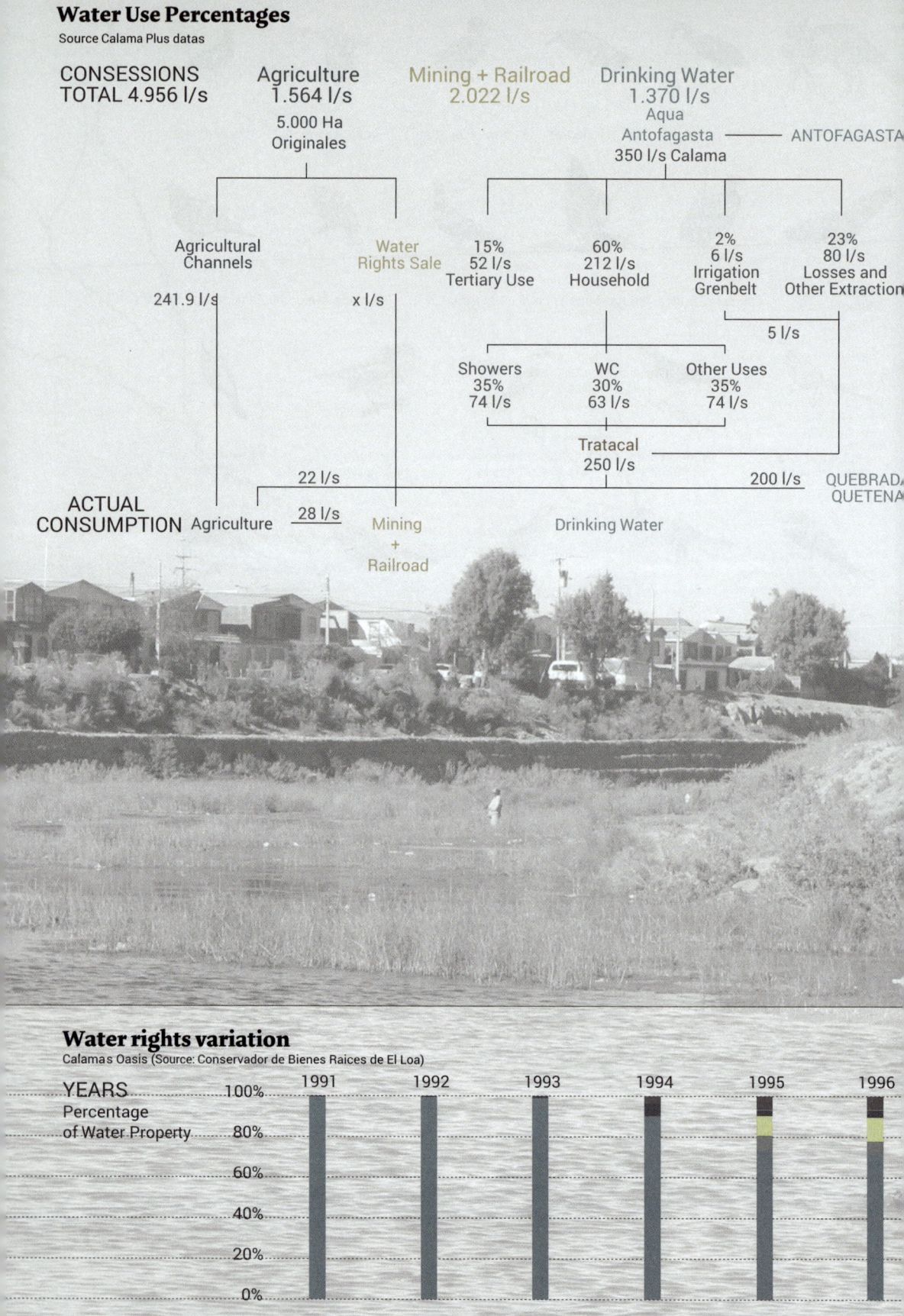

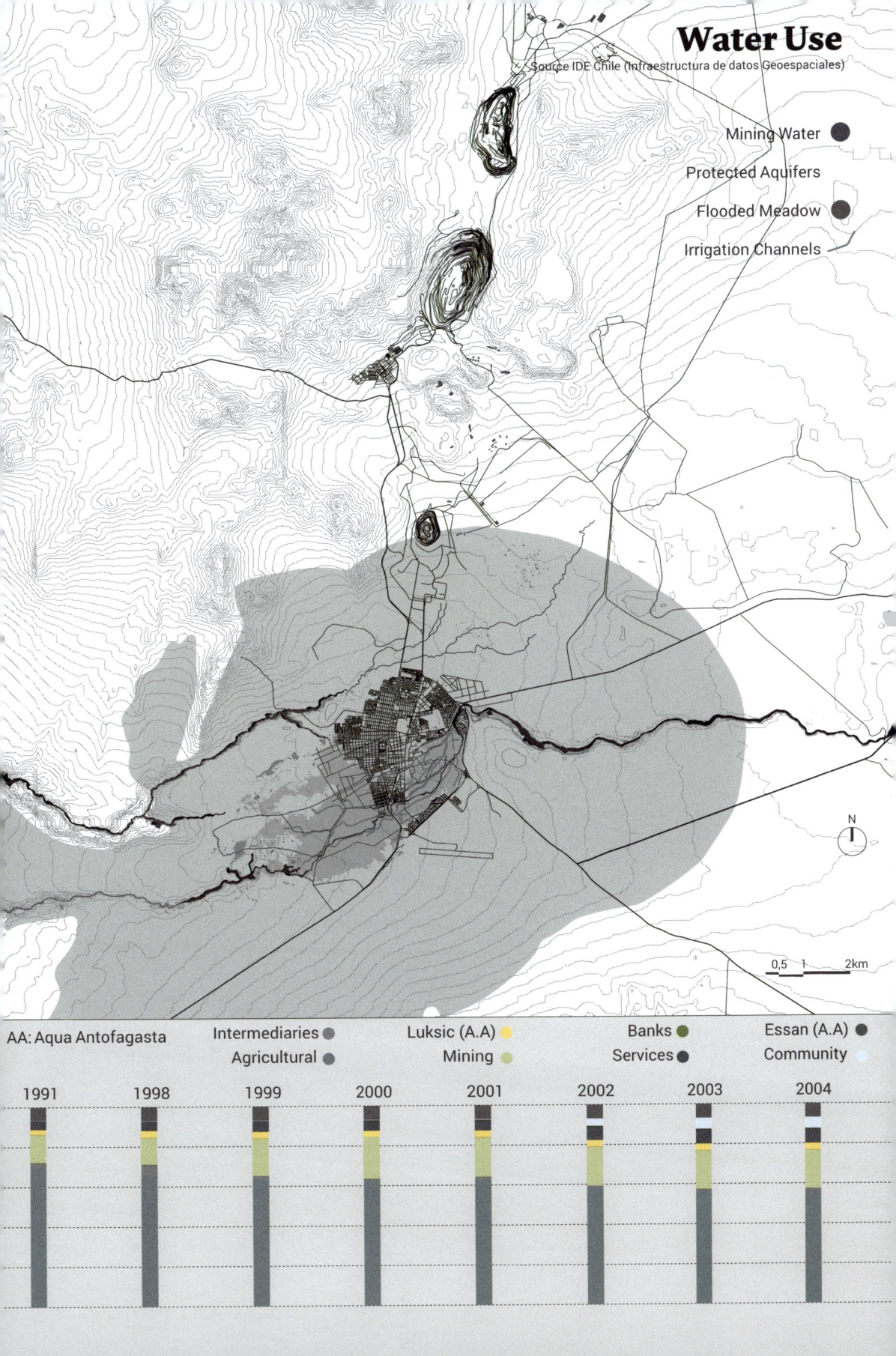

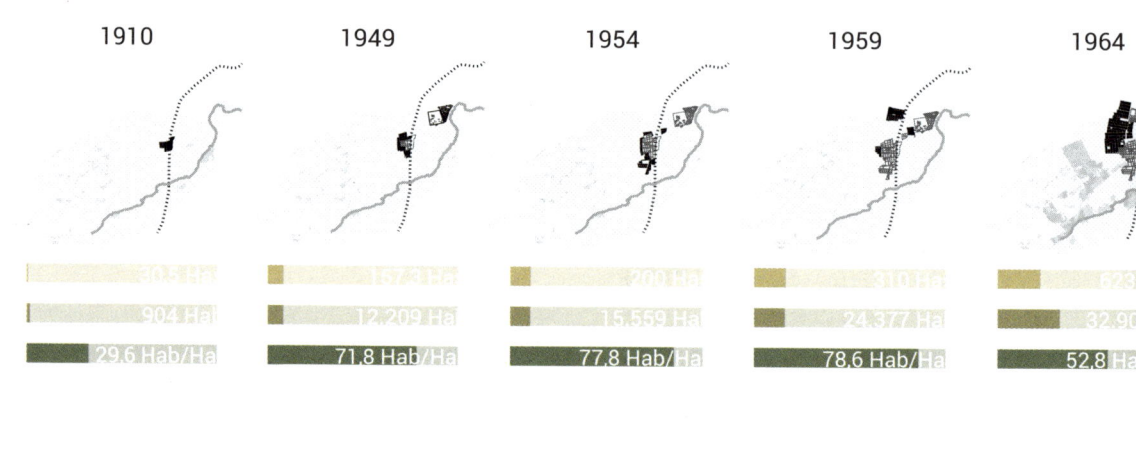

1910	1949	1954	1959	1964
30.5 Ha	157.4 Ha	200 Ha	310 Ha	623
904 Hab	12,209 Ha	15,569 Ha	24,377 Ha	32,90
29.6 Hab/Ha	71.8 Hab/Ha	77.8 Hab/Ha	78.6 Hab/Ha	52,8 Ha

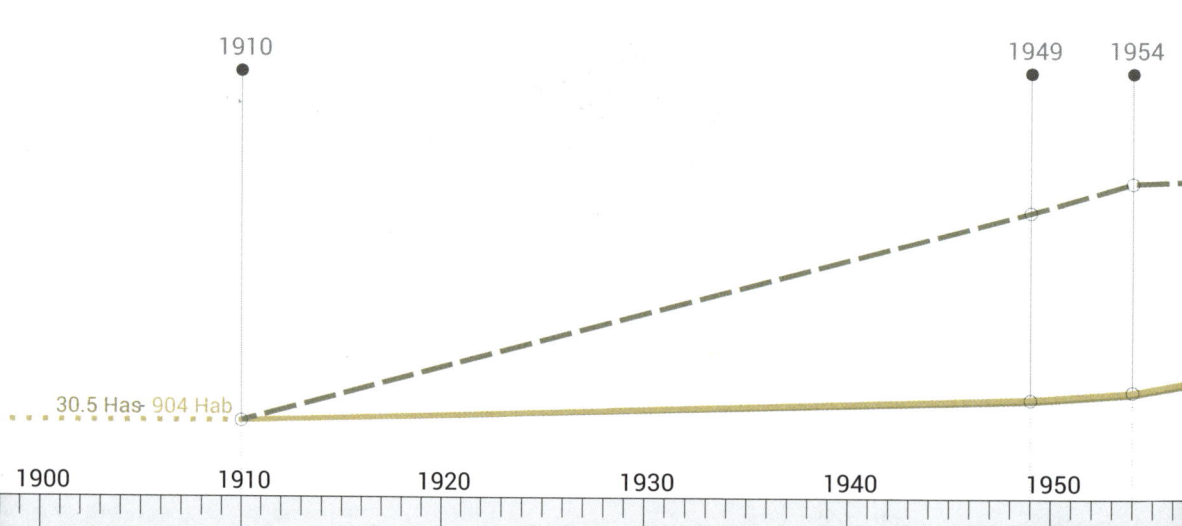

30.5 Has 904 Hab

Timeline

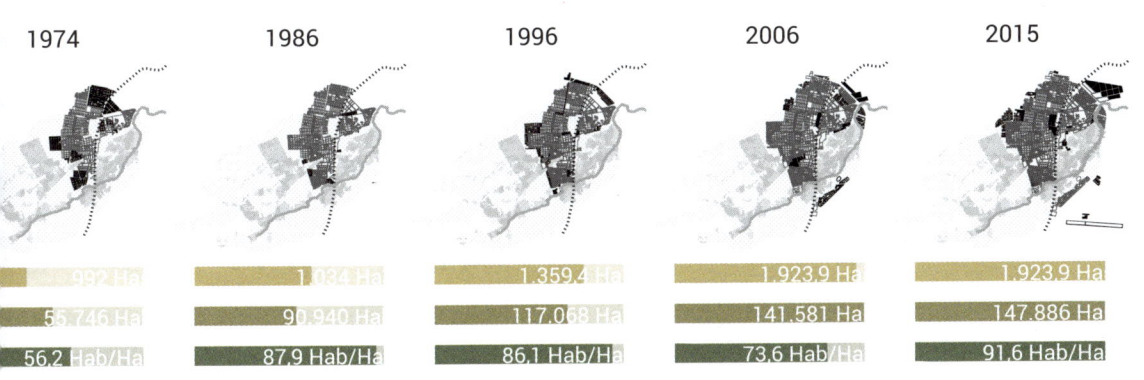

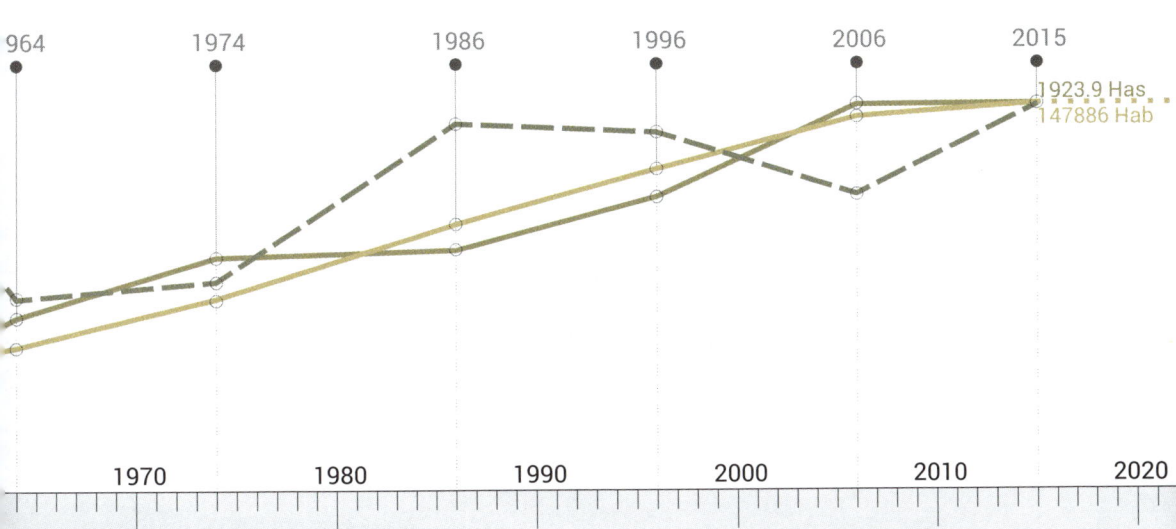

1923.9 Has
147886 Hab

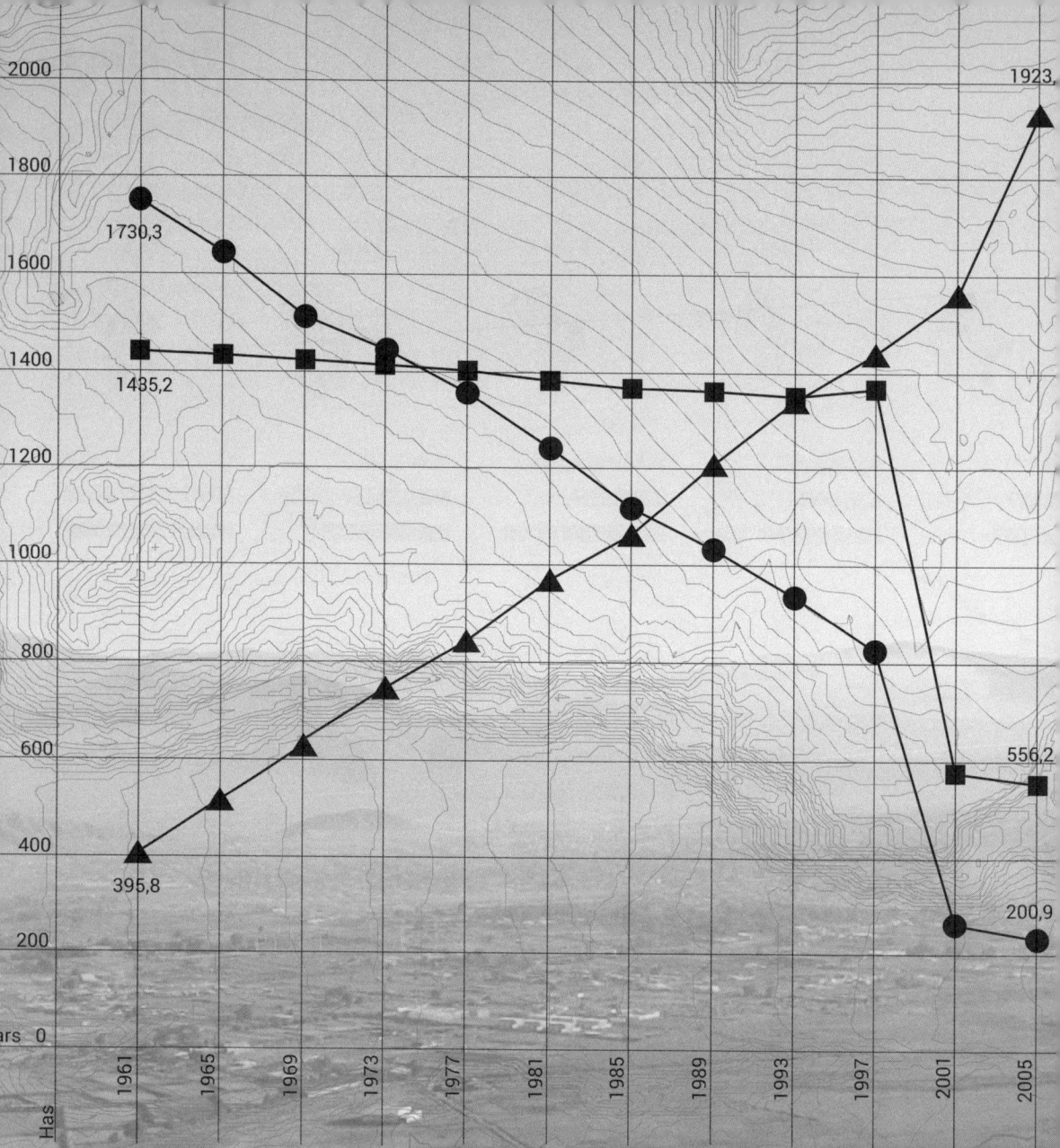

Oasis coverage variation

- ● Natural Vegetation
- ▲ Urban Growth
- ■ Active Agriculture

(Source : Thesis "Los derechos de agua de los agricultores de Calama son efectivos? by Luis Araya)

1985

Oasis Transformation

1990

Oasis Transformation

1995

Oasis Transformation

2000

Oasis Transformation

2005

Oasis Transformation

2010

Oasis Transformation

2015

Oasis Transformation

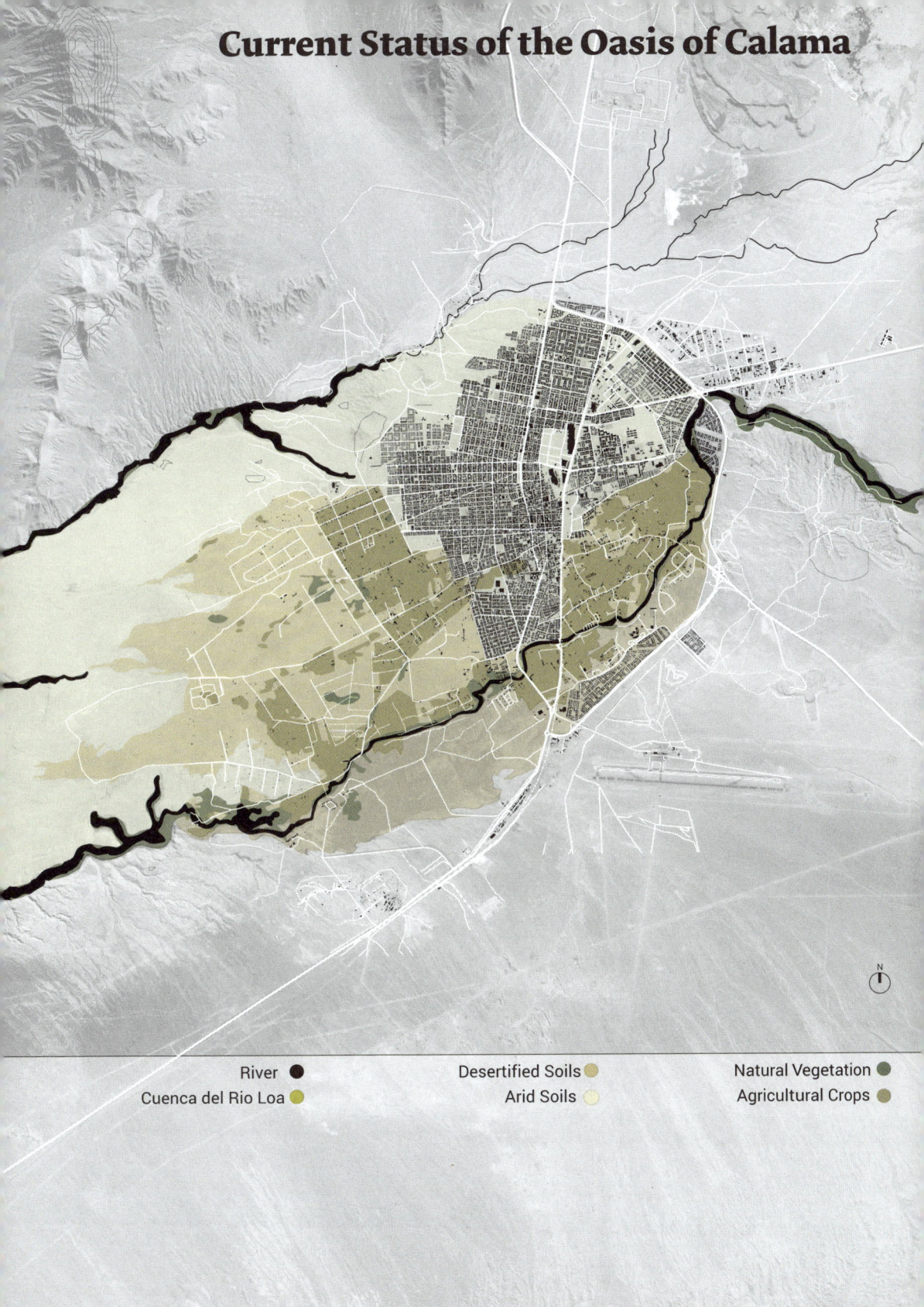

THE LAND OF EXTREME URBAN

Calama Oasis, Jeannette Sordi, 2015

The Landscape of Extractive Urbanization

Jeannette Sordi, Luis Valenzuela, Felipe Vera

Urbanization dynamics in contexts of extraction are difficult to conceptualize in disciplinary terms, but rather easy to understand in empirical ones. In a way, this happens because extractive configurations are urban contexts in which the inner dynamics of urban centers collapse with the expanded reality of operational territories serving mining activities. Extractive urbanization patterns, at a theoretical level, radically question the notion of the urban as a single and contained object, and invite us to find more complex conceptual rubrics for understanding dynamics and intervening within these geographies. This forces us to draw upon complementary sets of ideas, which are effective in framing an expanding territorial urbanization — a massive geographical flux. Here, the urban footprint extends across the territory as a productive transformational process, closely linked with the results of extractive operations facilitated by the presence of highly specialized labor and the apparatus needed for the management of resources. Such a type of urbanization is the result of strongly intertwined geographical production flows, territorially marked by the configuration of the movement of resources, the disposal of waste, and site-specific transformations occurring transversally along territorial scales and urban land limits, over administrative and political boundaries. With the acknowledgment that challenges posed by these urbanization processes do not necessarily coincide with the conventional quests of urban planning and design, one has to start a stream of applied research and develop innovative tools for the acquisition of capacities and knowledge that are specific and lead to the deep and operative understanding of extractive landscapes' dynamics. The real challenge would then necessarily be how to develop effective responses to site-specific problems and their demands in contexts of highly contested political and productive dynamics in tension. Along with any well-known capabilities that can contribute to this perspective, it also needs new forms of measure that lead towards effective solutions.

Several of these tools seem to gradually amplify the boundaries of design, and at the same time increasingly mark the need for evidence-based approaches that measure long-term results. Now, more than ever before, the value of territorial strategies needs to be strengthened as a more foundational aspect for the development of guiding principles around practices of data spatialization and more informed design and policy-making. In this sense, complex urbanization problems will be more and more strongly related to issues of spatial functionality in these territories of extraction. The availability of new strategies for territorial-scale interventions seems closer than ever, for example, such as for Calama Plus and Creo Antofagasta, however they yet still lack rigorous processes and analyses of evidence in their formulation of design strategies and impact forecasting.

In recent decades, extractive territories and cities have encountered strong pressures of different natures stemming from trends in social migration and other internal city stresses, together with the increasing demands of complex mining operations, a floating labor population, and other external globalized stresses. In these decades of intense extractive urbanization, conflicts strengthen around the assurance of data gathering and its argumentation as evidence of complex territories' spatial problems. We need new instruments and measurements to cognize the challenges posed by these problems, while at the same time evidence related to actual need and to building becomes increasingly critical in terms of achieving genuine progress toward real and effective problem-solving.

The city of Calama in Chile calls for working toward the development of better capabilities for spatially synthesizing and finding explanations for the development of the built environment. The extraction operation and production processes between the non-dense occupied territories and the densely occupied territories have built strategic infrastructures that link spatial dimensions of production without a necessary physical continuity. Unfortunately, despite some good intentions from the government and private companies, the damaging impact on natural resources, environments, local economies, communities, and indigenous people has also persisted and often times has been further aggravated. These analytical categories explain the massive transformation of spaces in extraction territories, yet it also makes evident the absence of any planning capable of coping with such a magnitude of changes. It becomes clear that adequate planning, in the sense of a strategic development instrument, has been absent from the overall process of mining installation and operation in intense territories of extraction such as Calama's mining enclave. Rather than a failure, it really has been a lack of reaction as well as a shortage of proper instruments focused on seizing other scales of territories than conventional inner urban developments.

In an intensive extraction enclave, the dispersion of decision-making, together with the concentration of power, makes for drastically uneven governance, especially because private extraction companies are usually the main stakeholders and role players. In this sense, it is broadly agreed that greater development and growth of localities that strongly depend on extraction, as well as their governance strength and institutional quality, become critical. In fact, local governments, alongside a diversity of public institutions, are an entity that struggles in its territorial negotiations with mining companies and any other natural resource economic sector. The main problem of the "Goliath" and "David" relationship arises when it is reduced to a monetary negotiation, and consequently institutions and governance decline as an effect of development dependent on extraction.[1] Then it is quite difficult to relate corporations' project-based response with long-term planning and even with the maintenance of initiatives. Logically, since companies are not meant to govern territories, then the question of to what degree conflicts arise because of a lack of governance is crucial.

Efforts in territories of extraction must be redoubled as well as reinforced; good and strong governments will be the first best step toward the coordinated multi-level governance required to seize the shifting relationship between different territorial scales and levels of government. The concept has two distinct characteristic trends: one is an explicit multi-level territorial governance focused on the regional level, dependent on the new spatial pattern of the mining enclave with a political and administrative decentralization, the other is having a greater scope of experimentation of new central-local and public-private relations along with the appropriate financial model. Among the schemes of governance, each territorial setting and situation of extraction must choose an appropriate political and financial model.

If public-private partnerships' well-known definition is a government determination of a quality and quantity of the service that it requires from a certain private partner, then public-private governance is intended to be a transfer of risks from the public sector to the private sector, and it is a transfer of resources from the private actors to the public sector. Relations of public and private are more commonly used today, yet how public and private entities build a governance alternative is less known, and even less so for the long-term implications of such an alternative. In extractive territories, mutual governance seems to be a logical choice in order to rely on the private sector's capacity to efficiently provide services and goods in a long-lasting relationship. Indeed, much of the proven public-private interactions happen in highly specialized and mature sectors. Now it is necessary to pass from a scheme in which the private sector determines the investments for operations and the public sector has a more supervisory role towards an integrated form of public-private governance with unified and agreed operations

---

1. Stella Tsani, "Natural Resources, Governance and Institutional Quality: The Role of Resource Funds," *Resources Policy* 38(2) (2013): 181-195.

based on public financing and control, but with shared authority. Such governance is meant to be set up in a form through which the institution gains the capacity to change the current situation. It must provide an opportunity for genuine political choice, and be hybrid in the schemes for coordination, flexible in the number of administrative functions, and driven by the design and implementation of strategic planning.

The spatial scale for implementing the understanding of the extended territory is its overall operational performance in an enclave. The enclave is the space of functional dependency of mining centers and their infrastructural capacity – such as airports, ports, highways, railways, and energy transmission lines – that they require from the beginning of mining processes, to waste disposal, up to the end product. Mining enclaves are therefore areas of operation that stretch over political administrative definitions such as urban limits, municipal boundaries, or eventually even regional areas. In this research project and book, we have identified the functional space of the operations as the "camp" of Calama, which expands its flows and elements over the territory. On the other side, the "city" of Calama is the functional command center that offers amenities and services to a large and intense economic sector. As a center, it tends to be the most intense and congested point of the enclave system. Multinational companies analyze and decide to which functional command center their mining extractions belong and set their operational bases there.

Mining outsourcing companies make a similar decision, many times taking into consideration what location logistically offers better services to the larger number of companies, even setting offices, workshops, or storage facilities in the command center cities. As outsourcing companies strategically relate to an enclave command center, mining services businesses are also located in same functional command city. The range of mining's environmental impact spans a vast range of intensity, from minor impacts such as indirect or imperceptible dust, vibration, and noise, to major ecological transformations of landscape, intense contamination, and other effects reflecting the scale of mining. Much of this impact does not quite disturb mineworkers as much as they are sensitive to salaries and bonuses. Miners tend to understand their spaces as a mining camp reality, where one must tolerate specific adverse conditions in order to extract the richness of resources.

Another factor to keep in mind when looking at territories of extraction is their temporal dimension. Actually the idea of "the ephemeral" is a notion evident in all discussions about mining, yet still not visible in the diverse instruments that refer to the territorial implementation of infrastructures for extraction. The ephemeral dimension has not yet permeated the values, concepts, and norms that motivate planning practices. Historically, temporal transformation has not greatly influenced spatial planning, but the innermost nature of mining infrastructure has always assumed a temporality or expiration date. The setting of a time span is always present in each debate about infrastructure investment. Mining camps are meant to be abandoned or disassembled as soon as extraction profitability changes; already in Chile, important mineral extraction sites such as nitrate mines have closed upon extensive railroad infrastructure and highly equipped mining company towns. Today, several of them remain as open museums of the past extractive landscape of northern Chile. Temporality then may at least have two meanings: first, the use of camps and infrastructure during a specific period of time until they are finally abandoned, and second, the use of camps and infrastructure as an intermediate stage to a further final outcome. This becomes even more important to this discussion when we acknowledge that ephemeral landscapes of extraction are comprised of an infinite number of towns scattered all over the world, serving as temporary settlements that support the exploitation of natural resources. These range from those related to agricultural production, mining for natural minerals, fisheries, tapping natural gas, and so on. These extractive activities generate all sorts of urban configurations that emerge within an incredible range of operations that constantly modify the topography of the natural landscape at a territorial scale. Most of them follow similar patterns of temporary spatial occupations and are either detached from pre-existing settlements or actually appropriate them — occupying and evolving their infrastructural presence and often dramatically increasing their footprint in the territory.

The "urban" in this case does not necessarily adhere to the traditional quest for permanence, but is rather configured as being momentary, assembling and disassembling itself in a reversible manner according to the flows of the material extracted, the market trends, and the availability of resources. Exaggerating the urban dynamics triggered by these ephemeral settlements is a visual metaphor — we might imagine these extractive territories as geographic platforms on and within which the temporary configuration of extractive settlements appear and disappear. Thus, they create ephemeral "exceptions" that allow and support the construction of and the consumption in the more permanent parts of the territory — "the city" as we usually know it. In extractive activities, when nothing is left, it is time to move on. In this sense, the development of settlements — towns or even cities that grow, fueled by economies of extraction — are intrinsically tied to the lifecycle of the resource they extract and its value as a commodity on the market. This fact tremendously affects the way in which the place develops, as well as the complexities that are present in such territories. In fact, many of these cities are born and grow dealing with a constant negotiation between people's aspirations and the fear of a certain or predictable expiry date — a fact that irrevocably imprints and limits the complete deployment of their potential. Many of these cities are designed, operated, and viewed from the outside as camps, while in the imagination of

---

2. Hugo Romero, Manuel Méndez, and Pamela Smith, "Mining Development and Environmental Injustice in the Atacama Desert of Northern Chile," *Environmental Justice* 5(2) (2012): 70-76.

their inhabitants they are actually experienced and perceived as active cities. Many of the dwellers' aspirations are not realized because of the fact that the lifecycle of these settlements can only extend as long as the duration of the extractive activity, following the availability of the resource and premises of implacable efficiency. One of the consequences of the booming mining development in Chile is the enormous revenue to the state as well as to the companies, yet it also has strong environmental impacts that trigger a forced migratory pattern of indigenous and resident populations from smaller villages faced with water scarcity.[2]

Calama is the gateway and strategic point for the world's copper and other minerals, yet experiences the lowest quality of life standards in Chile. Even the oasis, once one of the largest in Chile and the world,[3] is today shrinking and menaced. Despite the increasing accessibility of technological and communication devices and networks, there is still a persistent social and physical isolation of communities related to extractive territories, already detected in research from the mid-1980s.[4] Isolation is experienced as the lack of access to equal living conditions and results in uneven territorial equity in terms of access to public services such as health and education. Therefore, migration to larger cities in the region – in the Chilean case, migration towards the city of Calama – enables access to services and amenities that remote settlements cannot provide. Among all public services, education has become of increasing interest to migrant communities since their small villages have only elementary years of schooling.

Paradoxically, the camp dimension of the enclave has both city and settlement dimensions inside of it. In the case of the city of Calama, it has an additional intensity as the camp exerts more pressure than conventional urban tensions that could be found elsewhere. Segregation, inequality, poverty, crime, and other problems are increased inside the urban areas of the mining enclave. The functional factor of quality of life depends on the degree of access to public services and facilities that are intrinsically dependent on the spatial distance to them. Conceptually, the intention of a territorial equity discussion focuses on providing better spatial well-being as a way of addressing redistribution; in the case of extraction, this means resource richness as access to amenities and services. Empirically, the access to territorial welfare is the measurement for the analysis and decision-making about allocations of territorial social resources to residents and communities.

Traditionally, welfare has been understood as a government's overall expression of

---

3. Mary M. Poulton, Sverker C. Jagers, Stefan Linde, Dirk Van Zyl, Luke J. Danielson, and Simon Matti, "State of the World's Nonfuel Mineral Resources: Supply, Demand, and Socio-Institutional Fundamentals," *Annual Review of Environment and Resources* 38 (2013): 345-371.

4. Ricardo Godoy, "Mining: Anthropological Perspectives," *Annual Review of Anthropology* 14 (1985): 199-217.

political institutions' programs for its citizens as a guarantee of equal rights or for mediation in situations of social conflicts. In a different and complementary perspective, spatial acuteness of welfare unlocks accessibility, transferring the hierarchies of implementation from an institutional structure rationale to a spatial social demand rationale as an accurately and demonstrable framing for the output of public goods. The importance of welfare services such as free universal education, quality healthcare, and security are quite evident, and while the importance of territorial welfare is inferred, it nonetheless requires a larger capacity of measurement and analysis. For example, a group of individuals such as two families with the same income may have different levels of welfare because of their home's location compared to the geographic accessibility of public goods. If one of the families is closer to an urban park, they will have more accessibility to green areas per family member compared to the other group, which can establish significant quality of life differences. Calama is a case with great differences in territorial welfare, where neighborhoods with similar levels of income have dissimilar provisions of public goods, therefore creating disparities in the territorial welfare of their inhabitants.

While the measuring of indicators is an essential objective for future strategic planning and territorial welfare, an even more challenging and difficult task is to have adequate representation and spatial coherence in the indicators' measurements. The correlation of indicators and spatial units can generate an analysis with the ability to effectively influence the assessments and proposals for public policies, as a design of evidence-based public policy. To this end, a system of information and a methodological process is required, one that overcomes the limitations of conventional zoning planning used in geographical analysis. This means that the measurement of the proposed indicators is not expressed in a minimum territorial integrity or political unity, such as the administrative district or other administrative aggregation, but arises from a logic of spatial functionality.

A series of indicators can reveal the urban conditions of Calama on a detailed spatial level: i) indicators of functional accessibility that establish a coherent and comparable diagnosis of amenities and service levels at different scales in order to quantify the degree of accessibility that a certain territory has to public goods, services, or other offers in the arrangement of socio-demographic variables producing specific spatial measurement units, and ii) indicators of income segregation that serve to complement a consistent and comparable urban diagnosis.

The indicators of functional accessibility utilize several calculations such as Gravity-Based Accessibility Models, the Spatial Decomposition Method, the Two-Step Floating Catchment Area, and the Three-Step Floating Catchment Area. Quality of life was measured in relation to access to public facilities and services for each of the urban blocks compared to its population density in order to know the extent to which investments had increased the territorial welfare for different areas of the city. The resulting maps of Calama are the following: green areas accessibility, cultural amenities accessibility, public goods accessibility, and sport facilities accessibility; four levels of accessibility, for which a highly intense color represents urban blocks with higher accessibility, medium accessibility has an intermediate color, some accessibility has a light gray color, and dark gray represents almost no accessibility.

Calama has a north-south axis of historical development with considerable services and equipment. This divides a lower-income west side from an east side with a higher income and better quality of life. Calama Plus has fulfilled the main objective of shrinking the historical investment gap in improving the quality of life of the city. Yet almost all of the main investments articulated through Calama Plus have been largely concentrated in central areas or along the north-south axis of the city, the more peripheral areas with more density having less access to services and equipment, except sports equipment. Other peripheral investments are iconic school projects or parks on the outskirts. From a spatial perspective, it is quite possible that Calama Plus has exacerbated the territorial inequality of the city; it increased investment without an equitable spatial distribution of access for people.

In this sense, a meaningful discussion of visions for the city and enclave of Calama inevitably involves pursuing a dual vision to be implemented by strategic territorial planning whose main aim is to mitigate, compensate, and repair the extractive mining effects together with providing social license conditions for investments and operations. Additionally, it intends to foster social and knowledge-related development in the territory, and also provide a future path for development when resource reserves are extinguished or extractive production systems change. The strategic territorial planning must be sustained in values and seen as an opportunity to improve quality of life and the access to more and better services. The strategic plan will have significant effects on the living conditions of the residents in its territory, with mining projects whose impact can extend beyond the life of the project. The strategic plan will contribute to improving the environment and quality of life in those areas in which project operations will generate greater impacts, and to taking care of the aspirations of the local authorities and the community in general, thereby facilitating the social license for companies to operate.

A more strategic planning must integrate social concerns, community aspects, environmental dimensions, and the entire mining operation model over the territory. It also must build confidence in the design process and participation in the plan, elaborating in detail the ways the community will monitor the plan's progression and results.

Also, the territorial strategic planning can set up critical similarities and differences between the main two categories of stakeholders: the mining companies and the resident communities.

The future will seek answers for such issues in places like the city of Calama in the Chilean Atacama Desert, where emerging economies are building the incremental accumulation of social and spatial problems. Already in 2012, the Calama Sustainable Urban Plan was delivered to cope with the historical investment deficit, yet it seems it was not enough; new demands have escalated and caught up more quickly than all prognoses. The future will also seek answers not only in the fact of undertaking an initiative such as CalamaPlus or Creo Antofagasta, it will also require more thorough and accountable methods with which to intervene in the territory. In a sense, additional and better quality evidence-based design strategies must be constructed to tackle the diverse and distinctive dimensions of the challenges for functional landscapes of production.

Fostering innovations in spatial analysis and modeling, and GIS integrated applications, the research on this book has looked to provide new insights into an evidence-driven approach to territorial policy and design. The questions should be focused on the City's futures guided by three key questions: What forces will direct Calama's urban development and to which results? What can redefine urban life and urban evolution? And, how will this change the focus of urban development processes in Calama?

The city of Calama and its territory will be ground for exploring answers for the increasing demand to deliver public goods and services foremost occurring through city's urban infrastructures and systems. Design of public policy and projects' dependency to resourcefully increase the city's capacity toprovide benefits to each and all its inhabitants must be based in the certainty of the kind and nature of the problem attended.

Contributors

Pablo Allard

Doctor of Design Studies 2003, Harvard University GSD. Master of Architecture in Urban Design 1999, Harvard University GSD. Architect and Master of Architecture 1997 P. Universidad Católica Chile
Pablo Allard is Dean of the Faculty of Architecture and Arts at UNIVERSIDAD DEL DESARROLLO in Concepción and Santiago, Chile. He is also CEO at ALLARD & PARTNERS architecture, landscape and urban design (formerly known as URBANICA). Director at PATAGONIA SUR, dedicated to conservation and sustainable development in Chilean Patagonia, and NUEVA VIA consulting, focused on the development of transportation infrastructure projects. Allard was a founding partner of the *"Do-Tank"* ELEMENTAL along with Pritzker awardee Alejandro Aravena. He left ELEMENTAL in 2010 to serve as *National Urban Reconstruction Coordinator* at the *Chilean Ministry of Housing and Urban Development*, to lead the recovery efforts after earthquake and tsunami that destroyed more than 150 cities and towns that year.
Along with his academic and professional work, he is the author and editor of several books and papers, columnist for the newspaper *"La Tercera"*, Board member at the *Corporation for Infrastructure Policy* and also served as board member of the *National Council for Culture and the Arts*, the *Presidential Commission for Urban Mobility* and the *Presidential Commission for the National Urban Development Policy*.

Maria Arrasate

María Ignacia Arrasate is a Research Associate at the Zofnass Program for Sustainable Infrastructure at Harvard's Graduate School of Design (GSD).
Her research at Harvard is focused in promoting sustainable practices and improving resilience in large infrastructure projects across Latin American.
She recently graduated from the Master in Design program at GSD, focusing in the field of designing resilient projects and implementing public policies for post-disaster recovery. Before coming to Harvard, she worked as a Minister Advisor in the Chilean Reconstruction Program led by the Chilean government to recover thousands of houses and infrastructure, which were severely damaged after the earthquake and tsunami that partially devastated the South of the country in 2010. She has published several articles related to the experience in disaster recovery learned in Chile. Her career began in the construction sector as an architect practitioner, working for several years in project management and design, addressing different project scales, from individual housing to master plans. During her years in Chile, she combined her professional practice with academic work, giving courses both in Universidad Católica de Chile and Universidad del Desarrollo.
She holds a professional degree in architecture from the Pontificia Catholic University of Chile, as well as a Master's in Advanced Architectural Design from Columbia University.

Mariana Barrera
Licentiate in Economics and Masters in Finance by Torcuato Di Tella University. Master in Urban Planning from Harvard University, fully funded by Fulbright and World Bank, 2012-2014. She's Director of Habitat Studies and Investment Projects at Argentina's Ministry of Home Affairs. Lead Researcher for the project "Boom Towns and the effects of infrastructure investment: a case study of land use and socio-spatial patterns in Añelo, Argentina", Lincoln Institute of Land Policy, 2014-2016. Advisor on the design and coordination of Argentina's Habitat National Plan for 2015 Presidential Campaign. Since 2014 she's consultant on capacity building and urban development projects from international organizations. Research Assistant at Zofnass Program for Sustainable Infrastructure (IDB-Harvard), 2013-2014. Author of three publications on infrastructure investment and public spending in Argentina. Coordinator of several international events on project finance and public-private partnerships. Teaching fellow at Torcuato Di Tella University's Master in Finance and MBA, 2009-2011. Senior project finance analyst at international organizations and the public and private sectors in Latin-American, 2006-2012.

Sourav Kumar Biswas
Sourav Kumar Biswas is a research associate for Neil Brenner and Rahul Mehrotra at Harvard University Graduate School of Design. He is a Landscape Architecture graduate from Harvard University with a professional degree in Architecture from the University of Texas at Austin. His professional career in design and planning spans the cities of Mumbai, Copenhagen, Dallas, Austin, Doha, Auroville, Kolkata, and Cambridge working in diverse firms like Corgan Associates, Serie Architects, and SLA. He has complemented his professional experience with community outreach, curatorial and research experiences working with the BMW Guggenheim Lab and Observer Research Foundation in Mumbai, Interboro Partners in Cambridge, and the Zofnass Program for Sustainable Infrastructures at Harvard. He has also been a visiting faculty at the KRV Institute of Architecture in Mumbai.

Sourav's research focuses on the socio-ecological impact of extended urbanization on the landscape and its people, with a particular interest in community management of blue-green infrastructure and the intersection of working landscapes with land-water conservation. He is applying an understanding of land-water linkages and land-management frameworks towards integrated conservation goals for growing urban regions such as the Kolkata Metropolitan region and Pueblo County in Colorado. His project on agricultural landscapes around Mexico City received Analysis and Planning honor awards by the American Society of Landscape Architects and Boston Society of Landscape Architects. His current research project identifies urban governance challenges faced by transitioning settlements in India. A spatial deconstruction of Census datasets and global datasets is utilized to identify radical shifts in livelihoods within a highly populated agrarian field and rapidly transforming areas outside of large urban centers.

Diane Davis
Diane E. Davis, Charles Dyer Norton Professor of Regional Planning and Urbanism, and Chair of the Department of Urban Planning and Design, is the author of *Urban Leviathan: Mexico City in the Twentieth Century* (Temple University Press 1994; Spanish translation 1999) and *Discipline and Development: Middle Classes and Prosperity in East Asia and Latin America* (Cambridge University Press, 2004) as well as co-editor of *Irregular Armed Forces and their Role in Politics and State Formation* (Cambridge University Press, 2003) and *Cities and Sovereignty: Identity Politics in Urban Spaces* (Indiana University Press, 2011).

Her published works examine the relations between urbanization and national development, comparative international development, the politics of urban development policy, and conflict cities. She has explored topics ranging from historic preservation, urban social movements, and identity politics to urban governance, fragmented sovereignty, and state formation to planning theory.

Her current research focuses on the transformation of cities of the global south, particularly the urban social, spatial, and political conflicts that have emerged in response to globalization, informality, and political or economic violence. A prior recipient of research fellowships from the John D. and Catherine T. MacArthur Foundation, the Heinz Foundation, the Ford Foundation, the Social Science Research Council, the United States Institute for Peace, the Andrew W. Mellon Foundation, and the Carnegie Corporation of New York, Davis now coordinates a large scale project titled Urban Resilience in Conditions of Chronic Violence, funded by USAID. Currently, Davis is involved in various research projects hosted at the GSD. She directs a project funded by the Volvo Research and Educational Foundation titled "Transforming Urban Transport -- The Role of Political Leadership" (TUT); is the co-PI for the project "Rethinking social housing in Mexico" (ReSHIM), funded by Mexico s National Worker Housing Agency (INFONAVIT); and heads the "The Mexican Cities Initiative" (MCI).

Agustina González Cid
Agustina González Cid is a licensed architect and urbanist interested in a transcalar approach to territorial design. She holds a Master of Science in Architecture and Urban studies from MIT, funded by a Fulbright Scholarship. She also holds a diploma in Architecture and Technology from Torcuato Di Tella University and a professional degree of Architecture from the National University of Rosario where she teaches since 2010. González Cid is founder principal of I+GC [ar], developing projects that range from small furniture to housing and large-scale territorial designs. Her built work and competition submissions have been published in different national and international media.

González Cid's current research is focused on analyzing the urban condition of productive territories and designing new territorial logics based on the interaction between human actions and ecology. In 2015, she was funded by MISTI (MIT International Science and Technology Initiatives) to do research on copper mining in Chile at the Center of Territorial Intelligence at Adolfo Ibáñez University (Santiago, Chile). She now works at ECOM (Metropolitan Coordination Entity for the Rosario Metropolitan Area, Argentina) where she is in charge of establishing and designing productive peri-urban areas and their relation to other land uses of twenty municipalities and communes of the Rosario metropolitan region. She also teaches and conducts research towards the creation of an Atlas of Argentina's productive territory at Torcuato Di Tella University.

Rahul Mehrotra
Rahul Mehrotra is a practicing architect, urban designer, and educator and his firm, RMA Architects, was founded in 1990 in Mumbai. Mehrotra is a professor of urban design and planning at the Harvard Graduate School of Design (GSD) and a member of the Steering committee for the South Asia Institute at Harvard University. His writings include coauthoring *Bombay—The Cities Within*, *Banganga— Sacred Tank*, *Public Places Bombay*, *Bombay to Mumbai—Changing Perspectives* and *The Kumbh Mela — Mapping the Ephemeral Mega City*. He has also co-authored *Conserving an Image Center—The Fort Precinct in Bombay*, based on this study and its recommendations, the historic Fort area in Mumbai was declared a conservation precinct in 1995—the first such designation in India. His recent book Architecture in India, since 1990 inspired an exhibition he co curated titled The State of Architecture – Practices and Processes in India which was opened at the National Gallery of Modern Art in Mumbai in Jan 2016.

Rania Ghosn and El Hadi Jazairy
Rania Ghosn and El Hadi Jazairy are founding partners of the collaborative practice DESIGN EARTH. The practice engages the geographies of technological systems to open up aesthetic and political concerns for architecture and urbanism. Their work involves the coupled undertakings of writing about the earth and also writing on, or projecting again a world. DESIGN EARTH has been recognized with several awards, including the Architectural League of New York Young Architects Award, the Jacques Rougerie Competition, and the ACSA Faculty Design Award for their recently published Geographies of Trash (Actar, 2015). Some of his recent work has been published in Volume, Journal of Architectural Education, San Rocco, MONU, Avery Review, Thresholds, Bracket, and Perspecta. Ghosn and Jazairy hold doctor of design degrees from Harvard Graduate School of Design, where they were founding editors of the journal *New Geographies* and respectively editors of NG2: Landscapes of Energy and NG4: Scales of the Earth. Ghosn is an architect, geographer and currently assistant professor at Massachusetts Institute of Technology School of Architecture + Planning. Jazairy is a licensed architect and currently assistant professor of architecture at the University of Michigan.

Flavio Sciaraffia
Flavio is a professional Architect with a Master in Urban Design and a Master's Degree in Landscape Architecture from Harvard University, degree that was sponsored by a full scholarship from the Chilean Government. He is interested in larger scales involving coupled socio-ecological systems, in which urbanization and landscapes are a single entity and mutually dependent, making its management, design, and spatial understanding critical to address sustainability. Flavio's disciplinary scope is focused on addressing integrated conservation goals around land, water, biological and socio-cultural resources at the landscape level in growing urban regions with a particular concern in developing or underprivileged contexts. His work spans places such as Santiago-Chile, Mexico City, dwindling agricultural hinterlands in Colorado, and urban margins in Los Angeles-US. Flavio takes on spatial methodologies combining landscape planning frameworks and design to provide strategic. Integrating conservation and productivity is a priority in his approach when planning for a sustainable landscape change between urbanization processes, resource hinterlands and source landscapes. His skill set combines analytical methods in GIS and remote sensing, integrating them with design tools in a feedback loop to critically inquire, map and assess socio-ecological systems and landscape-level interactions. Flavio has acquired a theoretical and practical understanding of the linkages between urban and landscape processes through varied fields such as urban and social theory, landscape ecology, urban ecology, environmental management/planning, and geographic information science. Lately Flavio has been awarded in international competitions, such as the 2015 ASLA Awards and the 2016 BSLA Awards, and in cutting-edge venture programs, such as the Harvard i-lab Venture Incubation Program. His previous appointment was as a Research Associate at Harvard GSD. Currently he works at GeoAdaptive, LLC, a Boston based firm that specializes in geospatial technologies and analyses for critical planning issues.

Jeannette Sordi
Jeannette Sordi is Professor of Landscape and Urbanism at the Design Lab of Universidad Adolfo Ibanez, Santiago, Chile. She holds a PhD from the Polytechnic School of the University of Genoa (2014) and has been DAAD post-doctoral research fellow at Leibniz Universität Hannover (2014) and PhD Special Student at the Harvard Graduate School of Design (2011- 2012). Her research focuses on the investigation of recycling strategies for architecture, landscape, and urbanism and on the development of planning instruments and devices based on recycling, landscape, and ecology. She is the author of the book *Beyond Urbanism* (List, 2014) that reassembles the origins and theories of Landscape Urbanism, and co-editor of *Andrea Branzi. Ten Humble Suggestions for a new Athens Chart* (Arq, 2015).

Ricardo Truffello
Ricardo Truffello is Advisor on Geo-referenced Information Systems (GIS) and professor at Adolfo Ibánez University. He has taught Undergraduate courses at the Geography Institute of Chile's Catholic University as well as different diplomas and short courses on GIS.
He was project coordinator for the Cities Observatory at Chile's Catholic University, where he specialized on water efficiency. He has written in books "Urban Projects", "Building Chile: Public Policies in Social Housing" and different seminars on the topic. He has also published "Geographies of a Frontier Territory: La Chimba, Santiago de Chile XVII –XXI century" for Norte Grande Magazine.

Luis Valenzuela
Director for the Center of Territorial Intelligence and academic for DesignLAB at Adolfo Ibañéz University, professor at the school of business at Adolfo Ibañéz University and associated researcher at the Center of Conflict and Social Cohesion, COES.
He holds an Architecture diploma and a Master in Architecture from Chile's Catholic University and a Doctor of Design from Harvard's Graduate School of Design.
In 2014 and 2015 he was guest professor at Harvard's Graduate School of Design. In 2011 he founded the Center of Territorial Intelligence and worked as sub-director for the school of design. From 1997 to 2011 he was academic at the School of Architecture, Design and urban Studies of Chile's Catholic University, where he leaded the urbanism department for the School of Architecture and created the Master in Urban Project program. He was also academic of the Master in Building Administration at the School of Engineer at Chile's Catholic University. He was executive director of extension and external services at School of Architecture, Design and urban Studies and director of the Cities Observatory, both at Chile's Catholic University.

Felipe Vera
Architect, Universidad de Chile (2009). MDeS in Urbanism, Landscape & Ecology from Harvard Graduate School of Design (2013). Professor and co-director of the Center for Ecology, Landscape and Urbanism at the UAI DesignLab in Chile and Member of the Initiative for Sustainable and Emergent Cities at the Inter American Development Bank. He is editor of 'Kumbh Mela: Mapping The Ephemeral Mega City' (2014), 'Andrea Branzi: Ten Recommendations for a New Athens Charter' (2015) 'Rahul Mehrotra: Dissolving Thresholds' (2015), Ephemeral Urbanism (2016) and curator of the 'Radical Temporalities' Pavilion at the Shenzhen Biennale of Architecture and Urbanism (2015) awarded with the International Academic Award, and 'Ephemeral Urbanism Cities in Constant Flux' Pavilion at the Venice Biennale (2016). Felipe Vera was a faculty at the Department of Urban Planning and Design at Harvard University.

Published by
LISt Lab
info@listlab.eu
listlab.eu

Production
GreenTrenDesign Factory
Piazza Manifattura, 1
38068 Rovereto (TN) - Italy
T: +39 0464 443427
info@greentrendesign.it

Authors
Jeannette Sordi
Luis Valenzuela
Felipe Vera

Editor
Agustina González Cid

Editorial Director
Pino Scaglione

Editorial Assistant
Gioia Marana

Art Direction & Graphic Design
Blacklist Creative Partners, Barcelona
blacklist-creative.com

ISBN 97888898774753

Printed and bound in European Union,
April 2017

All rights reserved
© of edition LISt Lab
© of texts they authors
© of images they authors

Promotion and Distribution in Italy
Messaggerie Libri, Spa, Milano,
Numero verde 800.804.900
assistenza.ordini@meli.it

International Promotion and Distribution
ACC Distribution, United Kingdom
+44 (0)1394 389950
uksales@accpublishinggroup.com

List&Books Scientific Board
Eve Blau, Harvard GSD; Maurizio Carta, Università di Palermo; Eva Castro, Xi'an University of Architecture and Technology; Alberto Clementi, (già) Università D'Annunzio; Alberto Cecchetto, IUAV, Università di Venezia; Stefano De Martino, Università di Innsbruck; Corrado Diamantini, Università di Trento; Antonio De Rossi, Università di Torino; Franco Farinelli, Università di Bologna; Carlo Gasparrini, Università di Napoli; Manuel Gausa, Università di Genova; Giovanni Maciocco (già) Università di Sassari/Alghero; Mosè Ricci, Università di Trento; Roger Riewe, Università di Graz; G. Pino Scaglione, Università di Trento